"*Living the Lord's Prayer* is not, actually, about only the Lord's Prayer—it is about how we conceive of God, and what happens when we encounter God. Many of us have repeated the Lord's Prayer so often that we have ceased to notice what we're saying. Albert Haase's insights and reflections will help you not just understand the Lord's Prayer more deeply; this book will also help you pray those words that Jesus taught with more attentiveness."

Lauren Winner, Duke Divinity School, and author of *Girl Meets God*

"Prayer is the foundation of life, and for Christians all prayer is shaped by the words and spirit of the Lord's Prayer. In taking a fresh look at these familiar words, Albert Haase has engaged in a sparkling conversation with the great thinkers, writers and saints of the last twenty centuries; the result is a fascinating book which will provoke your thinking and leave you yearning to immerse yourself more deeply in our Father's presence."

Christopher Webb, president, Renováré

"Albert Haase combines a deep understanding of theology, keen insights into the human condition and observations about his own life's journey into a highly readable and helpful tool for personal devotion. *Living the Lord's Prayer* will help you deepen your relationship with Christ as you reflect on the prayer he taught us. You'll find yourself returning to this book after the first reading (as I have), and finding fresh insights every time you do so."

Sean Herriott, host of *Morning Air*™ on Relevant Radio

"Too often we fail to appreciate the depth of religious sentiment in the prayers with which we are most familiar. In this book, Albert Haase has brought together his extensive knowledge of spirituality, insights that have been honed by several years of pastoral ministry and spiritual direction, and his God-given talent for creative thinking as he reflects anew on the Lord's Prayer. . . . I'm sure that St. Teresa of Ávila would welcome this new look at the prayer she loved so well."

Dianne Bergant, C.S.A., professor of Old Testament studies, Catholic Theological Union, and author of *People of the Covenant*

"If your image of God needs healing, this book was written for you. *Living the Lord's Prayer* is a gift, a bright offering for today's seekers and disciples. It is a truly worthy guide for both prayer and study, embellished with theological, literary and contemporary reflection. I absolutely love it and joyfully recommend it."

Macrina Wiederkehr, O.S.B., retreat guide and author of *Seven Sacred Pauses*

"I have rarely been inclined to describe a book as superb, but in this case, no other word will do. *Living the Lord's Prayer* is so rich in story and holy conversation that, in conjunction with Scripture, it could make an almost complete library for those seeking authentic Christian formation."

Phyllis Tickle, compiler of *The Divine Hours* and author of *The Great Emergence*

Other books by Albert Haase, O.F.M.

Enkindled: Holy Spirit, Holy Gifts
coauthored with Bridget Haase, O.S.U.
(St. Anthony Messenger Press, 2001)

Instruments of Christ: Reflections on the
Peace Prayer of St. Francis of Assisi
(St. Anthony Messenger Press, 2004)

Coming Home to Your True Self: Leaving
the Emptiness of False Attractions
(InterVarsity Press, 2008)

LIVING THE LORD'S PRAYER

The Way of the Disciple

ALBERT HAASE, O.F.M.

FOREWORD BY GERALD L. SITTSER

IVP Books

An imprint of InterVarsity Press
Downers Grove, Illinois

InterVarsity Press
P.O. Box 1400, Downers Grove, IL 60515-1426
World Wide Web: www.ivpress.com
E-mail: email@ivpress.com

InterVarsity Press® is the book-publishing division of InterVarsity Christian Fellowship/USA®, a student movement active on campus at hundreds of universities, colleges and schools of nursing in the United States of America, and a member movement of the International Fellowship of Evangelical Students. For information about local and regional activities, write Public Relations Dept., InterVarsity Christian Fellowship/USA, 6400 Schroeder Rd., P.O. Box 7895, Madison, WI 53707-7895, or visit the IVCF website at <www.intervarsity.org>.

Scripture quotations, unless otherwise noted, are from the New Revised Standard Version of the Bible, copyright 1989 by the Division of Christian Education of the National Council of the Churches of Christ in the USA. Used by permission. All rights reserved.

Design: Cindy Kiple
Images: Eric Rorer/Getty Images

ISBN 978-0-8308-3529-4

Printed in the United States of America ∞

 InterVarsity Press is committed to protecting the environment and to the responsible use of natural resources. As a member of Green Press Initiative we use recycled paper whenever possible. To learn more about the Green Press Initiative, visit <www.greenpressinitiative.org>.

Library of Congress Cataloging-in-Publication Data

Haase, Albert, 1955-
    Living the Lord's prayer: the way of the disciple / Albert Haase.
        p. cm.
    Includes bibliographical references.
    ISBN 978-0-8308-3529-4 (pbk.: alk. paper)
    1. Lord's prayer—Criticism, interpretation, etc. 2. Christian
life. I. Title.
    BV230.H28 2009
    226.9'606—dc22
                                                                2008054474

P   23 22 21 20 19 18 17 16 15 14 13 12 11 10 9 8 7 6
Y   28 27 26 25 24 23 22 21 20 19 18 17 16 15 14 13

T he young hermit's excitement and self-satisfaction pushed his gait even before his forward foot had time to settle into the sand. He was on his way to see his elderly spiritual father and to report on this past month's spiritual practice. He had been instructed to pray exclusively the words of the Lord's Prayer.

"Father," the young hermit said, trying to contain the joy of his achievement, "as you counseled me, I have prayed continually the words our Savior taught us. This prayer has rooted itself in my heart and now, as I breathe, weave my mats or prepare a few biscuits for the daily meal, the prayer is constantly rising from my heart through my soul to the gates of heaven."

The spiritual father's face, baked by the sun and basking in the Son, betrayed disappointment as the young man began to speak of the worries and concerns that tormented every inexperienced hermit who had come to the desert. Would the sale of his mats be enough to support him? How could he make up for the time lost due to his previous life of sin? Would he be able to overcome the disturbance and distractions of pilgrims who found their way to his hut?

Pointing in the direction from which the young hermit had come, the spiritual father said, "Go back to your hut. You have not yet discovered how to live what you pray."

As the young hermit journeyed back and forth month after month, rumors circulated amid the sand and stone of a disciple who was living the Lord's Prayer.

Contents

Foreword

MOST PEOPLE, EVEN THE MOST IRRELIGIOUS, can recite it as if it were passed down from one generation to the next through the religious gene pool of humanity. Yet few of us, even the most religious, think much about it, though it has served as *the* prayer of the church since Jesus first taught it some 2000 years ago. Tertullian of Carthage was right when he said that the Lord's Prayer is "an abridgement of the entire Gospel."

Father Albert Haase, O.F.M, has written *Living the Lord's Prayer* to help us *think* about what we pray when we utter the most famous prayer in the world. But more than that, he challenges us to *live* the Lord's Prayer too. It is a novel idea, really. Accustomed, as we are, to pray it, we assume that it is God's responsibility to answer it. God is the one who acts; we are the ones who receive. Isn't that how prayer works? We ask God to do his will on earth, to give us our daily bread, to forgive our sins, to keep us from temptation, to deliver us from evil. Then we expect God to do what we ask. Not that Father Haase disputes that. But he dares to suggest that we should act, too, and thus be changed by our praying and perhaps even help change the world at the same time.

I have not known Father Albert (as his friends call him) for a long time. I met him in the spring of 2008, though we had corresponded on occasion before that. I remember his emails bursting with energy. When I met him face-to-face I discovered why. He is joyful, passionate and luminous. He has become a dear brother in Christ to me.

I make my living as a university professor, which means that I read many books, including books on spirituality. I assumed that *Living the Lord's Prayer* would be insightful and inspirational but not especially new and fresh. It is, after all, about the Lord's Prayer. Is it possible to write anything new and fresh about that subject? I discovered soon enough that I was wrong. Consequently, I found myself reading the manuscript more slowly than I had expected. There are three reasons why I think the book is compelling.

First, Father Albert challenges us to live what we pray, which will engender a seamlessness between out spiritual practices, narrowly understood, and our ordinary lives. What good is a spiritual life if it remains confined to formal religious activities? *Living the Lord's Prayer* advocates the proper kind of spirituality, one that is deeply Christ-centered, steeped in the historic faith and applicable to ordinary life.

Second, Father Albert has read the classics, which is abundantly clear throughout the book. Not that he is self-consciously learned. But he has breathed the air of the spiritual masters for so long, especially St. Francis (for obvious reasons), that he exhales their wisdom on almost every page. It is obvious that they have become his teachers and friends. The book therefore has a *gravitas* to it, even though it is also delightfully energetic and accessible.

Third, *Living the Lord's Prayer* is well written. Father Albert knows how to turn a good phrase. I have written enough myself to appreciate how difficult it is to write in a way that seems natural and effortless. Father Albert did not settle for worn-out phrases and ponderous prose. His writing is terse, lively and cogent. For example, there is this: "In our relationship with God especially, we are all infants, hitchhikers waiting for grace, beggars in need of a handout. To be human is to be in need." Or this: "Constantly reminding us of our sin, the ego then condemns us to forced labor in a cemetery where we are repeatedly exhuming skeletons only to bury them and exhume them again. This is the death camp of the ego." And this: "Indeed, the feeling of abandonment *by* God is a challenge to make an act of abandonment *to* God. That's putting blind faith into action."

I commend my dear friend Father Albert for writing this book on the Lord's Prayer, and I commend his book to you, the reader, to relish it, ponder it, pray it and live it.

Gerald L. Sittser
Professor of Theology, Whitworth University
Author of *Water from a Deep Well* and *A Grace Disguised*

Preface

Guiding Spiritual Formation

ONE DAY, A DISCIPLE SAW JESUS PRAYING. After Jesus finished, the disciple said, "Lord, teach us to pray, as John taught his disciples" (Luke 11:1). Surprisingly, Jesus did not respond with a method or technique. Rather, he responded with words that captured the essence of his teaching and ministry. This prayer quickly became a treasure of the early church. Jews and Gentiles preparing for Christian baptism found out about it rather late in their formation and then, like all Christians, committed to praying it three times a day.

The prayer is found in only two Gospels (see Matthew 6:9-13; Luke 11:2-4). All Christians today pray the longer version found in Matthew. The concluding doxology ("For thine is the kingdom and the power and the glory, now and forever") does not date back to Jesus; scribes of Matthew's Gospel added it later.

Many people have looked on this text as more than simply a prayer. In his commentary on the Lord's Prayer composed around 198–200 C.E., Tertullian, a priest of the Christian community of Carthage in North Africa, referred to it as a *breviarium totius evan-*

gelii, "an abridgement of the entire Gospel." Eighteen centuries later, Rowan Williams, the Archbishop of Canterbury, wrote, "If somebody said, give me a summary of Christian faith on the back of an envelope, the best thing to do would be to write Our Lord's Prayer." Clearly, the prayer encapsulates the good news of Jesus.

Down through history, great saints and mystics have commented and reflected on this prayer. The list of names is impressive: Augustine, Francis of Assisi, Julian of Norwich, Teresa of Avila, Martin Luther, John Wesley and Simone Weil, to name a few who instantly come to mind.

Living the Lord's Prayer: The Way of the Disciple is my commentary and reflection on this prayer of Jesus. I consider the prayer to be a trustworthy guide for spiritual formation and a compact handbook for holiness. Viewed in this way, the prayer offers both interesting insights and practical tips for growing more deeply in our baptismal commitment to become *Christian,* which literally means "little Christ." To *live*—rather than to simply *say*—the words of the Lord's Prayer is to walk in the way of the disciple.

Each chapter is a reflection on one phrase of this prayer. I have chosen not to reflect on the concluding doxology, since it did not come from the mouth of Jesus and was a later scribal addition.

For each phrase, I turn to Jesus and the rich Jewish tradition that he lived and breathed, to help grasp its significance. Indeed, the prayer traditionally has been called the "Lord's Prayer" precisely because its words, attitudes and actions come straight from Jesus' life. These words, attitudes and actions set the standard and are the benchmark for us disciples to reach our truest identity as little Christs.

I also turn to great people and classics of spirituality to help illustrate how these words, attitudes and actions have been lived in the past by the great witnesses who have trod the disciple's way before us. Sometimes I tell the stories of people I have met in my life and ministry as friar, priest, spiritual director and teacher. To respect the latter's privacy, I have changed their names and the details of their stories.

I have placed reflection questions at the end of each chapter; these questions can be used for personal meditation, for spiritual direction sessions or in small-group discussions. I have also placed two references to the Gospels at the end of each chapter; these passages capture an aspect of the chapter and can be used for personal prayer.

I first met Jerry Sittser in my office at Mayslake Ministries on a cold March morning in 2008. His sincerity, humility and self-depreciating humor were not only disarming but also made me realize he's the "real deal." Upon meeting Jerry and hearing his story, you know he's been tried and tested—and yet he continues to faithfully walk the way of the disciple. I am deeply humbled and grateful that he agreed to write the foreword to this book. I could think of no one better to write it.

I hope that as we continue to pray the Lord's Prayer, we give flesh to its words by the way we live. Then and only then will we be formed into our truest identity as little Christs.

Albert Haase, O.F.M.

1

God as Father

Shaping a Healthy Image of God

A healthy image of God reflects Jesus' experience of God as Abba. It should exude God's unconditional love for us and call forth selfless acts of sacrificial love for others.

WE DO NOT KNOW EXACTLY WHEN it happened to Jesus. As a child? In adolescence? As a young adult? Sometime during his life, an insight began to blossom as a sense of his identity emerged and matured: the best way to speak about the intimate love and unconditional acceptance he experienced from the God of Israel, the transcendent Creator of the universe, was to draw on the familiar language of his own family life. He called this God by the same name he called Joseph, "Abba!"

Abba is a Jewish child's name for a father. It is used when the child is calling for a father's attention. It is also an adult's name for an elderly person who has earned reverence and respect. In both cases, the name suggests immediacy, familiarity, approachability, trust, respect and love.

Jesus was not the first to call God Father. *Father* was used in both pagan and Jewish prayers. However, calling God Abba was so distinctive of Jesus' spirituality that the apostle Paul would repeat the Aramaic word when writing to Greek-speaking Romans and Galatians (see Romans 8:15; Galatians 4:6). And what made Jesus' use of it so distinctive was a "nuance of intimacy," suggesting a special understanding and closeness to the God of Israel as a loving sustainer and provider. Unfortunately, the English translation *Father* stumbles and blubbers in carrying the familial depth and emotional weight of the original Aramaic Abba.

By calling God Abba, Jesus was trusting his personal experience of God: a profound experience of divine love and undivided divine attention. Like a new parent contemplating a firstborn, the gaze of the God of Israel was riveted on Jesus and, Jesus insisted, on each one of us: "Even the hairs of your head are all counted" (Luke 12:7).

That experience of God—and Jesus' trust in it—would shape his entire personal spirituality and catapult him into ministry. Luke has an adolescent Jesus refer to the temple in Jerusalem as his "Father's house" (Luke 2:49). Many of Jesus' parables and sayings gave his followers insights into the lavish generosity and forgiveness of his Father (see, for example, Matthew 6:25-34; 21:28-32; Luke 11:5-13; 15:11-32). In fact, those attitudes of Abba became the benchmark for a disciple's life: "Be merciful, just as your Father is merciful" (Luke 6:36). Jesus' openness and table fellowship with sinners and the marginalized clearly modeled this image of God: someone not distant and aloof but as close as a father to his children. Indeed, without the experience of God as Abba, it is impossible to understand why and how Jesus did the things he did.

Jesus' childlike intimacy with the God of Israel must have confounded and challenged people like the scribes and Pharisees, sometimes burdened with external obedience to the law.

Jesus turned their approach to spiritual formation inside out: the interior quality of the heart superseded fatted calves and burnt offerings. From Jesus' perspective, divine closeness and intimacy overshadowed the divine majesty and transcendence advocated by the Pharisees.

With an assurance that might have scandalized many pious Jews, Jesus invited his disciples to join him in this intimate relationship with the transcendent One who is "my Father and your Father" (John 20:17). When they asked him for a way to pray, Jesus taught his followers the hallowed prayer that some Christians to this day refer to as the "Our Father."

Later, with fear and trembling in the Garden of Gethsemane and on the cross, Jesus might have agonized over whether or not he had deceived himself in trusting in this intimate experience of God as Abba. He prayed Psalm 22, which betrayed his feeling of being abandoned: "My God, my God, why have you forsaken me?" (v. 1; Mark 15:34). It also betrayed his hope of vindication: "In you our ancestors trusted; they trusted, and you delivered them" (v. 4). In the end, Jesus moved beyond his feelings and surrendered with trust: "Father, into your hands I commend my spirit" (Luke 23:46).

The Easter proclamation is a stunning declaration that Jesus was not disappointed or delusional: "Why do you look for the living among the dead? He is not here, but has risen" (Luke 24:5).

OUR IMAGE OF GOD

In a spiritual direction session, Edward shared with me the tragedy of a couple he had known for a long time. The story is so painfully heartbreaking that it seems fabricated; unfortunately, it is not. This couple lost their sixteen-year-old son in a hunting accident. As a result, the mother became a virtual recluse. For many months, she stopped attending both church services and family gatherings.

It took more than two years for the mother to return to her previous routine. Twenty years later, while her husband was hunting, the woman sobbed as she watched firemen trying to save her burning house. That same night she also learned that her husband had died of a heart attack.

Edward told me that he just couldn't understand why this woman had been suddenly visited with a tragedy of such magnitude. He decided that he would have a dialogue with God in his spiritual journal to see if he could make sense of this tragedy.

When he returned for spiritual direction a month later, I followed up on this issue. He told me that it all made perfect sense. "God clearly did not want the woman to become a recluse again and stop going to church. So, when He decided to call her husband home, He had her house destroyed. That way she wouldn't be able to hide from the world."

I challenged Edward on his rational explanation of this devastating tragedy. I told him that didn't sound like the God whom Jesus called Abba. I added that I personally would find it extremely difficult to believe in and trust—much less love—such a cruel, unfeeling God.

That spiritual direction session reminded me once again that our image of God is one of the most, if not *the* most, important aspects of our spiritual formation. Our God-image shapes and colors everything about our personal spirituality, from why we pray to how we understand personal suffering and evil in the world. Edward's explanation speaks volumes about his image of God: cold, aloof and apparently unfriendly.

Unhealthy images of God elicit unhealthy behavior and can be the very reason some of us walk at a snail's pace and drag our feet when it comes to spiritual formation. Frankly, some God-images leave us frightened and cowering in the corner.

I once attended the wake of a woman who had such a God-image. She died at the age of eighty-nine. Sadly, most of her life had been spent guilt-ridden over a promiscuous past, fearing death and terrified by the thought of facing God. At the wake, one of her friends commented to me, "You know, Irene would have been a different person if only she had had a different God. Unfortunately, the God she believed in carried a big stick and was hard as nails."

To name God as Father in the Lord's Prayer is to commit to having a healthy image of God. That is both a challenge and a grace. Such an image brings out the very best in us and helps us discover our truest identity. It coaxes us to be transparent, to lovingly open ourselves to every single moment that calls for self-sacrifice and self-forgetfulness. And indeed, that's the fingerprint of a Christian, "a little Christ," and an excellent way to define holiness: selfless, sacrificial love for others as an expression and response to God's love in our lives, to be as close to others as a father to his children. Again, the attitude of Abba becomes the measure and benchmark for the way of the disciple.

CHILDISH GODS

For us to live up to this call to holiness, our image of God must be able to draw out our deepest goodness and help us transcend the boundaries of the ego with its self-centered concerns. What kind of God-images do that?

Certainly, childish images of God as a stern teacher waiting to rap our knuckles with a ruler or a state trooper who sets speed trap after speed trap on the interstate highway of life do not. I encounter such images time and time again. As a Roman Catholic priest, my heart sinks when I meet the excessively scrupulous person who feels the need to go to confession twice a week "so I won't burn in hell." As a spiritual director, I raise an eyebrow when the Methodist pastor comes to me and says, "I had the car accident because God is punishing me for my inattentiveness to my wife and children." Such God-images leave us self-absorbed and self-centered.

So many of these images come to us from our childhood, our parents and what we heard preached from the pulpit at critical times in our lives. Remember how some were saying in the late eighties that AIDS was God's punishment on a sinful lifestyle? Or that the terrorist attacks of 9/11 were divine judgment on a secularist country that no longer trusted in God?

The late Basil Hume, a Roman Catholic cardinal of England, once told a story about the God-image offered to him in his childhood. His mother wanted to teach him self-discipline, so she called him into the kitchen and said, "Son, I have just finished baking some delicious cookies, and I've put them into this cookie jar. I'm going to leave this cookie jar right here on the table. But don't you dare sneak in here and eat any of them. Remember: God is watching you!"

For years, young Basil Hume lived in fear of the ever-watchful "God of the cookie jar." Then one day, long after he had become a Benedictine monk and was ordained a priest, it suddenly dawned on him: if he had snuck into the kitchen and put his hand into that cookie jar and secretly eaten one of those cookies, God would have looked down from heaven and said, "Basil, they're so good! Have another one!"

Cardinal Hume's story emphasizes a basic fact of spiritual formation sometimes inadvertently overlooked: God is vitally interested and invested in each one of us. God is as close to us as a father to his children. So much so, Jesus says, that Abba clothes us with a splendor greater than Solomon's and provides us with food and drink (see Luke 12:22-29). He says his Abba will respond with "good things" to those who ask (see Matthew 7:7-11). The depth of this caring interest and concern for us can be described only in the language of the deepest human experience: "[God] first loved us" (1 John 4:19). Hume's "God of the chocolate chip cookie" comes closer to Jesus' Abba than the cold, frightening "policeman of the cookie jar" some of us imagine God to be.

ADULT IMAGES OF GOD

We do not let go of our childhood images of God easily. They are rooted deep in our bones. If those early images are oddly distorted or downright unhealthy, our spiritual life in adulthood, if it exists at all, can be adversely affected.

Many people find themselves at the same crossroad as Hume: having to choose between "the policeman of the cookie jar" handed down to them or the "God of the chocolate chip cookie" revealed in their personal experience. This is similar to Jesus being taught about the distant, transcendent Creator of the universe, and yet having a personal experience of God as Abba, as close as a father is to his child. It is so much easier to believe in the God-image that one has been given in the home or classroom. That's why I have come to respect people who take the great leap of faith and place their trust in the personal revelations of God in their lives. My own experience revealed to me just how much of a gamble this can be.

As a child, I worshiped the ground my father walked on. Of his three sons and two daughters, I always felt I had a special bond with him. When I was thirteen, my father committed suicide. That gunshot wound not only killed my father, it also shattered the image of God I had been given early in life. The all-powerful, ever-present God given to me by my grammar-school education not only appeared powerless before my tragedy but also seemed coldly disinterested and far away.

One day in my mid-twenties, after years of searching for a father's love, I cried out in prayer to the God of my childhood, to that all-powerful, ever-present God of my youth. I demanded an explanation, reasons, an answer to the "why?" that continued to gnaw away at my soul.

And the response to my prayer? Silence. Cold indifference. An unconcerned, unsympathetic presence—maybe I should say absence. My childhood God seemed preoccupied with other concerns—or maybe even dead.

But then something happened. Out of the blue I felt myself surrounded by a loving comfort and a protective care I had never before experienced. It felt as if someone was cradling me in tender arms and holding me tight. I felt divine tears of compassion flowing over my heart. Though the pain and memory of my father's death were still very much present, I knew I wasn't alone in my suffering. And indeed, I wasn't. On a Thursday afternoon in 1981, my personal God—the Abba of Albert Haase—revealed selfless, unconditional love and compassion for me.

That experience has radically changed and shaped my personal image of God. I no longer think of God as a cold, aloof Creator who has abandoned me here on earth. I no longer believe God to be an insensitive judge who nonchalantly rules all creation heartlessly. My new God-image has been carved out of my wound and based on an experience of God's love and compassion for me. My image of God is getting closer to the Abba of Jesus—a God of selfless, sacrificial love and consolation who continually surrounds me in the protective air of the divine presence. God nurtures and nourishes me in times of pain and loneliness; God offers me strength and courage when I need them. God is so close to me that my other needs are often anticipated before I myself am aware of them.

And over the past twenty-five years, as I have crisscrossed the country preaching and have lived as a missionary among the Chinese in mainland China, my God-image has been touched up, refined and reformed. Just when I think I have grasped the reality of

God, I am reminded again that my image is just that, an image.

Our images of God change over time and with experience. We outgrow them like we do our clothes and shoes. Over and over again, we learn never to become too comfortable with our images, as if to suggest that we have captured God or figured God out. God-images are like photographs. They lamely capture in one dimension the most superficial aspects of the selfless, loving ground of reality that we know as God.

ABBA'S UNCONDITIONAL LOVE

It is crucial that our images of God exude the unconditional love of God that formed the cornerstone of Jesus' experience of God as Abba. Without that, our God-image is way off the mark and downright inaccurate. Or, to put it another way, if it does not convey unconditional love, our God-image is a hollow, plastic statue worthy of a yard sale.

The earliest Gospel tells us that at his baptism, Jesus had a profound experience of Abba's investment in his life, of unconditional love and of being the beloved: "You are my Son, the Beloved; with you I am well pleased" (Mark 1:11).

We, too, by baptismal incorporation into the life and death of Christ, share in Jesus' graced relationship to Abba. We are called and chosen as the beloved, who share in the same unconditional love Jesus experienced at his baptism. Divine adoption makes each one of us a child of God, having the freedom to address God as "Abba! Father!" (see Romans 8:15).

"But I'm a sinner! I don't deserve God's love! And how dare I call God a name steeped in such familiarity and intimacy?" Many of us say this in our own way. And it might be true. But we have already captured Abba's attention. We are indeed loved unconditionally as Abba's beloved.

This is one of the most difficult facts to absorb in spiritual formation. The unconditional love of Abba is so mind-boggling, in fact, that some people try to rationalize away the "unconditional" part. They say that God loves them *as long as* they are good, *as long as* they tithe, *as long as* they obey all the commandments. They believe that divine love is conditional and that they have to live up to certain requirements to be confident of it. "God cannot love me, because I struggle with anger" or "I'll have to change my ways before God could ever take a serious interest in me" or "How can God possibly love someone like me, who hasn't been to church in years?"

As the apostle Paul reminded the Romans, "But God proves his love for us in that while we still were sinners Christ died for us" (Romans 5:8). That demonstrates a startling fact: God loves us not because we are good but because God is good. It is as simple as that.

The American actor John Wayne was married three times and divorced twice. He had seven children. All his wives were Roman Catholics. His children were raised in the Catholic faith. But the "Duke" himself was never baptized.

However, a week before he died on June 11, 1979, while literally on his deathbed, he apparently had a spiritual conversion. He asked to be baptized a Roman Catholic. And he was given a full Catholic funeral.

Some conservative Catholics were shocked and scandalized: "How unfair!" they said. "How could any priest in good conscience baptize such a terrible person?" Others seemed to be envious: "That was one lucky cowboy! He was able to live a sinful life and then have a priest show up forty-eight hours before he died. It's amazing what money and fame can do."

John Wayne's deathbed conversion is a real-life example of God's lavish and generous love. And that was exactly the point of the parable of the workers in the vineyard (see Matthew 20:1-16). In that parable, Jesus compares the kingdom of heaven to a landowner who at five different times in a single day went out to hire laborers for his vineyard. When the laborers were paid, those hired at five o'clock, and who clearly had worked for only one hour, walked away with the full day's wage. Seeing this, those hired at dawn presumed they would get more money. They grumbled when they received exactly what had been agreed on as a daily wage. The landowner replied to their complaints, "Take what belongs to you and go; I choose to give to this last the same as I give to you. Am I not allowed to do what I choose with what belongs to me? Or are you envious because I am generous?" (Matthew 20:14-15).

Jesus' listeners would have known a version of this parable found in the rabbinical tradition. However, in that version, the workers hired last got a full day's wage *precisely because* they had worked extraordinarily hard.

Jesus' version, found only in the Gospel of Matthew, doesn't mention that crucial detail. The reason is obvious: Jesus' version is about the lavish generosity of God's unconditional love. That's why some scholars have suggested that the parable be titled "the good employer" or "the affirmative action employer."

Unlike our human love, the love of God is not fickle and conditional, based on expectations and hidden agendas. God's love is not some return for our hard work. Nor is it payment for services rendered, such as acts of charity. Rather, it is literally like the air we breathe in and exhale. God's love "makes his sun rise on the evil and on the good, and sends rain on the righteous and on the unrighteous" (Matthew 5:45). Indeed, its lavish generosity is celebrated in John Wayne's deathbed conversion and in Paul's passionate reminder to the Romans:

I am convinced that neither death, nor life, nor angels, nor rulers, nor things present, nor things to come, nor powers,

nor height, nor depth, nor anything else in all creation, will
be able to separate us from the love of God in Christ Jesus
our Lord. (Romans 8:38-39)

We, like Jesus, are first and foremost the beloved. Awareness of
such extravagant unconditional love calls forth from us selfless
acts of sacrificial love for others.

LOVE MADE FLESH

Anselm of Canterbury wrote *Cur Deus Homo?* ("Why Did God Become Man?") in the eleventh century. It had a monumental effect
on Christian theology. In this work, Anselm posited a rational
necessity for Christ's incarnation. He began by stating that human
sin wounded God's honor. Because God is infinite, the wound to
God's honor was infinite. Divine justice demanded satisfaction,
yet humanity's dilemma was that, being finite, it was incapable of
providing the required satisfaction for the infinite wound. Consequently, only God could pay any act of satisfaction. Yet, as a pen-
alty for humanity, it had to be paid under the form of human flesh.
Anselm then reasoned that satisfaction was possible only through
the sinless God-man. Because the God-man was exempt from the
punishment of sin, Christ's passion and death were voluntary. The
merit of the act was therefore infinite, God's justice was thus ap-
peased, and divine mercy was able to extend to humanity.

Anselm's theory has shaped so much of Roman Catholic and
evangelical theology. The image of God embedded in such a logical argument is a God who insists on justice and satisfaction and
yet, at the same time, is willing to provide the very means to have
both justice and satisfaction rendered. Anselm's God seems better
suited for the courtroom than for the heart of a disciple. More
strikingly, God's greatest gift to the universe, the Son, is only occasioned by the sinfulness of humanity.

Two centuries after Anselm, the great Franciscan theologian of the thirteenth century, John Duns Scotus, offered a radically different understanding of Christmas that has framed Franciscan spirituality down through the ages. Scotus believed that the incarnation was not a divine after-thought, occasioned by human sin. Rather, from the very beginning of creation, when the Spirit of the living God breathed over the abyss and drew forth light, Jesus as the light of the world was already in the mind of God. "God's Masterpiece," as Scotus called the incarnate Person of the Son, was always intended, even before the historical creation of the universe and the reality of human sinfulness. Without Christ, creation would be incomplete. Indeed, according to Scotus, Christ is the beginning, middle and end of all creation. This is technically known as the "Doctrine of the Absolute Primacy of Christ in the Universe" and demonstrates that God-made-flesh is first and foremost a demonstration of self-effusive divine love. Because human sinfulness did in fact become a reality, the incarnation took place in the mode of a suffering, crucified and glorified Christ who overcame, as one scholar puts it, "the humanly constructed obstacles to achieving God's first aim: the sharing of divine life and love with creation."

The Franciscan image of God is a fountain-fullness of selfless love, of a divine love whose very nature is to move beyond and outward. Clearly, divine love comes before divine justice. That love is experienced in daily life and calls forth the same selfless, sacrificial love from the heart of every disciple. Again, the attitude and actions of the Father become the disciple's measure and standard of living.

SEEN WITH THE EYES OF GOD

When twenty-seven-year-old Joseph first sought me out for counseling, he was very depressed. He was drinking too much and pushing his luck at the casino. His self-esteem had clearly hit rock bottom. We met only twice. He never showed up for his third appointment.

Then, a year later, I happened to run into Joseph in a shopping mall. I was surprised. The Joseph I had worried about and so often prayed for seemed no longer to exist. Here was a new Joseph: confident, at peace with himself and with a wonderful sparkle in his eyes. The more we talked, the more my curiosity got the best of me.

"Joseph, what's happened to you? You seem different." I really wanted to say "changed."

He coaxed me with a bag of popcorn to sit down on a bench in front of a department store. And with the reverence of a newly ordained minister proclaiming the Scriptures, Joseph began telling me about Mary Jo.

"I guess she just took a shine to me at first. It really wasn't mutual. And it certainly wasn't love at first sight. But we talked on the phone, did some dating and, somewhere along the line, she blurted out, 'I think I'm in love with you, Joseph.'

"To be honest, Father, that's when I first really noticed Mary Jo. And a funny thing started happening after she said that. It was like a heavy weight was suddenly taken off my shoulders, like someone freed me from prison. I stopped fighting against life and came out of my depression. I started going back to church. Her love not only challenged me to accept myself but, as a result of it, I gradually became the person I guess I'm meant to be. I went for professional counseling and that opened up the whole new world of feelings and emotions for me. And the next thing I knew, I was in love!"

A few minutes later, with tears in his eyes, Joseph added a profound statement that initially passed me by. "When I now think about that first time Mary Jo told me she loved me, I can't help but think that she was seeing me with the eyes of God."

And indeed, she was. Joseph's experience of Mary Jo's love—anyone's experience of human love—is not somehow "like" the experience of God's love. It *is* the love of God, though always incomplete and at times even distorted. Loving hearts are the opened floodgates of God's love. Whenever a person says to us, "I love you," we catch a glimmer of how God looks on us.

A number of years ago, while visiting the United Kingdom, I heard an Anglican priest preach a beautiful insight in her Christmas sermon. She mentioned that the story of the incarnation betrays the divine disposition toward us and reveals the divine dynamic that continues to go on in this life: Abba's unconditional, selfless love for each one of us takes on flesh and blood in our spouses, our families and our friends. That awareness gets us walking the way of the disciple with selfless, sacrificial love for others.

THE MOTHERHOOD OF GOD

The ancient Hebrews did not balk at using feminine imagery to speak of God. Their term for a woman's womb was often used to describe divine compassion. Furthermore, the prophet Isaiah compared God's selfless, sacrificial love for us to that of a mother's for the child of her womb (see Isaiah 49:15). He also stated that God comforts us as a mother comforts her child (see Isaiah 66:13).

In spite of the patriarchal society in which he was reared, Jesus had an appreciation for his ancestors' sensitivity to the feminine dimension of God. He compared the forgiveness of God to a woman who woke up late at night and swept her house in search of her lost coin (see Luke 15:8-10). Speaking of divine providence, Jesus said God feeds the birds and helps the wildflowers to grow (see Matthew 6:26, 28-30; Luke 12:22-31), two traditional tasks of women in Jewish, Greek and Roman society. He compared God's reign over us to the yeast kneaded into dough by women (see Matthew 13:33; Luke 13:20-21).

Like Isaiah and Jesus, many Christians have continued to use feminine imagery to speak of God. In the second century, Clement of Alexandria described the eternal Word of God as both a father and a mother. In the fourteenth century, the English mystic Julian of Norwich wrote at length about God's maternal love and fertile creativity, about God being our "natural Father" and our "natural Mother." Pope John Paul I, in his noontime Angelus address of September 10, 1978, said, "God is our Father. Even more, God is our Mother."

In fact, neither the image of God as father nor the image of God as mother says everything there is to say about the nature of God. Each actually focuses our attention on just one divine trait and, as a result, can distort the divine nature. Like the seven blind men who each touched a different part of the elephant's body and then thought their particular description of the animal was accurate, we think our images for God describe the reality of the Divine. But they don't. In fact, when we think we have discovered the perfect image for God, we have discovered only a carnival mask that hides more than it reveals.

> *All the perfections of created things are also in God; and therefore He is at once Father and Mother. As Father He stands in solitary might surrounded by darkness. As Mother His shining is diffused, embracing all His creatures with merciful tenderness and light.*
>
> THOMAS MERTON

The Abba of Jesus transcends all human gender characteristics, categories and distinctions. And yet, only an image of God that absorbs and incorporates what we traditionally refer to as masculine *and* feminine characteristics can approximate the God whom Jesus experienced. The Abba of Jesus is strong, yet tender; loving and compassionate; indulgent, yet protective—the very best of the masculine and the very best of the feminine. God is selfless, sacrificial love, who incarnates that unconditional love in human flesh.

THE CONVERSION OF FRANCIS OF ASSISI

Our knowledge of the young Francis of Assisi is unfortunately colored by the pen of an author writing the story of a newly canonized saint. Literary convention and medieval writing techniques play critical roles. Nevertheless, scholars are still able to get a sense of the external events of his conversion. And perhaps not surprisingly, Francis's emerging image of God was an important factor in it.

For twenty-five years, the young Francis squandered both time and money. He outdid his friends in vanity, vainglory, popularity and fine clothes. Francis focused his creative energies on making a name for himself. His proud, extravagant father must have been pleased to see his son living according to the values he was given.

A member of the rising merchant class by birth, Francis wanted the prestige of the nobility. Though his common blood would deny him the fulfillment of that desire, he could attain it superficially by becoming a knight. And so he did. However, in the battle with the rival town of Perugia, Francis was taken prisoner and spent a year in jail.

Upon his release, he returned home. He was depressed, restless and searching. The story goes that he spent an inordinate amount of time alone, struggling to find meaning in life.

An encounter with lepers, the most marginalized and feared of all the societal outcasts of his day, softened his heart and challenged the value system given to him by his father. In a dramatic scene, Francis stood before the bishop of Assisi and renounced the clothing, possessions and inheritance given him by his father. A short, telling speech placed in the mouth of the saint speaks to the fact that he was surrendering himself to an emerging image of God:

> From now on I will say freely: "Our Father who art in heaven," and not "My father, Pietro di Bernardone." Look, not only do I return his money; I give him back all my clothes. I will go to the Lord naked.

We do not know what image of God Francis possessed before his conversion. If he had one at all, it probably did not elicit any great emotional response from him. What did elicit a response, though, was his father's lesson that happiness was found in experiencing and hoarding the pleasures and treasures of the world. The young Francis had believed that.

However, at twenty-five, Francis's own experience began to betray the lie of his father's selfish values. So Francis began to renounce those values. In doing so, he began to open himself to an experience of God as the divine Almsgiver who provided for all his needs, both physical and emotional. Like Jesus' and many of our own, Francis's image of God was carved from his own personal experience.

THE POWER OF AN IMAGE

Sunday after Sunday we go to church. And there we find as many different images of God as there are people in the congregation. Whether we are consciously aware of it or not, each of us has painted an image of God on our heart. That image is framed by the experiences of our past and shaped by our present situation.

If our God-image is healthy and rooted in Jesus' teaching of an unconditionally loving God being as close to us as a father to his child, it can change and transform us. That's what happened in the life of Francis of Assisi. A healthy God-image will call forth selfless, sacrificial love for others and thus lead us to our truest identity as little Christs.

And so, as different as our personal God-images are, nevertheless, we stand united as the beloved as we pray and live the words "Our Father . . . "

REFLECTION QUESTIONS

1. How has my image of God changed over the years? What experiences have challenged and shaped it?

2. How does my present image of God elicit selfless, sacrificial love for others?

3. What experiences in my life have reminded me that I am the beloved of God?

4. What role do I believe God plays in my personal suffering and the tragedies witnessed in the world?

5. What experiences in my life suggest the masculine dimension of God? The feminine dimension of God? The fact that God transcends all human gender characteristics?

Gospel Passages for Meditation and Prayer: Matthew 6:26-34; Luke 15:8-10

"Our" Father

Recognizing the Family of All Creation

The first word of the Lord's Prayer reminds us of our relationship with others and with the wider family of creation. The way of the disciple is the way of love, intercession and hospitality.

I HAVE PREACHED ON THE AFRICAN continent a couple of times. Its exotic beauty and the way human beings and animals live side-by-side continually move me. As a Westerner, I am always disarmed and challenged by the practical implications of the African understanding of community.

Traditional African culture, unlike Western culture with its emphasis on individualism, believes relationships are critical in the discovery of who we truly are. This belief is enshrined in the concept of *Ubuntu*, which states that through our interaction with others, we discover what it means to be human. According to a Zulu expression, a person becomes a person through other people. Archbishop Desmond Tutu says that *Ubuntu* points to what is best about the human condition:

[Ubuntu] is the essence of being human. It speaks of the fact that my humanity is caught up and is inextricably bound up in yours. I am human because I belong. It speaks about wholeness, it speaks about compassion. A person with Ubuntu is welcoming, hospitable, warm and generous, willing to share. Such people are open and available to others, willing to be vulnerable, affirming of others, do not feel threatened that others are able and good, for they have a proper self-assurance that comes from knowing that they belong in a greater whole. They know that they are diminished when others are humiliated, diminished when others are oppressed, diminished when others are treated as if they were less than who they are. The quality of Ubuntu gives people resilience, enabling them to survive and emerge still human despite all efforts to dehumanize them.

Nelson Mandela explained the practical consequences and ramifications of *Ubuntu*:

A traveller through our country would stop at a village, and he didn't have to ask for food or for water. Once he stops, the people give him food, entertain him. That is one aspect of Ubuntu but Ubuntu has various aspects. Ubuntu does not mean that people should not enrich themselves. The question therefore is: Are you going to do so in order to enable the community around you to improve?

Clearly, from Mandela's point of view, this traditional concept points to a sensitivity and awareness of the needs of others. Indeed, it is humanity focused on others. It therefore suggests self-forgetfulness as the highest expression of humanity—the "fingerprint" of Christ's disciple. Mandela's rhetorical question also suggests that *Ubuntu* points to the common good, to improving the life of the entire community.

The first word of the Lord's Prayer honors *Ubuntu* as a critical factor in spiritual formation. It confronts and challenges the belief that the Christian life is a quaint little individualistic affair between "me and Jesus." It also reveals one of the great illuminations in spiritual formation: all creatures, both rational and irrational, are our brothers and sisters.

GOD AS TRINITY

One of the first mysteries of the faith that many of us were taught as children is that God is Trinity: Father, Son and Holy Spirit. This mystery alerted us to the relational quality of divinity. The Father loves the Son; the Son loves the Father; and their very relationship is bonded together by the Holy Spirit. The very essence of our God is loving relationships. "God is love" (1 John 4:8).

That doctrine makes an important statement about the way of the disciple. For if we are created in the image and likeness of this trinitarian God, we too must be in loving relationships. This insight lies at the very heart of the oldest account of creation found in the Hebrew Scriptures. Eve is built up around one of Adam's ribs. Adam and Eve complement and complete one another. In relationship to each other, they discover their truest identity: "Therefore a man leaves his father and mother and clings to his wife, and they become one flesh" (Genesis 2:24). This is *Ubuntu*.

Jesus also emphasized the importance of relationships in his understanding of spiritual formation. He combined two Mosaic laws into the "greatest commandment": love of God (Deuteronomy 6:5) and love of neighbor (Leviticus 19:18; Mark 12:29-31). One love complements and completes the other love. In the words of the first letter of John,

Those who say, "I love God," and hate their brothers or sisters, are liars; for those who do not love a brother or sister whom they have seen, cannot love God whom they have not seen. The commandment we have from him is this: those who love God must love their brothers and sisters also. (1 John 4:20-21)

In other words, love of God is expressed in love of neighbor; love of neighbor celebrates the experience of God's love. They are the two sides of the coin of spiritual formation. This speaks directly to my understanding of holiness and the way of the disciple: performing selfless acts of sacrificial love for others in response to the love of Abba experienced in our lives. This is the self-forgetfulness and orientation toward the common good that *Ubuntu* is all about. And this brings us to the very threshold of God's kingdom, as Jesus remarked to a wise scribe (see Mark 12:28-34).

ENGAGEMENT WITH THE WORLD

An unorthodox strain of Christianity that is suspicious of the world, the neighbor and the flesh continually rears its head. It suggests that the world and the flesh tie us down and hinder us from experiencing God. It is cloaked behind the simple statement that Christians are to be "in the world, but not of the world." This expression has its roots in John's Gospel (see John 17:14, 16) and has subsequently been misinterpreted to mean the world is Satan's playground and Christians should not invest themselves in it. Instead, Christians should emotionally and psychologically withdraw and disengage from the world.

A spiritual work of the early fifteenth century, *The Imitation of Christ,* attributed to Thomas à Kempis, is probably the best-known text of spiritual devotion in the Western world, second only to the Bible. Its influence on spiritual formation has been enormous. In the Roman Catholic tradition, it has played a central role in the spiritual formation of people like Thomas More, Ignatius Loyola,

Francis de Sales, Alphonsus de Liguori and Thérèse of Lisieux. Within the Protestant tradition, John Wesley and John Newton mentioned its influence at the time of their conversions.

The influence of *The Imitation of Christ* has also been unfortunate. In reacting against a medieval spirituality that had become highly speculative and intellectual, the text promoted an inward-looking spirituality based on withdrawal from the world and a strong negative view of oneself, other people and things. Two short quotes from the text give a sense of its perspective on spiritual formation:

> The greatest saints guarded their time alone and chose to serve God in solitude. Someone has said, "As often as I went out among men, I returned less of a man." We often experience this when we have spent a long time in idle chatter. It is easier to stay at home than to be properly on guard outside the monastery. A person whose goal is the inward, spiritual life must cast his lot with Jesus and not follow the crowd.

> That person is truly blessed who understands what it is to love Jesus and to serve him with deep humility. Jesus wishes to be loved above all things; everything else must come second. The love of anything other than Jesus is deceptive and fickle; the love of Jesus is faithful and enduring. The person who clings to anything other than Jesus falls with its falling; the person who embraces Jesus stands firm forever. Love Jesus and keep him as your friend. When all things fade he will not abandon you, nor will he allow you to perish in the end.

Though solitude and a single-hearted love of Jesus are laudatory and necessary for spiritual maturity, as these two passages suggest, they become suspect when they promote an expression of Christianity that is blatantly dualistic ("God and the world are incompatible"), individualistic ("me and Jesus") and disengaged from the world ("not of the world"). Surprisingly, as we mature in our vocation as little Christs, we find ourselves becoming more and more engaged with the world and its struggles.

When Thomas Merton entered the walled cloister of the Cistercian monastery, he was a severe young monk who had truly renounced the world. His choice for God and the monastery meant a renunciation of humanity and Madison Avenue. Typical of the Catholic piety of the 1940s, this early period of his religious life was marked by a rigid and arbitrary separation between God and the world.

As Merton matured spiritually, however, he realized that the monk is called to a relationship with the world. Also created in the image of God, the monk is meant to be relational. Living as a hermit for the last two years of his life, Merton kept the windows of his hermitage open to the world. He wrote about the scandal of nuclear arms, the Vietnam War and the volatile race relations between African Americans and whites in the South. His vocation as a Christian demanded that he be in the world and relating to the world. He prayed with one eye on Scripture and the other on the daily newspaper. To quote the title of one of his poems, Merton lived his life "with the world in [his] blood stream."

THE PRAYER OF INTERCESSION

We, too, are called to stand before Abba with the world in our blood streams. Our truest identity feels pity and compassion for the worries and concerns of others—and as little Christs, we intercede for the world.

Many people mistakenly believe that the purpose of intercessory prayer is to change the mind of God or to make God aware of a particular problem that needs special attention. We might even think of it as a rain dance, as praying through a megaphone, as strong-arming God or saying "abracadabra" to pull a rabbit out of a hat. But that understanding is rooted in the image of a distant, aloof God, not our Abba, who is as close to us, the beloved, as a father to his children.

Intercessory prayer is an expression of our engagement with the world. It is one of the many ways to take a stand against war, to dispel our suspicions and fears about the so-called enemy and to strengthen our resolve to work for justice, peace and the integrity of creation. Intercessory prayer is an expression of *Ubuntu*. It proclaims that Abba is "our" Father and spiritual formation is about God, others and me.

The absence of the prayer of intercession in our daily devotions is a poignant indicator that we have veered off the way of the disciple. Christian disciples are incapable of praying with eyes closed to the sufferings of the world, with ears deaf to the cries of the hungry and with hearts insensitive to the sobs of those who have lost a lifetime in a tsunami, a forest fire or a hurricane. The first word of the Lord's Prayer reminds us that our prayer must move beyond the egotistical boundaries of "me."

SPLANCHNIZEIN

The importance of compassionate intercession was one of the points Jesus was trying to make in his parable about the good Samaritan (see Luke 10:29-37). A man is robbed and left to die in a ditch. Two law-observant Jews, a priest and a Levite, perhaps fearing that the man is dead and not willing to risk ritual impurity should they touch him, deliberately pass him by. But then a foreigner, a Samaritan, comes along. Considered an outcast by Judaism, this Samaritan no doubt knows the feeling of being left behind to die. He offers a hand of mercy and a heart of compassion that go beyond mere charity and philanthropy. We can almost hear him say to the man in the ditch, "I know what it's like. I've been there."

This parable challenges any kind of "institutional piety" that is content to reduce the spiritual life to an individualistic, private affair. With an incisive critique, Jesus highlights the inability of rigid observance of the law to bring forth selfless acts of sacrificial love for others. In many ways, this parable is a commentary on the words written later in the first letter of John, "Those who say, 'I love God,' and hate their brothers and sisters, are liars" (1 John 4:20).

So many people are currently left behind in the ditch by institutional churches, governments and society. There is always a group of people marginalized in such a way that so-called Christians consider them "untouchables," unworthy of Abba's unconditional love. Perhaps that is why Jesus, in the very center of institutional Judaism, the temple, challenged the sense of legalistic and institutional holiness of the chief priests and elders when he said, "Truly I tell you, the tax collectors and the prostitutes are going into the kingdom of God ahead of you" (Matthew 21:31). Abba's selfless, sacrificial love breaks through the dikes and surges over the levees put up by any institution. It was this very insight, perhaps, that motivated the Canaanite woman to challenge Jesus' initial understanding of his mission as only and exclusively to Israel (see Matthew 15:21-28); it was also at the heart of the early church's understanding that "God shows no partiality," which led to the baptism of Gentiles (see Acts 10:34-48).

The Greek verb Jesus uses for the good Samaritan's mercy and compassion is *splanchnizein*. It is the same word the writers of the Gospels use to describe Jesus' pity and compassion (see Matthew 9:36; 15:32; 20:34; Mark 1:41; 6:34; 8:2; Luke 10:33).

The Greek *splanchnizein* is derived from the noun for "entrails," "bowels," "guts," as the seat of the emotions. The Greek word also connotes a feminine quality because it is occasionally associated with the Hebrew word *rechem*, "womb." Compassionate intercession therefore emerges from the place where life begins.

Authentic compassion and intercession are the natural and spontaneous responses of disciples as they live in and relate to the world. They feel in their depths the pains and sorrows of others as they struggle to live a fuller dimension of life. Disciples respond with the power of prayer and love. This response helps to lift up those left behind in the ditch. Disciples are constantly in labor as they struggle to perform selfless acts of sacrificial love for others in response to Abba's love and compassion.

TRANSFORMING STONE INTO FLESH

Because I was left behind by suicide, I have experienced compassion's life-giving power as I listen to others struggling to get on with their lives after the suicide of a loved one. Delores was left behind by an older brother whom she loved dearly. Shirley was tangled in guilt over the suicide of her son, Michael. Peter struggled to survive after the suicide of his wife, Alice. In each and every instance, I simply sat, listened and lived through the pain of my own father's suicide all over again. And my com-passion ("suffering with") brought forth a fuller experience of life for Delores, Shirley and Peter.

Every day the labor pains of intercession and compassion are giving life to others. Ed acts as a sponsor for another recovering alcoholic in Alcoholics Anonymous. Julia, widowed last year, pauses to write a tender note of sympathy to Ruth, who has just lost her husband. Through a multitude of twelve-step programs and support groups, people help one another sort through the emotional damage that has them feeling as if they are left in a ditch. In each and every case, one person's pain and suffering becomes life giving, "redemptive," for someone else.

Remember your suffering. It need not be in vain. It can become the womb of compassion.

Compassion makes us aware of who we truly are as it bonds us to others in relationships. We experience the African concept of *Ubuntu* as our eyes are opened to our truest identity and to the family of humanity. Such compassion makes our hearts more loving, more tender and, in the end, more human. Compassion changes a heart of stone into a heart of flesh. It is a practical witness to the world that God is "our" Abba.

THE HEART OF HOLINESS

Jesus demonstrated the communal nature of holiness, challenging the very foundation of traditional Jewish piety, the observance of the law. The Gospels note instances when Jesus disagreed with the legalistic interpretation of one of the commandments or the cultural and social restrictions forbidding public conversations with foreigners and women (see Mark 2:23–3:6; John 4:4-30). He touched those considered "untouchable," like the dead and lepers, and allowed the marginalized, like a hemorrhaging women and children, to get close to him (see Matthew 8:3; 9:20-23; 19:14).

Such transgressions against a legalistic mentality were deliberate. When questioned about his disciples' lack of attention to the ritual purity laws of Judaism, Jesus explained his perspective:

> Listen to me, all of you, and understand: there is nothing outside a person that by going in can defile, but the things that come out are what defile. . . . For it is from within, from the human heart, that evil intentions come: fornication, theft, murder, adultery, avarice, wickedness, deceit, licentiousness, envy, slander, pride, folly. All these evil things come from within, and they defile a person. (Mark 7:14-15, 21-23)

These sins originate from the lack of loving relationships or caring involvement in the lives of others; from the unwillingness to perform selfless acts of sacrificial love in response to the love of

Abba in our lives; from a loss of *Ubuntu*. They point to a selfish, insensitive, possessive and defensive heart.

According to Jesus, holiness is about living the two sides of the "greatest commandment": love of God and love of neighbor. That is the way of the disciple. The more our hearts are open and attached to the needs and desires of the poor, the hungry, the disadvantaged and the marginalized, the more we reflect our truest identity as little Christs. And the more we express our heart's attachment in any form of intercession or compassion, the more we show our gratitude for the unconditional love that Abba has, in fact, shared with us, the beloved.

Jesus challenges us to move beyond a "contract approach" to holiness. Legalistic concerns about obeying laws and commandments are not enough. Indeed, there is something more important than obedience to the law. On at least two occasions, Jesus drove this point home with the Pharisees (see Matthew 9:10-13; Mark 2:23-28).

The apostle Paul understood this. To those Galatians tempted to place their religious justification on the fulfillment of the law of circumcision, he wrote:

> You who want to be justified by the law have cut yourselves off from Christ; you have fallen away from grace. For through the Spirit, by faith, we eagerly wait for the hope of righteousness. For in Christ Jesus neither circumcision nor uncircumcision counts for anything; the only thing that counts is faith working through love. . . . For you were called to freedom, brothers and sisters; only do not use your freedom as an opportunity for self-indulgence, but through love become slaves to one another. For the whole law is summed up in a single commandment, "You shall love your neighbor as yourself." (Galatians 5:4-6, 13-14)

Spiritual formation must move beyond a skin-deep, cosmetic spirituality—focused on external behaviors that are obedient to commandments—to a cardiac spirituality rooted within the heart and expressed through selfless acts of sacrificial love.

In Christian spiritual formation, the maturity of obedience is love: "Love is the fulfilling of the law" (Romans 13:10). Selfless acts of sacrificial love are rewarded with the kingdom (see Matthew 25:31-46). In the words of the medieval Franciscan Margaret of Cortona, "The way of salvation is easy. It is enough to love."

HOSPITALITY

Christian love is expressed in a multitude of ways: friendship, charitable acts, sharing our time, talents or treasures with a worthy cause. It is limited only by one's creativity, vision and attitude.

Hospitality is one practical way to express the love of neighbor that reflects our experience of Abba's love. It is also an important witness to the conviction that God is "our" Father and we are all one family. From Cameroon to China, I have experienced its two essential elements: welcome and acceptance.

Part of hospitality is simply welcoming another as sister or brother into the circle of our attention. We do this with welcoming words and by calling the other by name; by a firm handshake, embrace or kiss; and sometimes by letting a person feel noticed by a silent, friendly nod, wink or smile. Think of Mary being attentive to Jesus as she sits at his feet; compared to Martha's frenzied food preparations and anxiety, Jesus called Mary's attitude the "better part" (Luke 10:42). We sometimes go through all the motions of hospitality, laudable as they may be, and miss the most fundamental attitude of welcoming a guest: offering our undivided attention.

However, hospitality not only acknowledges the other person

but also accepts the person without judgment or criticism. Indeed, it is the human expression of God's acceptance of us. Think of Jesus calling unworthy Zacchaeus out of the tree or Jesus' acceptance of the sinful woman washing his feet with her tears (see Luke 19:1-10; 7:36-50).

I still remember attending an eightieth birthday celebration. Sitting together at the same table were an African American, an Asian, a Catholic priest and a single parent of two children. I was touched when the birthday grandmother announced after grace was prayed, "Don't forget, my friends: we are all family around my table."

"We are all family . . . " The early Christians expressed this familial reality in two ways that were thoroughly unique to them: they addressed one another as brother and sister, and following the custom practiced by members of the same family, they greeted one another with a kiss on the lips (see Romans 16:16; 1 Corinthians 16:20; 2 Corinthians 13:12; 1 Thessalonians 5:26; 1 Peter 5:14). This witness to the family of humanity continues today as we open ourselves to others through compassionate intercession, love and graceful hospitality.

THE FAMILY OF CREATION

Francis of Assisi's understanding of God as our Father included *all* creatures—not just human beings. Put another way, he expanded the concept of *Ubuntu* to include not only animate but also inanimate objects. From that stance, he rediscovered his rightful place amid the family of creation. Indeed, as the world shrinks to a global village, the saint of Assisi becomes a symbol of the human heart that is open not just to our brothers and sisters in the flesh but also stretches to include the stars, the California redwoods, even the smallest fish swimming in a stream.

Such a posture was the original stance of Adam and Eve. The

Garden of Eden is a biblical symbol for the ecological balance and familial harmony God originally intended for creation. From hickory trees to human beings, all of reality formed an elegant tapestry, with each created thing an essential thread. Everything was interrelated and interdependent.

The wise stewards of Eden, Adam and Eve, tended this garden with wonder and awe. And they saw their Creator reflected in this divine handiwork.

But the moment Adam and Eve looked on that offered fruit with the eyes of desire, devoid of original awe, everything changed: "the woman saw that the tree was . . . to be desired to make one wise" (Genesis 3:6). They now looked at creation with self-centered concerns, observing its elements as threads *for* a tapestry, no longer threads *of* a tapestry.

Utility replaced childlike wonder. The mind supplanted the heart. Many descendents of Adam and Eve to this day do not see a tree until they have need of paper.

Of course, our utilitarian and pragmatic approach to nature has performed miracles that, in days gone by, would have been considered worthy only of God. Irrigation has transformed deserts and wastelands into places of foliage and human habitation. Technology and science have opened up the mysteries of the moon and stars to the human mind. Computers, satellites, the Internet and transportation have helped the human community better cope with the tragedies and natural disasters of the world. The wonders of medical science give hope for healing diseases once thought incurable.

Such blessings, however, have cost Mother Earth and her dependents dearly. Since the Industrial Revolution, we have been burning fossil fuels (oil, coal and gas), the by-products of which have been collecting around the globe and forming a blanket that causes the earth to warm beyond the normal temperatures of the past. This "greenhouse effect" is wreaking havoc on many places of the planet. Some of God's more fragile creatures have disappeared due to the destruction of natural habitats. Synthetic chemicals dumped in rivers, streams and lakes threaten the food chain. Some have suggested that the "sixth extinction" (the fifth being when the dinosaurs disappeared some sixty-five million years ago) will be caused by human selfishness. Sadly, our oversized, selfish and pragmatic hands have become intruders in the Garden of Eden—the original bull in a china shop.

Now, with so much china broken, what are we to do?

The great Franciscan theologian Saint Bonaventure believed that Francis of Assisi had rediscovered our original and rightful relationship to the things of creation and to God as our Father. According to Bonaventure, Francis clearly saw the world as a way to God:

> In beautiful things [Francis] contuited Beauty itself
> and through the footprints impressed in things
> he followed his Beloved everywhere,
> out of them all making for himself a ladder
> through which he could climb up to lay hold of him
> who is utterly desirable.

CREATION AS GOD'S FOOTPRINTS

In his short, mystical work *Itinerarium mentis in Deum* ("The Soul's Journey into God"), Bonaventure shows how we too can experience creation as that ladder to God. He maps out the journey in six stages, culminating in the seventh stage of ecstatic wisdom and mystical rest.

Only the first two stages are pertinent here. They clearly show that the purpose of animals, vegetables and minerals is to awaken us to God—to love, praise and give thanks. Consequently, we are not to flee from the world. Rather, we are to be hospitable toward all creation and immerse ourselves in contemplation of it so we can be led to an experience of the Creator, our Father.

These first two stages are unique to the Franciscan tradition and deal with the contemplation of God's vestiges, or "footprints." Vestiges consist of all created reality. According to Bonaventure, when we think about things that our five senses perceive, we recognize divine power, wisdom and goodness. It's as if all creation is a neon arrow pointing to the majesty of God. That's the first stage. We are led "through" the vestiges to God.

Think about seeing a shooting star or a comet streaking across the night sky. Have you ever smelled a gardenia bush in blossom or heard frogs croaking in the morning? Touch a newborn's finger. I still remember the taste of a mountain spring in the hills of Tibet. Bonaventure believes that every "footprint" perceived by one of our senses, rather than tying us down here to earth, actually raises us up to God.

The second stage challenges us to accept Bonaventure's thirteenth-century theory of sensation. According to this theory, any object perceived by the senses leaves a copy of itself, an "impression," inside us that evokes feelings and some type of judgment.

Bonaventure believes that, in this second stage, this process of sensation, impression and judgment replicates in a less-than-perfect way exactly what goes on in the Trinity, and especially the incarnation. The Father and the Son behold one another and take the Other in perfectly. This is not a mere impression, as in our human experience, but is, in fact, the total openness of Divinity to Divinity. This second stage reveals God's essence, power and presence "in" the vestiges, since our senses are lamely doing what the Father and Son constantly and eternally have been doing in a perfect way.

Our memories and reactions to seeing shooting stars, smelling gardenia blossoms, hearing a pond wake up with frogs, touching a newborn or tasting water gushing from the earth are faintly and vaguely analogous to the eternal gaze of Father and Son that gives birth to the Spirit.

From the first two stages in which we are led to behold God in vestiges . . . we can gather that all creatures of the sense world lead the mind of the contemplative and wise [person] to the eternal God. For these creatures are shadows, echoes and pictures . . . of that eternal Source, Light and Fullness . . . They are vestiges, representations, spectacles proposed to us . . .

SAINT BONAVENTURE

Bonaventure shows us that our engagement with the world reveals creation to be an epiphany of the power, wisdom and goodness of our Abba. Like Francis of Assisi, by following the footprints left behind in creation, we too can come into the presence of the divine Creator.

MYSTICAL MARVELS

One of my relatives shows me how to rediscover creation as the ladder to God and how to climb it. Surprisingly, it comes more naturally than we might think.

Aunt Margaret is sixty-eight years old and has a senior citizen's card to a local zoo. About six times a year, during the summer and autumn, she treats herself to a visit. She sits in front of the giraffes and is amazed at their grace and elegance. The nervousness of the coyotes tickles Aunt Margaret. She gazes into the eyes of the baboons and wonders what they are thinking. And she takes utmost delight in watching children as their parents introduce the animals. In the midst of all these creatures and people, Aunt Margaret experiences her connectedness to all creation—and to her Abba, who graciously and generously allows her to experience such "mystical marvels," as she calls her friends in the zoo.

When we gaze on the majesty of creation with the original wonder and awe of Adam and Eve, we are pulled out of our utilitarian self-centeredness and led into the presence of our Abba. Contemplative reverence and hospitality toward creation are two of the many ways of the disciple. Hence we do not hesitate to champion a form of hospitality toward creation: giving due attention to nature and allowing it to be what it is without judgment or criticism.

Creatures like giraffes and turnips, in being what the Creator intended them to be, offer God glory and provide a reminder: the more a creature is what God intends it to be, the more it is a clear reflection of the Creator.

Rabbits were busily eating all the vegetables in the monastery garden. While the other monks were trying to devise ways to protect their crops, Thomas Merton commented that the rabbits were simply doing what rabbits do. He continued by saying that if we saw them for what they are, we would see the "rabbitness of God" shining through them.

Each thing of creation points to the hands of its Creator and becomes a reflection of the Divine. Creation mirrors God like a Wisconsin lake reflecting the sunset. In the "Canticle of the Creatures," Francis sings that Brother Sun "bears a likeness of You, Most High One."

Creation's reflection of divinity does not mean we cannot use creation for our own needs. Creation is, after all, God's gift to us: "See, I have given you every plant yielding seed that is on the face of all the earth . . . ; you shall have them for food" (Genesis 1:29). Even Francis mentions in his "Canticle of the Creatures" that Sister Water "is very useful."

But "use" does not imply "abuse." Stewardship means we respect creation for what it is: a gift, a ladder, an intricate tapestry in which we ourselves are woven. We respect its integrity. We don't unravel the threads.

Our respect for and use of creation are founded on the fact that creation is a ladder leading to God. Creation and Creator are in a relationship as close as the footprints left behind by a beachcomber. To waste water is to wash away a trail to God. To ignore the Creator is to be sucked into the black hole of selfish pragmatism. The way of the disciple meanders through creation because it is a reflection of and a path to our Father.

THE WOLF OF GUBBIO

A marvelous little story in the Franciscan tradition vividly highlights the fact that all creation forms one family. According to this fourteenth-century text, the town of Gubbio was haunted by a large and fierce wolf that devoured both its animals and its citizens. So petrified were the citizens that when they journeyed beyond the walls of the town, they armed themselves as if they were going to war.

When Saint Francis visited Gubbio, he felt compassion for its citizens and decided to go out and confront the beast. When he stepped into the animal's territory, the wolf charged with mouth wide open. Francis stopped the beast and immediately acknowledged his relationship to the wolf: "Come here, Brother Wolf. I command you on behalf of Christ that you do no harm to me or to anyone." Then, as the animal lay at the feet of Francis, the saint declared,

> Brother Wolf, you do much harm in this area, and you have done great misdeeds, destroying and killing the creatures of God without His permission. . . . For this reason you are worthy of the gallows as a thief and the worst of murderers. And all the people cry out and complain against you, and all

this town is your enemy. But I, Brother Wolf, want to make peace between you and these people, so that you do not offend them any more, and they may pardon your every past offense, and so neither the people nor the dogs will persecute you any more.

The wolf agreed to the peace initiative. As a result, the saint promised that the townsfolk would feed the animal every day "since I know very well that you did this harm because of hunger." The pact was sealed by paw in hand. Then Francis and the wolf, "like a tame lamb," went to the marketplace of the town, where the terms of the pact were again publicly stated and accepted. Francis pledged himself as trustee for the beast.

The story concludes like this:

Afterwards that same wolf lived in Gubbio for two years, and he tamely entered the houses, going from door to door, without doing harm to anyone and without any being done to him; and he was kindly fed by the people, and as he went this way through the town and the houses, no dog barked at him. Finally after two years Brother Wolf died of old age, at which the citizens grieved very much, because when they saw him going through the city so tamely, they better recalled the virtue and holiness of Saint Francis.

The story of the taming of the wolf of Gubbio is a myth about rediscovering the harmonious balance and familial relationships in the Garden of Eden, a land where a son of Adam could call a wolf "Brother." It highlights the transforming power of love and compassion. It shows how even the most savage and untamed of beasts can become downright endearing, "like a tame lamb."

The story recognizes that wolves will be wolves. Hunger was the reason for Brother Wolf's crimes. So Francis creatively restored the wolf to a more familial balance in the food chain. In the end, this tale shows how reverence and respect can restore dignity to a creature as mangy as a wolf. And in regaining his dignity, Brother Wolf became a ladder leading the townspeople of Gubbio to the holiness of God.

Whether it is a bald eagle silently gliding across the sky, an erupting volcano or the stunned cry of a newborn infant, each is a deliberately written musical note. As the disciple listens with reverence in the spirit of *Ubuntu*, the genius of the maestro is revealed. Indeed, the disciple is only too aware that our Abba is the composer and conductor of the symphony of creation. And living that reality leads to the way of compassion, intercession and hospitality toward the family of all creation.

REFLECTION QUESTIONS

1. How do I measure up to Archbishop Desmond Tutu's description of *Ubuntu*?

2. What role does the prayer of intercession play in my daily devotions? How do I stay informed about wars, famine, poverty, unemployment, racial injustice, incurable diseases and so on?

3. What circumstances and situations challenge me to move beyond legalistic obedience to the obligation of love?

4. How do I express a contemplative reverence for the integrity of creation in my everyday life? In what areas has my use of creation become an abuse?

5. How do I express hospitality?

6. Who are the wolves in my life? How can I be reconciled with them?

Gospel Passages for Meditation and Prayer: Matthew 15:21-28; Luke 10:25-37

Who Art in Heaven

Experiencing the Extraordinary
in the Ordinary

Language is incapable of accurately describing the transcendent God. The God who lives in heaven has taken on human flesh, thus making holy all human flesh.

MY UNITED AIRLINES FLIGHT WAS approaching Tokyo's Narita Airport. It was a clear, beautiful morning. I nonchalantly looked out of the left side of the plane and there it was: Mount Fuji!

My eyes were wide opened, and I was filled with wonder. A silent awe came over me as I beheld what I consider to be a mystical marvel. My interior being was moved to adoration of the Creator.

And then I chuckled.

All my life I had had a curious fascination for photographs and pictures of Mount Fuji—its mysterious beauty, its snowcapped grandeur. But my experience of Mount Fuji instantly revealed to me how far off the mark the photographers and artists had been.

THE MYSTICISM OF MOUNTAINS
Perhaps of all created beauty, nothing points more directly to the

transcendence of God than mountains. No wonder they are a frequent symbol in spiritual and mystical literature. In primitive so-
cieties, mountains were believed to be the home of the gods.
Mount Olympus, the highest mountain in Greece, was considered
the home of the Twelve Olympians, the principle gods of the Greek
pantheon. The worship of mountain gods for ancient Tibetans was
fundamental to their entire belief system and spirituality. I think
of the snow-capped peak of Mount Huaytapallana, which looms
over the landscape of Huancayo, Peru, and how the Quechua people of the central Andes to this day consider it a symbol of God
and a source of life.

Mountains are also prominent within our own Judeo-Christian tradition. Isaiah speaks of "God's holy mountain" as the
place where God dwells (see Isaiah 11:9; 56:7; 57:13). There are
Mount Sinai, Mount Tabor and the Mount of Olives (see Exodus
19:16-25; 24:16; Mark 9:2-8; Matthew 26:30). In the letter to the
Hebrews, the beautiful eschatological image of Mount Zion is
called the "city of the living God," where Jesus, the angels and
the souls of the just made perfect are gathered together (see Hebrews 12:22-24).

By their very nature, mountains continue to proclaim the awesome and tremendous power of God, the other-worldliness of the
divine, the fact that we have an Abba "who lives in heaven."

When we locate the presence of God "in heaven" in the Lord's
Prayer, we are not confining God to a snail-mail address or physical location. Though the Hebrew Scriptures suggest that God
dwells in a place (see, for example, Genesis 11:5; Psalms 11:4;
18:10; Isaiah 66:1; Micah 1:2), they also make clear that heaven
and earth cannot contain God (see 1 Kings 8:27; Jeremiah 23:24).
And so, to pray to God "in heaven" is to admit the totally incomprehensible nature of God. The first letter to Timothy says that
God "dwells in unapproachable light" (1 Timothy 6:16). And in

his Earlier Rule, written for his friars, Saint Francis says that God
is the One who is

> without beginning and end,
> is unchangeable, invisible,
> indescribable, ineffable,
> incomprehensible, unfathomable,
> blessed, praiseworthy,
> glorious, exalted,
> sublime, most high,
> gentle, lovable, delightful . . .

Our words and images stagger, wobble and stumble before God.
No word or image can accurately describe this ineffable, unapproachable and incomprehensible God who lives in heaven. Our
presumptuous attempts to definitively name or describe God
bring us to a dead-end street. Indeed, when describing Divinity,
our language is a straightjacket that confines us to sometimes
cruel characterizations rather than to accurate expressions. As if
we are trying to describe an Hawaiian sunset to a person blind
from birth, our adjectives and analogies instantly become gobble-
dygook and gibberish before the reality of the Divine.

DARKNESS AND LIGHT, SILENCE AND WORDS

The desire to describe the God who is in heaven and the inability
of language to do so points to the two main currents of mysticism
that have always flowed in opposite directions in the history of
Christian spirituality. The first is apophatic spirituality. It is sometimes referred to as the "negative way," and its chief symbol is
darkness. It tries to experience something of the divine presence
without using the five senses and without language or imagery.

One of the best and earliest articulators of apophatic spirituality in the Christian spiritual tradition is the fourth-century bishop

and Cappadocian father Gregory of Nyssa. In his seminal work *The Life of Moses*, the prophet's calling by God, his guidance of the Hebrews out of Egyptian slavery and his ascent up Mount Sinai to receive the law are symbolically interpreted as progress in spiritual formation and knowledge of God.

Using the image of a mountain, Gregory writes,

> [Moses] teaches, I think, by the things he did that the one who is going to associate intimately with God must go beyond all that is visible and—lifting up his own mind, as to a mountaintop, to the invisible and incomprehensible—believe that the divine is there where the understanding does not reach.

And so, the journey to God—"where the understanding does not reach"—is a journey up the mountain into darkness. The believer must follow Moses into the dark cloud, and when the senses cease their sensing, the believer contemplates a darkness "and there . . . sees God." Gregory continues:

> This is the true knowledge of what is sought; this is the seeing that consists in not seeing, because that which is sought transcends all knowledge, being separated on all sides by incomprehensibility as by a kind of darkness. . . . When, therefore, Moses grew in knowledge, he declared that he had seen God in the darkness, that is, that he had then come to know that what is divine is beyond all knowledge and comprehension.

For Gregory of Nyssa, this darkness is not a meaningless emptiness but the ultimate fullness, a darkness caused by the dazzling brilliance of divine light. God's presence is so complete that its ineffability comes as blindness to the senses.

Many people like myself are attracted to apophatic spirituality.

We find the use of candles, devotional pictures or statues, music, incense and even Scripture a distraction. "Less is more" when it comes to prayer for people like me. Our actual prayer is very simple; one might even say dark. We might slowly and deliberately repeat a single prayer word called a mantra. Or we might simply have a wordless interior gaze on the divine presence, sometimes called "centering prayer."

Those of us who are attracted to apophatic spirituality need to be on guard lest, while praying, we end up in some kind of "never-never-land" where our prayer circulates around an impersonal great abyss, an empty void or a meaningless darkness. When that happens, we have simply "stilled the mind" and are no longer encountering the Abba of Jesus, who is as close as a father to his children yet lives in heaven.

The opposite current in the Christian spiritual tradition is kataphatic spirituality. It is sometimes referred to as the "positive way," and its chief symbol is light. This spirituality is very comfortable using words to describe God, even though human words, of their very nature, are inadequate and miss the mark. "God is love." Indeed, God is—but God is also so much more than what the human word *love* means.

A typical example from this current is found in Francis of Assisi's "Praises of God." If we are to believe a notation made on the original copy by his longtime companion, Brother Leo, this prayer was written very soon after the experience of receiving the stigmata, the wounds of Christ on Francis's body. In this short prayer of five verses, which was composed on a mountain, Francis uses more than thirty adjectives and nouns to describe the reality of God. Just one verse gives a true sense of the joy of kataphatic spirituality in describing God and yet, at the same time, the frustration in realizing the inadequacy of any one description:

You are love, charity; You are wisdom, You are humility,
You are patience, You are beauty, You are meekness,
You are security, You are rest,
You are gladness and joy, You are our hope, You are justice,
You are moderation, You are all our riches to sufficiency.

People like Francis of Assisi, who are drawn to kataphatic spirituality, love to "pull out all the stops." They revel in the "smells and bells" of high-church liturgy. They are different from apophatic people, for they believe "more is better." They find the use of music, litanies, walks in nature and even the prayers of others helpful for making them aware of God's presence.

The moment we think we have captured God in an image, metaphor or description, however, our very words turn and betray us. We become idolaters like the ancient Israelites. This is the great temptation of kataphatic spirituality.

In Exodus 32, the Israelites worship a golden calf. Some Scripture scholars have suggested that the sin here is not in worship of a man-made object but in thinking that the reality of Yahweh could be contained in something built of human hands:

> He took the gold from them, formed it in a mold, and cast an image of a calf; and they said, "These are your gods, O Israel, who brought you up out of the land of Egypt!" (Exodus 32:4)

God refuses to become an object that can be contained by the human mind—whether that's a golden calf or a literary image. God lives in heaven! God dwells in unapproachable light. God is indescribable, ineffable, unfathomable, incomprehensible. God is like the air we breathe: we can never grasp it in our hands. God is like the horizon: we can never take in its length in one single glance. God is like the universe with its black holes and quasars: we will never comprehend it. Indeed, it is an arrogant presumption to think that God can be captured, photographed, contained or described by the human mind or heart. God is God: totally other, totally transcendent. In the words of the first letter to Timothy, "No one has ever seen or can see [God]" (1 Timothy 6:16).

POVERTY OF SPIRIT

Meister Eckhart, the fourteenth-century Dominican mystic, once said that it is possible to be so poor that one does not even have a God. What he meant is that the poor in spirit have abandoned all mental images of God. When the poor in spirit pray, they consistently renounce any image or metaphor because they want to avoid any temptation toward idolatry.

Such a stance in the life of prayer reveals a profound realism and poverty. It constantly smashes the golden calves that claim to contain the living God. That is the practical wisdom of the apophatic tradition.

Though language is crippled before the reality of the Divine, it does have a place. As human beings, we use words to communicate and for prayer; we use images to process reality and for understanding. That is the practical wisdom of the kataphatic tradition.

And so there is a constant tension between the kataphatic and apophatic traditions. The kataphatic tradition reminds us that words, images and metaphors help to lead us up the mountain of God. However, once there, the apophatic tradition reminds us that we must leave our images and descriptions of God behind as we enter the dark cloud of the divine presence. Awe-filled silence and hands empty of all images and metaphors make us receptive to experience the God who lives in heaven.

SACRED READING

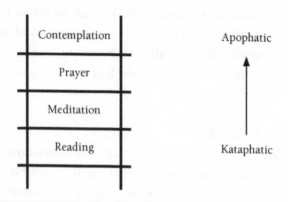

Figure 3.1. The rungs of *lectio divina*

A practical example of experiencing the God in heaven through the kataphatic and apophatic traditions, though flowing in opposite directions but actually supporting one another, is the ancient practice of *lectio divina,* or the sacred reading of Scripture. Practiced as early as the fourth century among the desert fathers and mothers, it was the twelfth-century Carthusian monk Guigo II who is credited with delineating its four steps. Though he does not use the image of a mountain, he does, nevertheless, speak of this prayer in terms of an ascent, using the image of Jacob's ladder (see Genesis 28:10-22). Guigo writes that this practice of sacred reading becomes a "ladder for monks by which they are lifted up from earth to heaven. It has few rungs, yet its length is immense and wonderful, for its lower end rests on earth, but its top pierces the clouds and touches heavenly secrets." The four rungs are reading, meditation, prayer and contemplation. The first three are kataphatic; the fourth is apophatic.

Sacred reading traditionally begins with *reading* a passage of Scripture. We read the text slowly and attentively with the goal of finding out its literal meaning. What exactly is going on in this Gospel scene? What point is the apostle Paul making to his readers? A Bible commentary can sometimes be helpful as we seek to understand the historical circumstances behind the scene or letter.

Reading leads to *meditation*, to ruminating, or "chewing," the text interiorly. We delve into the implications and ramifications of text. We might compare the text to others that come to mind. We climb higher as we go from the external found in the literal meaning to the internal, to the very heart of what the text is actually saying. This meditation can be challenging as we begin to apply the text's deeper meaning to our daily lives.

As we begin to apply the meaning of the text to our lives, we are led to *prayer*. Depending on the circumstances, this might be a prayer of praise and thanksgiving for Abba's generous love or forgiveness discovered in the meaning of the text. It might lead to the prayer of intercession—for a dear friend or the marginalized of society, or for a special grace of which the text speaks and which we are lacking. We do not authentically encounter Scripture if we are not moved to some type of prayer—be it praise, gratitude, intercession or forgiveness.

Occasionally, our prayer will lead to the gift of silent *contemplation*. Sooner or later, the kataphatic has to admit its inability to make sense before God and must give way to the apophatic. This is not to suggest that apophatic spirituality is somehow "better" than kataphatic spirituality; rather, it is just a vivid reminder that our loving God is totally incomprehensible and cannot be contained in words or imagery.

Contemplation is a grace from God as we are, to use Guigo's words, "sprinkled with sweet heavenly dew, anointed with the most precious perfumes." When this happens, Guigo says, God slakes our thirst, feeds our hunger and makes us forget all earthly things. Indeed, following the angels ascending Jacob's ladder into heaven, we momentarily bask in the presence of the God in heaven with a profound sacred silence. This is the essence of contemplation.

THE WORD BECAME FLESH

Judaism, Christianity and Islam all acknowledge the one God who is in heaven. Each of these great religions has a profound respect and reverence for the transcendent nature of the Divinity.

From the Christian point of view, however, the transcendent God who is in heaven "became flesh and lived among us" (John 1:14). This is the great Christian insight: the God of the heavens has come down to earth in human flesh.

Christ was made sharer of our mortality, that we might also be partakers in His divinity.

AUGUSTINE

And with that incarnation, human flesh became a tabernacle and dwelling place for the ineffable divine Word of God. One dimension of the miracle of Christmas is the affirmation of the goodness and sanctity of human flesh. Paul had an intuition into this when he asked, "Do you not know that your body is a temple of the Holy Spirit within you?" (1 Corinthians 6:19). Unfortunately, some Christians still look at flesh and blood as instruments of the devil and threats to their spiritual formation.

When the God who is in heaven became the God of human flesh, the flesh of every human being was consecrated and made holy. Christ represents the potential of every disciple. Indeed, by virtue of our baptism, each one of us is a Christian, a little Christ.

THE SACRAMENT OF MY NEIGHBOR

Because the God who is in heaven has taken on flesh and blood, we Christians are challenged to adopt a deeply contemplative vision of one another. We are called to look beyond the superficial appearances of hairstyles and first impressions, to see and reverence in our neighbor another dwelling place for the Divine, another temple of the Holy Spirit, another incarnation.

Yuri Gagarin was the first Soviet cosmonaut to orbit the earth in 1961. Upon his return, he held a news conference in which he arrogantly proclaimed, "Comrades, I have circled far above the earth and have discovered that there is no God in heaven." The story goes that a Russian Orthodox priest immediately stood up and said, "Sir, you will never find God in heaven unless you first find God here on earth."

That is the great challenge of spiritual formation for the twenty-first century. I failed the test on Good Friday, 1979.

I had just finished shopping at a sporting-goods store in downtown Chicago. Since it was getting near one o'clock, the time the Good Friday Service was to begin, I would have to walk fast to get to the church on time. As I left the store and started down the street, a beggar approached me for a handout.

"Hey, Mister, how about a quarter for some food? I haven't eaten in two days."

I could tell by the alcohol on his breath that he was telling me a half-truth. I pretended not to notice him and quickly stepped up my pace. After all, I had to get to the church on time.

But after I had walked about thirty yards, something told me to turn around. I looked over my shoulder and froze in my tracks. There was Jesus standing where the beggar had been. And though the street was crowded and I was thirty yards away, I heard Jesus whisper ever so clearly, "Albert, you couldn't give me a quarter? Not even today—on Good Friday?"

On Good Friday, 1979, I encountered God in the flesh, and I failed the test.

To confine God to an image or metaphor is idolatry; to ignore God in my neighbor is a sacrilege.

A whole tradition of spirituality emphasizes the need to become aware of the sacrament of the neighbor. Martin of Tours gave half his cloak to a beggar who, that same night, appeared to the saint in a dream as Christ himself. Benedict of Nursia begins chapter fifty-three of his *Rule of Saint Benedict*, "The Reception of Guests," with the unequivocal declaration: "Any guest who happens to arrive at the monastery should be received just as we would receive Christ himself, because he promised that on the last day he will say: I was a stranger and you welcomed me." Bonaventure, interpreting Isaiah 53:3 in terms of leprosy, suggests that Francis of Assisi's early ministry to lepers was a direct result of the saint's devotion to the crucified Christ. In an essay on love, Thomas Merton wrote, "Our faith is given us not to see *whether or not* our neighbor is Christ, but to recognize Christ in him and to help our love make both him and ourselves more fully Christ." Mother Teresa of Calcutta, who spent the vast majority of her life working with those dying on the streets of India, once said, "I see God in every human being. When I wash the leper's wounds, I feel I am nursing the Lord himself."

An important aspect of spiritual formation is growing in the awareness that the world and my neighbor are to be embraced and engaged, not simply endured. It is recognizing that our God who is in heaven has taken on flesh and walks this earth in the poor, the sick, the marginalized, the forgotten—indeed, in everyone.

INCONVENIENT ANNUNCIATIONS

During my first year of ministry as a deacon at St. Jude's Church in New Lenox, Illinois, my frustration must have been quite evident. Most professional ministers learn sooner or later that the primary focus of ministry is people. But that was a hard lesson for me.

I remember Sister Marcia asking me how I was adjusting to ministerial life "in the real world." I told her it was much tougher than I would have ever imagined. I complained how every time I sat in my office to begin working on the Sunday homily or my adult-education presentation, inevitably the phone rang, someone knocked on my door, or I got sidetracked with somebody needing something. I never seemed to make any headway with all the stuff piling up on my desk.

Marcia's response was downright practical. She reminded me that God never makes an appointment.

Incarnation is not only the basic Christian insight but also the basic ministerial priority. Ministry is about people—not paper, processes or procedures. The God who is in heaven has taken on human flesh. And that God has the terrible habit of showing up at the most inopportune times.

Divine annunciations are so inconvenient. It is wise to heed the advice of Meister Eckhart. When asked by a sinner for a way to make up for lost time in the spiritual life, Eckhart replied, "One ought to become a God-seeker in all things and a God-finder at all times."

AMNESIA OF THE PRESENT

To seek and find the God in heaven here on earth demands that we be awake and alert to the here and now. Tragically, many of us do not live in the present and thus, according to Merton, suffer from amnesia.

Many people have lost touch with the present moment because they prefer to live in the past. They are forever mulling over yesterday—regretting it, analyzing it or glorifying it with nostalgia. Sentimentality, regret and guilt are the prices we pay when we live yesterday today.

Other people are always jumping ahead to the future: anxious about next weekend, planning next month, wondering about next year. With antacids in their pockets and ulcers in their stomachs, they race toward tomorrow. Anxiety and worry are the prices we pay when we live tomorrow today.

So much of our suffering originates in our lack of attention to the present. We are rarely present to where we physically are. Convinced that the real action is someplace else, we rarely experience just this particular moment, pregnant with its own annunciations.

THE SACRAMENT OF THE HERE AND NOW

Our schizophrenic existence of being in one place physically and in another place mentally is aided and abetted by the traditional dichotomy between the secular and the sacred, between the natural and the supernatural. This Western dualistic thinking can lead to the view that God must be elsewhere, since nothing worthy of the Divine can be found in the ordinary, present moment.

Dualistic thinking belittles the ordinary routine of life, sometimes offering a false sense of control and security. By dividing, categorizing and compartmentalizing, it makes reality seem manageable. Everything becomes ordered. Everything has its determined place. "God is up there. I am down here." We can then sit back as a proud master and gaze on the castle we have built with fine theoretical distinctions.

But that house of cards collapses when confronted with the incarnation. Finely ordered distinctions cannot make sense of the awesome reality of God-made-flesh, of Divinity-on-earth. The incarnation frustrates our dualistic thinking process by revealing the sacred in the secular, the God in heaven walking on earth, the presence of God within us. Mental categories and images suddenly become a burden, the fuse box of the mind explodes, and we are challenged to start the journey back home to where we physically are because this is where we encounter God.

The medieval dictum *agi quod agis,* "do what you are doing," speaks volumes about the sacrament of the here and now. The "action" is nowhere else but right here, right now. One of Merton's friends recounts this story that the famous Trappist monk liked to repeat:

> Once [Merton] met a Zen novice who had just finished his first year of living in a monastery. Merton asked the novice what he had learned during the course of his novitiate, half expecting to hear of encounters with enlightenment, discoveries of the spirit, perhaps even altered states of consciousness. But the novice replied that during his first year in the contemplative life he had simply learned to open and close doors.
>
> *"Learned to open and close doors."* The quiet discipline of not acting impetuously, of not running around slamming doors, of not hurrying from one place to another was where this novice had to begin (and perhaps end) in the process of spiritual growth. *"Learned to open and close doors."* Merton loved the answer and often retold the story, for it exemplified for him "play" at its very best—doing the ordinary, while being absorbed in it intensely and utterly.

We mature in the spiritual life the more the wall dividing the sacred from the secular comes down. Or to put it more accurately, when we realize that there is no wall in the first place! To pray to the Abba "who art in heaven" drives us deeper into the world, into relationships and into the present moment. Because we experience the extraordinary in the ordinary, we disciples continually strive to be utterly and intensely attentive to the present moment. Any other response is not authentic Christian mysticism but pagan escapism.

I had a Chinese calligrapher make me a scroll bearing an oft-repeated dictum of Zen: "After enlightenment, do the laundry." A more accurate rendering would have been, "Enlightenment is doing the laundry." Or perhaps the most accurate, "Do laundry."

The way of the disciple leads to the sacrament of the here and now. It is to return to the hallowed earth where we experience the God who is in heaven, to the place where the bush burns brightly with the presence of God. It is to break through the lie of Western dualism with its schizophrenic anxiety. It is to experience God enfleshed. This experience is a rediscovery of what is *within*: "It is no longer I who live, but it is Christ who lives in me" (Galatians 2:20). It is also a rediscovery of what is *without*: "In [God] we live and move and have our being" (Acts 17:28).

To be precise, there is no "within" or "without." There is only Christ, the "fullness of him who fills all in all" (Ephesians 1:23), both in heaven and on earth. No wonder Christ said to the thirteenth-century mystic Angela of Foligno, "You are I and I am you."

REFLECTION QUESTIONS

1. At what times in my life have I confused my images of God with the reality of God?

2. Am I more apophatic or kataphatic in my personal spirituality? How do I find it expressed?

3. How can the practice of sacred reading enhance my spiritual formation?

4. How can I further grow in sensitivity to the daily divine annunciations in my life?

5. How can I continue to cultivate an authentically contemplative vision that sees in my neighbor a sacred vessel of Divinity?

6. How do my actions show that I am living in the sacrament of the present moment? At what times am I tempted to dwell on the past or worry about the future?

Gospel Passages for Meditation and Prayer: Matthew 25:31-46; John 1:1-18

Hallowed Be Thy Name

Walking in the Presence of God

To hallow God's name is to walk the way of humility as we adore God's presence with the awareness of our sinfulness. Praying the name of Jesus has the power to open us to the experience of unceasing prayer.

I WAS NAMED ALBERT AFTER MY GRANDFATHER. Within hours after my baptism, however, an elderly Ursuline nun pronounced my name in her native French, "Al-bear"—with no T pronounced. It was a smash hit! "So unique, so different," the shoe salesman of Russian descent and his wife thought. So my parents decided to adopt the French pronunciation.

Growing up, I developed a "thing" about my name. I liked the way it sounded. It set me apart. It also had an air of sophistication that occasionally fed my ego. And it's been the source of a laugh or two. When I first introduce myself, people often reply, "Nice to meet you, Father Al." And I always have to tell them, "No. It's Father *Al-bear*—like 'Teddy bear.'" I've stopped counting the number of letters I've received addressed to "Father Al Bear." Ah, the price of sophistication!

Names are precious and sacred. Indeed, a person's relationship to us is expressed in the name he or she calls us. A name can throb with intimacy when used by someone who loves us. My mother was the only person on earth who could get away with calling me her "Sugar Pie." Or a name can be a formal means of address replete with all appropriate honor and respect: "Mrs. Michaels," "Pastor Jones."

People sometimes ask our permission to address us in a personal way. The first question my new eye doctor asked me was, "Father, may I call you by your first name?" I am sometimes a bit surprised when someone I have never met before just presumes that level of intimacy, for names are special. They should express the appropriate level of familiarity and depth of relationship.

THE NAME OF GOD

To pray, "hallowed be thy name," in the Lord's Prayer is to open ourselves to a rich Jewish tradition. According to the Hebrew Scriptures, name and existence are closely associated. To have no name is to have no existence in reality. To have a name is to have an existence; it reveals one's character, identity and how one's life is lived. And to know a name is to have knowledge and a relationship with that person.

With this in mind, we can see how the revelation of the different names of God at different times suggests a deepening relationship between God and God's people. As God becomes more intimate and gets closer to the chosen people, God reveals more and more of the divine identity in the holy name. And with that revelation of the name, the chosen people could approach and know God.

Up to the time of Abraham, God is known as Elohim. But to the patriarchs God is known by the obscure title El Shaddai, perhaps meaning, "God, the One of the mountain."

God revealed to Moses a new name that appears 6,828 times in the Hebrew Scriptures. It was considered so sacred that the Jews never wrote the new name in full nor ever pronounced it. They wrote only its four consonants, YHWH, known as the Tetragrammaton and substituted the more distant Adonai (Hebrew for "my great Lord") in public reading.

The revelation of this divine name occurred at the burning bush in the third chapter of Exodus. Thomas Merton considered this text to be one of the most important in the Bible.

> But Moses said to God, "If I come to the Israelites and say to them, 'The God of your ancestors has sent me to you,' and they ask me, 'What is his name?' what shall I say to them?" God said to Moses, "I AM WHO I AM." He said further, "Thus you shall say to the Israelites, ' I AM has sent me to you.'" God also said to Moses, "Thus you shall say to the Israelites, 'The LORD, the God of your ancestors, the God of Abraham, the God of Isaac, and the God of Jacob, has sent me to you':
>
> This is my name forever,
> and this my title for all generations. (Exodus 3:13-15)

Scholars are not sure of the exact meaning and translation of the divine name, Yahweh. Possibilities include "I am who [or what] I will be," suggesting divine mystery or God's presence along with an association of future liberation from slavery, or "He causes to be what exists [or happens]," suggesting the Creator and ruler of history. In either case, the name subsequently became a "succinct expression of this faith" in God as Creator, ruler and liberator.

According to the Hebrew mentality, Moses' knowledge of this holy name would serve as proof to the Israelites of his direct experience of God. Furthermore, knowledge of the divine name also meant a relationship.

Jesus revealed a new name for God, Abba. This name, suggesting almost scandalous familiarity and given such prominence by Jesus, must have raised an eyebrow or two among the more conservative ranks of Judaism. It spoke of God's closeness, no longer "the One of the mountain" but a God as close as a father to his children. Jesus' sense of personal intimacy with this God was unparalleled in its time.

From the biblical perspective, the divine name has a sacramental quality because it is weighted with the divine presence. Every time we say Abba, we become aware of the divine presence surrounding us and dwelling within us. Thus we do not say God's name flippantly or absent-mindedly. It must be "hallowed"—kept holy.

HALLOWING THE NAME

Francis of Assisi sings in his "Canticle of the Creatures" that God is so glorious that "no human is worthy to mention Your name." The first dimension of hallowing the name of God, then, is to recognize God's very presence when the name is pronounced. That's what we do when we say "hallowed be thy name" in the Lord's Prayer.

The spontaneous response to the presence of God in the proclamation of the name is awe-filled adoration. We open up our hearts and souls to the God whose selfless, sacrificial love surrounds us like the air we breathe. Our very being is filled with wonder as the loving, compassionate eyes of God probe our being.

But there is a second—and sobering—dimension to hallowing the divine name. It means recognizing our own unworthiness before such a loving God. Our sinfulness is exposed like open sores. Here arises one of the great sources of tension in the spiritual life.

Jesus invites his disciples to join him in calling God Abba. Now calling God Abba is like meeting Her Majesty, Queen Elizabeth, and having her say, "Call me Beth." We would feel uncomfortable and embarrassed by such familiarity. A tension immediately emerges between feeling undeserving and, at the same time, wanting to accept the invitation to intimacy.

We see this tension played out in the lives of Moses, Isaiah and the apostle Peter. Moses responded to the call of God in a burning bush on Mount Horeb and immediately hid his face "for he was afraid to look at God" (Exodus 3:6). In a similar vein, Isaiah had a vision of God and exclaimed, "Woe is me! I am lost, for I am a man of unclean lips, and I live among a people of unclean lips; yet my eyes have seen the King, the LORD of hosts!" (Isaiah 6:5). Witnessing the miraculous catch of fish, Peter fell at the feet of Jesus and said, "Go away from me, Lord, for I am a sinful man!" (Luke 5:8).

In keeping God's name holy, we experience the paradox between the awe-inspiring presence of God and our awful unworthiness, between the adoration of the divine presence and the abomination of our sinful presence. Adoration and abomination walk hand-in-hand in spiritual formation. This paradox gives birth to the virtue of humility.

> *Our proud attempts at upward climbing will really bring us down, whereas to step downwards in humility is the way to lift our spirit up towards God.*
>
> BENEDICT OF NURSIA

THE LADDER OF HUMILITY

God's holiness is the foundation of the seventh chapter of the *Rule of Saint Benedict*, probably the most famous explanation of the virtue of humility within the history of Western Christian spirituality. Using the image of Jacob's ladder, Benedict reminds us that the way toward God is the way of downward mobility.

Benedict says that the ladder of humility consists of twelve rungs. These rungs "mark the decisions we are called to make in the exercise of humility and self-discipline." The first rung is living with a sense of awe in God's presence. The ladder continues with renunciation of our own desires and will. After accepting difficult conditions and acknowledging ourselves as "poor workers" in any given task, we come to the crucial seventh rung: an honest acknowledgment and belief in our inferiority when compared to others. The twelfth and highest rung is manifesting in action the humility of our hearts.

Though expressly written for a sixth-century monastic setting, Benedict's practical explanation of this virtue hits home and is uncannily contemporary. He notes that humility is a "decision," an act of the will. One chooses to live in this way and with this attitude, especially in light of the very first rung: the awareness of being in God's presence. That awareness comes through the recitation and subsequent hallowing of God's name.

Humility comes from the Latin word *humus*, which means "dirt" or "ground." Humility is the paradoxical virtue that, according to Benedict, lifts our spirits toward God by keeping our feet on the ground as we call God Abba. It is the fruit of an honest self-appraisal and self-knowledge that comes by the time we reach Benedict's seventh rung and acknowledge our inferiority before others.

One of Jesus' parables speaks directly to that seventh rung. Luke tells us that Jesus addressed a parable to listeners "who trusted in themselves that they were righteous and regarded others with contempt." It is the parable of the Pharisee and tax collector (see Luke 18:9-14). It is surprising—and shocking—that the Pharisee has the audacity to bring his inflated ego before God and to tell God that he is not like others, who are "thieves, rogues, adulterers, or even like this tax collector" (v. 11). He self-righteously defends himself before God and places himself above others. The tax collector, on the other hand, knows himself too well. In the divine presence, all he can do is beat his breast and beg for God's mercy. We can feel the awe of adoration and the sting of abomination in the tax collector's behavior. Jesus says the tax collector was the one who went home "justified" (v. 14).

Pharisaical pride takes personal credit for everything: talents, gifts, accomplishments and abilities. It commands an audience for what it perceives to be its own creation. It demands to take a bow and have an encore. The deformed, proud ego claims itself a self-made success: "God, I thank you that I am not like other people. . . . I fast twice a week. I give a tenth of all my income" (Luke 18:11, 12). A good way to think of the ego is E-G-O: Easing God Out. Pride raises the ego up as it lowers the grace of God. It clearly steers us off the path of the disciple.

The humility of self-knowledge keeps us from being puffed up with such pride and on the way of the disciple. As the fourteenth-century author of *The Cloud of Unknowing* says, "In itself, humility is nothing else but a man's true understanding and awareness of himself as he really is." Or as Saint Francis used to say, "What a person is before God, that he is, and no more." And who we really are before God, as the tax collector reminds us, is a shameful, undeserving creature steeped in the insignificance of our own existence.

FALSE AND TRUE HUMILITY

But such humble self-knowledge and self-acceptance, if they are to be authentic, must be in communion with reality and truth. Unfortunately, what sometimes passes as humility is, in fact, a neurotic form of low self-esteem. It's seen in the man who believes he has nothing of value to say and is unassertive; it's found in the woman who becomes "a doormat for Jesus" and allows people to walk all over her. This is false humility. It deflects all compliments and praise and promotes a tragic feeling of worthlessness. Such forms of false humility often implode into self-humiliation.

Greg is a very successful computer programmer. He has an uncanny ability to design and develop customized programs for a wide and diverse clientele. This talent has given his wife and four children a very comfortable lifestyle.

Surprisingly, because he struggles with bouts of anger and impatience that cause him to say things he later regrets, he is blind to this gift. His struggles with anger and impatience have the first and final word on his self-esteem. In fact, Greg continually loads himself down with guilt and regret, which paralyze him to the point of tears. Rather than raising his spirit to God as Benedict's humility does, Greg's disappointment in himself and virtual self-contempt drag him down into depression.

Always putting ourselves down is just as wrong and just as sinful as always raising ourselves up.

Authentic humility faces reality squarely. The first seven rungs of Benedict's ladder of humility help to illuminate reality and unmask our obsession with being king of the hill and queen for a day. Those rungs challenge us to renounce our desires, our wills, to patiently accept unjust conditions, to confess our faults and to accept the most menial tasks as "poor workers." Our ease or struggles with these decisions expose the stranglehold of low self-esteem or pharisaical pride and help to keep our feet firmly planted on the ground.

A good friend of mine is a very popular motivational speaker. Many businesses and corporations turn to her for help in influencing their employees. Surprisingly, many churches often ask her to speak as well, since so much of what she has to say is rooted in Christ's Sermon on the Mount. From all appearances, my friend is an outstanding citizen, a committed Christian and very successful. But she has a more realistic image of herself. She struggles at times with the temptation to use her speaking talent and notoriety for personal gain and self-aggrandizement. She is well aware of her personal challenge to spend more time with her husband and children, since she is away from home so often. My friend really is a humble person; she knows only too well the attraction of her ego and the extent of sin and darkness in her life.

But truly humble people also know the light. They hallow the divine name by recognizing who God created them to be, what gifts and talents God has graciously bestowed on them, and how God has acted in their lives. People often remind me of what I am only too aware: that I have a gift for preaching God's word; it's a talent God bestowed on me. A friend's son is very conscious that his athletic ability is a God-given gift; he did not earn it. A friar in my community delights in his untrained talent for sculpting clay; it's a skill he was born with. In the words of the Virgin Mary, "The Mighty One has done great things for me, and holy is his Name" (Luke 1:49).

Keeping the name of God holy, in the tradition of Mary of Nazareth, is to put God where God belongs: at the very center of life. To hallow the divine name is to be aware of and stunned by the fullness of God's grace and action everywhere. It is to remain aware that God is the One who does the speaking and acting through us. God is the One who accomplishes all the good in our lives in spite of our sinfulness. As Saint Francis wrote,

Let us refer all good
to the Lord, God Almighty and Most High,
acknowledge that every good is His,
and thank Him,
from Whom all good comes,
for everything.

Meister Eckhart once preached, "If the only prayer I ever say is Thank You . . . that is enough." Contemporary spiritual writer Ronald Rolheiser goes even further when he writes, "To be a saint is to be fuelled by gratitude, nothing more and nothing less." To paraphrase Mary's statement in contemporary terms, "God writes straight with our crooked lines and holy is the name!"

Authentic humility lives with the awareness that we are simply earthen vessels—*humus*—through which the surpassing power of God acts (see 2 Corinthians 4:7). Adoration of the surpassing power of God and the abomination of our earthen vessels are inextricably bound together. The experience of this interplay between grace and nature, between adoration and abomination, is the very ground of the humble disciple's path.

THE NAME OF JESUS

Our Christian tradition goes one step further in hallowing the divine name. Not only is God's name holy, so is the very name of our brother and savior, Jesus. This name effects what it means. In first-century Judaism, the name Jesus in Hebrew, "Jeshua," literally meant "Yahweh helps." This was often interpreted as "Yahweh saves." Thus the angel tells Joseph that Mary "will bear a son, and you are to name him Jesus, for he will save his people from their sins" (Matthew 1:21).

The early church recognized the power of Jesus' name. To the crippled man at the Beautiful Gate, Peter said, "I have no silver or gold, but what I have I give you; in the name of Jesus Christ of Nazareth, stand up and walk" (Acts 3:6). Peter later proclaimed to the Sanhedrin that it was by the name of Jesus Christ that the crippled man was able to walk (see Acts 4:10-12). He concluded with a statement that astonished his listeners: "There is salvation in no one else, for there is no other name under heaven given among mortals by which we must be saved."

In what might have been the conclusion of an early hymn appropriated by the apostle Paul or, in fact, a poetic narrative composed by the apostle himself, the letter to the Philippians states,

Therefore God also highly exalted [Jesus]

and gave him the name
that is above every name,
so that at the name of Jesus
every knee should bend,
in heaven and on earth and under the earth,
and every tongue should confess
that Jesus Christ is Lord,
to the glory of God the Father. (Philippians 2:9-11)

The name of Jesus has been kept holy by Christians down through the centuries. Western Christianity developed the custom of bowing the head at the mention of the name of Jesus. Pope Gregory X had this formally written into law in 1274 at the Second Council of Lyons. Echoing the letter to the Philippians, the council stated, "Whenever that glorious name is recalled, especially during the sacred mysteries of the Mass, everyone should bow the knees of his heart which he can do even by a bow of his head."

The Eastern Orthodox tradition of Christianity gave birth to the Jesus Prayer: "Jesus, Son of God, have mercy on me, a sinner." And Orthodox spiritual writers have insisted on the power inherent in the very name of Jesus. A great Russian Orthodox saint of the nineteenth century, Theophan the Recluse, said, "The Jesus Prayer is like any other prayer. It is stronger than all other prayers only in virtue of the all-powerful Name of Jesus, Our Lord and Saviour." Another Orthodox saint said, "The Name of our Lord Jesus Christ is divine—divine are the force and virtue of this Name—all-powerful and salvific, beyond our understanding." And still another, "The Name of the Lord is the Lord Himself. . . . The very Name of God is power."

Interestingly, this emphasis on the divine character of the name of Jesus became a subject of controversy from 1912 to 1913 on Mount Athos, the great monastic republic of Greece. Two monks began promoting the doctrine that the actual name of Jesus is the Divinity. Those who followed this teaching were called "glorifiers of the name." Though the Patriarch of Constantinople, Joachim III, condemned this as heretical, the "glorifiers of the name" refused to back down. Finally, in 1913, the imperial Russian government sent a ship to Mount Athos and, violating Greek territorial waters, arrested the recalcitrant monks. To this day, the question of the orthodoxy of their doctrine remains unresolved.

Some Orthodox writers believe that the name of Jesus is so sacred, precious and powerful that it should never be pronounced or prayed by itself. Rather, it should always be watered down with an adjective or an invocation: "Jesus, save me!" "Loving Jesus!" "Jesus, remember me!" From the Orthodox Christian perspective, the intensity and power of the name of Jesus could overwhelm the one who pronounces it unaccompanied by a modifier. In Christian spirituality, this hallowing of Jesus' name has given rise to a way of praying at all times and living continually in the divine presence.

THE WAY OF A PILGRIM

The Way of a Pilgrim is the journal of an anonymous nineteenth-century Russian Christian that teaches one way of keeping holy the name of Jesus. At the Divine Liturgy on the twenty-fourth Sunday after Pentecost, the Russian heard these words in the day's epistle: "Pray without ceasing" (1 Thessalonians 5:17). Curiosity about these words inspired the pilgrim to wander the steppes of his motherland in search of a method of unceasing prayer.

After a year, the pilgrim arrived at a monastery where an elder taught him the Jesus Prayer. He was initially told to limit his recitation of the prayer to three thousand times a day. Then six thousand times a day. Finally, after ten days of laborious recitation, he could increase it to twelve thousand times a day. One day, during this last period of practice, he woke up, and what had been previously a labor for him was suddenly second nature. From that moment on, the Jesus Prayer became the constant prayer of his heart.

Recitation and hallowing the divine name of Jesus changed the pilgrim's relationship with all creation. In the words of the pilgrim,

> When I began to pray with the heart, everything around me became transformed and I saw it in a new and delightful way. The trees, the grass, the earth, the air, the light, and everything seemed to be saying to me that it exists to witness to God's love for [all] and that it prays and sings of God's glory.

Praying the name of Jesus opened the pilgrim's eyes so that, like Francis of Assisi, he rediscovered creation's original purpose: the glory and praise of God. The Jesus Prayer moved the pilgrim to a contemplative hospitality toward inanimate objects. Thus all creation became a ladder leading him to the awareness of divine love in the present moment.

The prayer also transformed the pilgrim's relationship to others:

> I spent the rest of the summer reciting the name of Jesus vocally and I enjoyed great peace. If I happened to meet people during the day they all seemed as close to me as if they were my kinsmen, even though I did not know them. . . . The calling on the name of Jesus Christ comforted me on the road; all people seemed good to me and I felt that everyone loved me. . . . When someone offends me, I remember how sweet the Jesus Prayer is and the offense and anger disappear and I forget everything.

The power of the name of Jesus acted as a healing balm for the wounds and divisions among people caused by the selfishness, blindness and prejudice of the ego. The pilgrim's was an experience of *Ubuntu,* of coming to know himself *through* others and focusing his humanity *for* others. He thus rediscovered the family of humanity. The faithful recitation of the Jesus Prayer led the pilgrim to the very heart of spiritual formation: performing selfless acts of sacrificial love for others in response to the experience of God's love in his life. In doing that, God's name was hallowed as the pilgrim lived with awe and reverence in the divine presence.

So much of my own devotional life is focused on the recitation of the Jesus Prayer. Every morning during my prayer time, I recite it slowly and deliberately. It helps me to open up and center my attention on God's presence, which surrounds me and dwells within me. As I slowly recite it, I am sometimes moved just to be silent and to sit in the presence of God. And so I do. And when I find the silence becoming distracted by the wandering of my mind, I return to the slow recitation of the prayer. I also have found it helpful to finger a *chotki,* an Eastern Christian prayer rope designed specifically for the Jesus Prayer, as I pray the prayer. Fingering the prayer rope is another way of keeping me attentive to the sacredness of this devotion. On days when my prayer seems especially dry or I am sleepy or distracted, the slow recitation of the Jesus Prayer becomes a prayerful refuge. I also find the prayer useful when I want to "catch God on the run" as I wait in the checkout line at the grocery store or walk through a shopping mall.

UNCEASING PRAYER

I once heard someone say that God is like radio music playing in the background of life. I find the analogy helpful. Though I am not always consciously aware of it, the music continues playing. Once in a while, a particular melody grabs my attention. Then I stop what I'm doing and hum along with the music. After a few moments or at the conclusion of the song, I go back to what I am doing. Sometimes my activity—some manual labor or enjoying a cup of tea—can proceed hand-in-hand with my singing for an extended period. At these times, the activity of the present moment and attention to the background music are bound together in one and the same act.

Unceasing prayer is the traditional goal of the recitation and hallowing of the Name in the Jesus Prayer. It is analogous to our relationship with the radio music playing in the background. Periodically, the divine presence commands our attention. So we stop what we are doing and momentarily bask in the presence of God. Or we continue what we are doing but with the conscious awareness that we are doing it in God's presence. In either case, we have reached the first rung of Benedict's ladder of humility, which is the awareness of the divine presence.

Set periods of prayer when we make deliberate use of techniques such as the Jesus Prayer should make us more prayerful, more attuned to the presence of the Divine that at this and every other moment enfolds and surrounds us. Scheduled prayer times hopefully provide us with a deeper sensitivity to and awareness of God's presence when we are not praying. This opens us to receive the graced gift of unceasing prayer.

As we become prayerful and contemplative in our stance toward reality through the recitation of the Jesus Prayer, we become more attentive to God's presence in the ordinary routine of everyday life: in God's footprints of creation, in the sacrament of others whom we encounter, in solitary moments of waiting, driving, sitting on the bus or doing dishes. Thus, unceasing prayer is never dissociated from respect for creation, hospitality toward others or the sacrament of the present moment.

Finally, there comes a point when our prayerfulness makes us aware of a startling reality: at every single moment, no matter where we are or what we are doing, Abba is contemplating us with the wonder and awe of a father or mother gazing on the beloved firstborn.

The experience of God as the constant *subject*—not object—of prayer is the blossoming of unceasing prayer. We forget ourselves and enter into communion with the very prayer life of God. "Pray in the Spirit at all times in every prayer and supplication" (Ephesians 6:18). Such rare moments resonate with our truest identity: we are the beloved "with whom I am well pleased" (Matthew 3:17).

BERNARDINE OF SIENA

No preacher was more aware of the power of the name of Jesus than the great fifteenth-century Franciscan, Bernardine of Siena. He was a zealous promoter of the veneration of the name of Jesus throughout Italy. In his day, many Italian city-states were torn by different rival factions, each with its own party emblem or logo. As a way of breaking down those divisions and bringing people together, Bernardine made banners emblazoned with the emblem "YHS," the abbreviation of the Greek word for Jesus. He then organized processions behind these banners to symbolize the surpassing of old allegiances, the destruction of all rivalries and the unity that Christians share in the name of Jesus. And so, through the power of the holy name as well as Bernardine's creative—one might even say superstitious—maneuvering, many people in rival factions were brought together in unity and peace.

His own words remind us how the name and ministry of Jesus are bound inextricably and effect the salvation of God:

> Jesus, Name full of glory, grace, love and strength! You are the refuge of those who repent, our banner of warfare in this life, the medicine of souls, the comfort of those who mourn, the delight of those who believe, the light of those who

preach the true faith, the wages of those who toil, the healing of the sick. To You our devotion aspires; by You our prayers are received; we delight in contemplating You. O Name of Jesus, You are the glory of all the saints for eternity. Amen.

When we disciples pray, "hallowed be thy name," we commit ourselves to the path of humility as we come into the divine presence. We realize our unworthiness and recognize God as the source of all our gifts, accomplishments and talents. We are privileged not only to call God Abba but also to be given God's power and salvation "on account of [Jesus'] name" (1 John 2:12).

REFLECTION QUESTIONS

1. What are my God-given gifts and talents? How do my words and actions demonstrate that such gifts and talents have their origin in God?

2. When am I tempted to "ease God out" of situations?

3. What helps me to keep my feet on the ground in spite of my talents, gifts and accomplishments?

4. What advantages can the practice of the Jesus Prayer have in my daily devotions?

5. How can I open myself to receive the gift of unceasing prayer, the experience of God as the subject—not object—of prayer?

Gospel Passages for Meditation and Prayer: Luke 1:46-55; 18:9-14

Thy Kingdom Come

Promoting God's Intention for the World

The kingdom can come in the slightest of circumstances. All it takes is an awareness of God's love for us, the love of others in a manner appropriate to our lifestyle, surrender to the present and living joyfully and peacefully.

THE GARDEN OF EDEN IS A SYMBOL OF the realization of God's intention for all creation. It represents an idyllic paradise where all creation was woven together into an intricate tapestry and Adam and Eve had all their needs met. The first couple basked in the blessings and banquet laid out before them—and God was pleased: "God saw everything that he had made, and indeed, it was good" (Genesis 1:31).

Divine attention was riveted on Adam and Eve. The fountain-fullness of God's presence overflowed in selfless love expressed in the delights and pleasures of the Garden. God so marveled at Adam and Eve that God placed all creation into their laps and made them its stewards. They were to nurture this world with tender care, all the while preserving it as a place where there would be no war, violence or distrust; a place where there would be no racism, inequality or prejudice; and a place where each member of creation's family would rely on one another. Adam and Eve were entrusted with and became the guardians of God's magnificent creation.

ORIGINAL SIN

But this graced reality was soon fractured. Adam and Eve, by choosing to follow their own egotistical agendas, committed the original sin. And with that, they "eased God out" of their lives and usurped the throne of God.

The intricate web of creation was broken and thrown into disarray. Adam and Eve lost the immediate awareness of God's all-embracing presence and were expelled from the Garden of Eden (see Genesis 3:24). God's intention had suddenly been relegated to a hope, a dream.

Over hundreds and hundreds of years, God raised up prophets to remind the chosen people that their present situation was far removed from the paradise God had intended. Social injustice, the worship of other gods and sinful ethical behavior were all symptomatic of the human ego masquerading as the lord of creation. God hoped, with human cooperation, to once again restore creation to a place of blessing. Indeed, the prophets spoke of a time to come when all the nations would live in peace and together worship Yahweh (see Isaiah 2:2-4; 19:19-24; Micah 4:1-3). Ezekiel, as Isaiah and Hosea before him, prophesied about God's intention, using images suggestive of a return to the Garden of Eden (see Isaiah 11:6-9; Ezekiel 34:25-30; Hosea 2:18).

THE KINGDOM OF GOD

More than a prophet, Jesus enfleshed God's intention. He called it the "kingdom of God" and reiterated, in his preaching and ministry, its essential characteristics: peace, love and justice. The earliest Gospel begins with Jesus proclaiming, "The time is fulfilled, and the kingdom of God has come near; repent, and believe in the good news" (Mark 1:15).

Its justice can be seen in Jesus' friendship with the social and religious outcasts of his day and Jesus' mission to the marginalized proclaimed in the synagogue of Nazareth (see Matthew 11:19; Luke 15:1; 4:16-21). The kingdom's justice was expressed in the way Jesus raised the status of children and women, both considered second-class citizens in his patriarchal society (see Mark 9:33-37; Luke 7:36-50). Clearly people were being restored to the condition his Abba had intended from the very beginning.

The kingdom's love and peace found voice in parables about fathers welcoming home wayward children without retribution, punishment or apology, and foreigners showing compassion toward people left behind to die (see Luke 15:11-32; 10:25-37). Love and peace were the cornerstones of teachings about stopping the cycle of violence and turning the other cheek, doing good to our enemies and forgiving without limitations (see Matthew 5:38-43; Luke 6:27-37; Matthew 18:22). Selfless acts of sacrificial love paved the way of the disciple: "I give you a new commandment, that you love one another. . . . By this everyone will know that you are my disciples, if you have love for one another" (John 13:34-35).

Surprisingly, Jesus never used big, splashy images or esoteric language when he talked about God's kingdom. Rather, he often compared the kingdom to ordinary things that are rather small: seed, yeast, a hidden treasure, a pearl, a fisherman's net (see Matthew 13:24-50). And yet, each of these objects, small as it is, can have a profound effect on the field, the flour or a person's future. Perhaps this was Jesus' subtle way of validating the influence of an individual believer's life and how it can actually foster and promote the realization of God's intention for the world.

Luke's description of the early church shows what happens when individual believers live out their commitment to the kingdom's peace, love and justice:

> Awe came upon everyone, because many wonders and signs were being done by the apostles. All who believed were together and had all things in common; they would sell their possessions and goods and distribute the proceeds to all, as any had need. Day by day, as they spent much time together in the temple, they broke bread at home and ate their food with glad and generous hearts, praising God and having the goodwill of all the people. And day by day the Lord added to their number those who were being saved. (Acts 2:43-47)

The early church lived out the practical implications of the kingdom's characteristics. Consequently, everyone thrived because all were again woven in the tapestry of relationships. God's intention, sometimes with effort and labor as we read elsewhere in Acts, had once again become a reality—and it all started with each individual walking the way of the disciple.

When we twenty-first-century Christians pray, "Thy kingdom come," we remember Abba's intention for us and how Jesus incarnated this kingdom of peace, love and justice in his preaching and ministry. We also call to mind how the early followers of Christ lived out its implications.

Remembering is just the beginning, though. One of the challenges in spiritual formation is to live out the kingdom characteristics as the early Christians did—in our individual lives, in our daily routines. As Augustine preached, "When you say, 'Thy kingdom come,' you pray for yourself, because you pray that you may lead a good life." The kingdom comes to realization when each one of us individually engages the world and brings peace, love and justice to it. That's why Jesus challenges us to "strive first for the kingdom of God" (Matthew 6:33).

I know three people who each strives to realize one characteristic of the kingdom in a unique way. The first is Michael. He has
purposely chosen to work for a minimal salary in a nongovern-
mental organization of the United Nations that specializes in
peacemaking. His challenge is to bring his skills of reconciliation
to warring factions on the African continent. Michael is very
aware that the kingdom can come only through listening, dialogue and mutual understanding.

Marilyn volunteers once a week at an AIDS hospice. She sometimes worries that people have forgotten that this disease continues to spread and affect the lives of countless people in her Midwestern hometown. The kingdom comes as she continues Jesus'
ministry of touch with the so-called untouchables of our day (see
Matthew 8:3).

The third person is Julie. She doesn't hesitate to drive down to
Georgia the weekend before every Thanksgiving. She joins thousands of people marching down Victory Drive in Fort Benning,
Georgia, to demand the closing of the Western Hemisphere Insti-
tute for Security Cooperation. Formerly known as the School of
the Americas, this United States government facility trains foreign
military officials, primarily from Latin America, who return to
their home countries only to oppress their fellow citizens. Julie
believes her protest is a witness to the kingdom's justice.

I am only too aware that our God depends on the contribution,
collaboration and cooperation of such women and men—and each
one of us—for the fullness of the kingdom to be realized. The letter to the Colossians speaks of "co-workers for the kingdom of
God" (Colossians 4:11). Though we might think ourselves powerless before the insurmountable problems of the world, we can still
plant the seed of the kingdom or knead the kingdom's yeast in the
dough of daily living by leaving behind the "fingerprint" of a little

Christ, namely, selfless acts of sacrificial love.

This is certainly one of the implications of John's version of the feeding of the five thousand (see John 6:1-15). Philip was clearly overwhelmed by the size of the hungry crowd and even noted, "Six months' wages would not buy enough bread for each of them to get a little" (v. 7). And yet, one boy's offer of five loaves and two fish becomes an occasion for Jesus to celebrate the abundant potential of one selfless act of sacrificial love.

My oldest sister spent a year in the desert of Sudan, feeding starving children during the famine of the mid-1980s. She told me how, after one week of her arrival, she was overcome by the magnitude of human misery and the thousands of children who needed to be fed at the refugee camp of Wad el Hileau. An American doctor who was also a volunteer noticed her depression and discouragement. "Bridget," he advised her, "remember: we just focus on the single child in front of us. We feed this particular boy or girl and leave the others in the hands of God and the other volunteers. One-on-one is how it's done."

Like a seed or some yeast, we have the ability as individuals to transform the present situation into an experience of the kingdom's peace, love and justice. One-on-one is how it's done. We offer our selfless act of love and then trust that, as happened in the feeding of the five thousand, God will make up for what is lacking.

Christ has no body but yours,
No hands, no feet on earth but yours,
Yours are the eyes with which he looks compassion on this world,
Yours are the feet with which he walks to do good,
Yours are the hands with which he blesses all the world.

ATTRIBUTED TO
TERESA OF AVILA

The kingdom becomes reality whenever and wherever we commit to being a little Christ—to be the hands, feet, eyes and body of Jesus. As "ambassadors for Christ," (2 Corinthians 5:20), we stand on his behalf and continue his ministry. That is the commitment and way of the disciple.

The kingdom emerges and is established as our hearts become hungry and are willing to die for the peace the world cannot give, as we are ready to be broken out of a selfless love that is pure gift and as we are bold enough to renounce the ego and work for justice. Indeed, the way of the disciple is oriented for and by the final coming of the kingdom.

KEEPERS OF THE KINGDOM

My friend Alice's fidelity to her husband, Ronald, is second to none. For forty-four years, she cooked for him, did his laundry and loved him as a devoted wife. But when his short-term memory loss with its resulting confusion and anger became severe, she knew she could no longer single-handedly give him the care he deserved. She then made the agonizing decision to put him in a nursing home.

Every day, she goes to feed him lunch and talk with him before his afternoon nap. Ronald still recognizes his wife of forty-six years and has some recollections of the past. In many ways, Alice has become the guardian of his memories and the keeper of his dreams. When she reminds him of their honeymoon in New York City, Ronald nods. He smiles with delight and blurts out a "yeah!" when she tells him again how he had surprised her with an automobile for their silver wedding anniversary. Alice talks about their three grown children and how she feels they did a good job raising them.

Alice is only too aware that one day Ronald will no longer recognize her. His memories of the past, his hopes and their dreams as a couple will fade as his own sense of self recedes into the ocean of Alzheimer's disease. But she plans to continue to guard the memories, honor the dreams and keep both of them alive in her own life as Ronald's wife. One-on-one is how it's done.

In a very similar way, we are called to be "keepers of the kingdom." We go through life praying "Thy kingdom come," all the while planting its seeds of peace, love and justice in our own small way. Like Alice, we guard and honor God's intention—we keep it alive—by what we say and how we live.

Though the list is far from exhaustive, there are four characteristics of keepers of the kingdom: awareness of God's love, love of others in a manner appropriate to one's lifestyle, surrender to the present, and peace and joy. Let's take a look at each one.

CHARACTERISTICS OF DREAM KEEPERS AND KINGDOM PEOPLE

- Awareness of God's love
- Love of others in a manner appropriate to one's lifestyle
- Surrender to the present
- Peace and joy

Awareness of God's love. Before I began teaching fifth-grade religion during the summer Bible camp, I had been warned about Tommy Nicholson. Eleven-year-old Tommy was seen by all as a holy terror. The more anyone punished him, I was told, the more Tommy would yell, fight and generally turn the classroom into a pressure cooker for everybody.

The camp coordinator told me that Tommy was simply trying to get the attention and love he did not get at home. So I decided to take a different approach with him. I continually showered him, to the point of favoritism, with love and attention. I let him erase the blackboard. I encouraged him to collect the drawings of his classmates and made a point of giving his picture special recognition. Not once during those three weeks did I raise my voice at him or publicly embarrass him.

And it worked! The camp's holy terror was transformed into a guardian angel who not only became the teacher's pet but also a model of conduct for his fifth-grade classmates.

What was the secret? Love. For the first time in his eleven years of life, Tommy Nicholson felt noticed and knew he was loved. One-on-one is how it's done.

The first characteristic of keepers of the kingdom is this: they know in their bones that they are first and foremost the beloved of Abba. The experience of divine love grounds them in the present moment. Indeed, divine love *is* the experience of the present moment. Keepers of the kingdom know God's love not as some intellectual abstraction or theory but as the very air that surrounds them and gives them life.

This awareness drives them deeper and deeper into the world, relationships and the present moment. Their lives overflow with awe as they experience divine love touching them in the family of creation. Each moment has the potential to be an annunciation; each creature, a ladder to God; each person, a sacrament of the Divine.

Some saints and mystics have written of this experience of divine love as if they were God's bride or lover. This is called "bridal mysticism" or "love mysticism." The scriptural text often used is one of the shortest books of the Bible, the Song of Solomon, sometimes called the Song of Songs or the Canticle of Canticles. This love poem, describing a bride's longing as she waits for the return of her bridegroom, found itself within the Hebrew Scriptures. Though unabashedly vivid and erotic for its times, the Song of Songs was viewed by the Jewish tradition as sacred because it reflected the relationship between God and the Israelites. The first-century Jewish rabbi Akiba ben Joseph wrote of it, "Heaven forbid that any man in Israel ever disputed that the Song of Songs is holy. For the whole world is not worth the day on which the Song of Songs was given to Israel, for all the Writings are holy and the Song of Songs is holy of holies."

In the third century, Origen, though not the first to interpret the book as applying to the love between Christ and the church, furthered the mystical interpretation by suggesting it symbolized the relations between Christ and each individual soul. This elevated the Song "to the mystical text par excellence in Christian history." The list of people who subsequently wrote commentaries or preached on the Song of Songs reads like a "Who's Who" of spiritual giants: Gregory of Nyssa, Bernard of Clairvaux, William of St.-Thierry, John of the Cross and Teresa of Avila, to name just a few.

Bridal or love mysticism, drawing from the Song of Solomon, often uses erotic imagery to describe the experience of divine love. Quotes from the thirteenth-century Mechtild of Magdeburg and the sixteenth-century John of the Cross and Teresa of Avila, respectively below, are classic examples:

"You (the soul) are like a new bride whose only love has left her sleeping from whom she cannot bear to part for even one hour. . . . I (God) await you in the orchard of love and pick for you the flower of sweet reunion and make ready there your bed." The soul replies, "Ah my beloved! I am hoarse in the throat of my chastity but the sweetness of your kindness has cleared my throat so that now I can sing."

There he taught me a science most delectable;
And I gave myself to him indeed reserving nothing;
There I promised him to be his bride.

But when this most wealthy Spouse desires to enrich and

comfort the Bride still more, He draws her so closely to Him that she is like one who swoons from excess of pleasure and joy and seems suspended in those divine arms and drawn near to that sacred side and to those divine breasts. Sustained by the divine milk which her Spouse continually nourishes her and growing in grace so that she may be enabled to receive His comforts she can do nothing but rejoice.

One scholar has noted that these metaphors are clearly drawn from bodily functions sometimes condemned by the church and show an integration of the erotic with the holy. Those attracted to love mysticism clearly see the beauty and sacredness of sexual desire as just another way to describe the selfless, sacrificial love of Abba.

The experience of unconditional love changes our lives drastically—just like eleven-year-old Tommy Nicholson's. We no longer have the emotional need to prove ourselves, gain the attention of others or make a name for ourselves. Our obsession with self-concern, self-image, self-preservation and self-gratification dissipates. In effect, God's love sets us free from the ego's stranglehold and gives us the freedom to respond with selfless acts of sacrificial love.

Love of others in a manner appropriate to one's lifestyle. The beloved of God are impelled to become lovers of others. That is the second characteristic of keepers of the kingdom. Acceptance of others, hospitality and love are the "fingerprints" of these people. Indeed, there is no surer sign of the way of the disciple than a tender heart of selfless, sacrificial love. "Love is from God" (1 John 4:7). Indeed, love *is* God's presence in the world.

The measure of a disciple's love for others cannot be overemphasized, since it is *the* acid test for authentic Christian spiritual formation. There is no dichotomy between love of neighbor and love of God. Human love for another does not take away from love for God. Rather, love of another person completes, rather than competes with, the love of God. Writing of the fourth-century Christians who went out into the desert to live solitary, God-centered lives, Thomas Merton notes their insistence on the primacy of love over asceticism, contemplation and everything else in the spiritual life. He then summarizes, "Love in fact *is* the spiritual life, and without it all the other exercises of the spirit, however lofty, are emptied of content and become mere illusions." Merton is simply repeating what Paul had stated centuries earlier: without love, we are "a noisy gong or a clanging cymbal" (1 Corinthians 13:1).

Authentic love moves us beyond our feelings and our self-centered desires. It is truly selfless—that is, it focuses on the other without looking in the mirror or counting the cost. It is a decision, a commitment like Alice's faithful care of Ronald, Michael's efforts for peace in Africa, Marilyn's ministry to those with AIDS and Julie's dedication to justice. The measure of authentic love is the degree of self-forgetfulness.

The expression of this selfless donation of ourselves must be appropriate to our chosen lifestyle. That includes God's sacred gift of sexuality, a topic some of us are uncomfortable discussing candidly. And yet, the sexual dimension of our life often reveals the depths of our selflessness or selfishness. Singles, celibates and spouses know this reality. Fidelity to a lifestyle as a single Christian, a celibate or a married spouse—each has its own unique struggles and temptations with regard to sexuality and love of others. And so we pray for the coming of the kingdom in the sexual dimension of our lives as in all others.

Singleness. Single Christians are often tempted to think they are at a great disadvantage because "there's no sex outside marriage."

They sometimes fantasize about having a spouse in order to experience and celebrate God's gift of sexuality. However, this fantasy promotes the illusion that equates sexuality with genitality. Sexuality goes far beyond what is below our waists. In fact, it has more to do with what is above the waist than below. It includes how we see God, others and the world—and how we experience and relate to them as men or women. Far from being at a disadvantage, the single Christian can offer an appropriate love of others that witnesses to a deeper appreciation and understanding of what it means to be a female or a male.

In coming to that deeper appreciation and understanding, however, single Christians will experience sexual temptations. They will be enticed and seduced by the false, fleeting seduction of togetherness that a noncommitted sexual relationship with another sometimes provides. This feeling fizzles with the sunrise, when two people realize they are alone again and one has been treated as an "object" that was used for pleasure. The challenge for single Christians is to bring God's peace, love and justice to their relationships with others.

As they explore the depths of what it means to be a man or woman faithful to God's kingdom, single Christians would be wise to cultivate varied and deep friendships with others. As the concept of *Ubuntu* suggests, we come to know ourselves only through our relationships with others.

Celibacy. As a celibate, I am tempted to become "asexual for Jesus." I want to run yellow caution tape around my waist and only give God what is above it. My spiritual director often reminds me that repression and attempts at suppression smack of a dualistic spirituality that denigrates my sexual desires.

When vowed celibates repress their sexual urges or keep people at a distance in order to "preserve" their vow, they become mimics in ministry. Their lives become petty, sterile and lonely. Our appetites, whether for food, sleep or sex, must be faced and given appropriate respect; otherwise they go underground and find release in unconscious or unhealthy ways.

To face sexual desires appropriately in the celibate lifestyle means accepting them as part of our humanity and respecting them as a divine gift. The drive for union, the ultimate aim of the sexual appetite, can be celebrated and sublimated through deep, loving friendships with others and a daily, consistent prayer life. Sexual energy can be released in a healthy way through exercise and recreation.

However, celibacy is not just about "negotiating" the sexual appetite; such an attitude also degrades God's gift of sexuality. Celibacy is one expression of the kingdom's unconditional love, especially for the poor, marginalized and forgotten. Celibates are challenged to open their arms and stretch their hearts for any person in a most unique way. One-on-one is how it's done. Without love, celibacy is much ado about nothing.

Marriage. The Roman Catholic tradition of Christianity has seven sacraments. By definition, they are "efficacious signs of grace, instituted by Christ and entrusted to the Church, by which divine life is dispensed to us." To the surprise of many non-Catholics, the Roman Catholic tradition considers marriage with its sexual expression of love as one of the seven dispensers of divine life.

To think that God's life is enfleshed in and through marital spouses excites me. That suggests married people are challenged to live out bridal mysticism in their very flesh.

I still remember how, during a spiritual direction session, Andy told me that he felt he had his priorities in line. "It's God first," he said, "then my wife comes second and finally my family." I had to disagree. Such a pecking order smacks of a dualistic approach to spiritual formation that does not respect the incarnation—divine love made flesh. I suggested to Andy that he might want to become more aware of how he experiences divine love and shows love for God *in* and *through* the love for his wife. It's all about the experience of "God's-love-in-my-spouse." To use the language of the Catholic Catechism, divine life "is dispensed" in and through marital love.

For married keepers of the kingdom, any mental walls that separate divine love from sexual love must be torn down. Indeed, an appropriate celebration of sexual love in marriage gives a rightful place to all that is material, sensuous, emotional and passionate between the spouses. The aim of sexual love is fundamentally to call forth and celebrate the most fleshly expression of God's life and love. After all, divine love continues to be made flesh in the sacrament of the beloved.

This is not to suggest an attitude of "if it feels good, do it." Indeed, anyone in love knows only too well that motivations can sometimes be mixed and self-centered. But like all godly love, sexual love is pure when the lover dies to the demands and desires of the self for the sake of the beloved.

Marital love attends to and incorporates the particular needs of each partner and the unique history shared between them. The kingdom comes every time a married couple gives free, creative and joyful sexual expression to the selfless love that God has incarnated in and through the gift of the other. One-on-one is how it's done.

Surrender to the present. Trusting surrender to the present moment is the third characteristic of kingdom people and forms the backbone of the spiritual teaching of eighteenth-century Jesuit Jean-Pierre de Caussade. De Caussade spent roughly a decade of his priesthood doing spiritual direction for the Visitation nuns of Nancy, France. In that capacity, he sometimes gave spiritual conferences to them. He also wrote letters of direction, advice and encouragement. About 110 years after his death, some of those letters as well as notes taken during his spiritual conferences were put together, edited and became the perennial spiritual classic *Abandonment to Divine Providence,* a book de Caussade himself did not know he had written!

De Caussade's approach to spiritual formation is as simple as it is challenging. It is based on abandonment to the will of God that is found in what he described as "the sacrament of the moment."

Abandonment for de Caussade means a continual self-surrender to every single circumstance of every single moment of our lives. He offers Mary of Nazareth as the example par excellence of abandonment as she proclaims her *fiat,* "Here am I, the servant of the Lord; let it be with me according to your word" (Luke 1:38). True spirituality, he writes, "is the ready acceptance of all that comes to us at each moment of our lives." With startling simplicity, he continues, "What God arranges for us to experience at each moment is the best and holiest thing that could happen to us." And still later, he writes, "There is never a moment when God does not come forward in the guise of some suffering or some duty, and all that takes place within us, around us and through us both includes and hides his activity."

This abandonment is partly active and partly passive. It suggests an active discernment of the presence of God in the here and now and an active response of selfless, sacrificial love based on the certainty of God's love. De Caussade compares us to a tool that is totally useless until it is placed within the hands of a workman; it then begins to perform the task for which it was designed. He writes, "To sum up: we must be active in all that the present moment demands of us, but in everything else remain passive and abandoned and do nothing but peacefully await the promptings of God."

At the root of this approach to spiritual formation is the conviction that Abba's love comes to us at every single moment of our lives. This is the meaning of de Caussade's expression "the sacrament of the moment." Indeed, every moment presents its own duty, some task to be completed. This is an expression of God's will. To surrender to that will found in the present moment's duty is to abandon ourselves to divine providence. "It is the fulfilling of this duty," he writes, "no matter in what guise it presents itself, which does most to make one holy." And so, holiness is not found somewhere else or in some more dramatic or specifically spiritual practice. He writes,

> Let [people] realize that all they have to do to achieve the height of holiness is to do only what they are already doing and endure what they are already enduring, and to realize, too, that all they count as trivial and worthless is what can make them holy.

In other words, the kingdom comes and blossoms right here, right now when we respond to what the present moment is asking of us. As Jesus' imagery suggests, it comes in the smallest and most ordinary of ways.

De Caussade is adamant that feelings, the five senses and intellectual reason are utterly useless as guides in this mysticism of everyday life. Faith and faith alone is the guide and light—though at times it seems like a blinding darkness. With utter simplicity, he writes, "There is nothing safer and less likely to lead us astray than the darkness of faith." When it comes to spiritual formation and promoting the kingdom, "we walk by faith, not by sight" (2 Corinthians 5:7).

There is a profoundly moving paragraph in *Abandonment to Divine Providence* that sums up de Caussade's spiritual teaching and is well worth quoting at length:

My dear souls, you are seeking for secret ways of belonging to God, but there is only one: making use of whatever he offers you. Everything leads you to this union with him. Everything guides you to perfection except what is sinful or not a duty. Accept everything and let him act. All things conduct you and support you. Your way is lined with banners as you advance along it in your carriage. All is in the hand of God. His action is vaster and more pervasive than all the elements of earth, air and water. It enters you through every one of your senses so long as you use them only as he directs, for you must never employ them against his will. God's action penetrates every atom of your body, into the very marrow of your bones. The blood flowing through your veins moves only by his will. The state of your health, whether you are weak or strong, lively or languid, your life and death, all spring from his will, and all your bodily conditions are the workings of grace. Every feeling and every thought you have, no matter how they arise, all come from God's invisible hand. There is no created being who can tell you what his action will achieve within you, but continuing experience will teach you. Uninterruptedly your life will flow through this unfathomed abyss where you have nothing to do but love and cherish what each moment brings, considering it as the best possible thing for you and having perfect confidence in God's activities, which cannot do anything but good.

Surprisingly simple and yet profoundly challenging, de Caussade's spiritual teaching is ranked on the same level as the Spanish mystics Teresa of Avila and John of the Cross.

As de Caussade teaches, keepers of the kingdom live in the present moment, accepting what it brings them, surrendering to the unexpected and unknown. They embrace the mysterious ways of God even when they do not understand. "My thoughts are not your thoughts, nor are your ways my ways, says the LORD" (Isaiah 55:8). They renounce the compulsion to dominate and control every moment, to pray, "Not your will, Lord, but *mine* be done!" They trust in the reality of divine love that surrounds them like the air they breathe.

Fostering this kingdom characteristic is just like learning how to float in water—and just as tricky. The more we actively try to float, the more we sink. Our need to be in charge of the floating is our greatest obstacle. Floating requires trust and surrender. We give ourselves over to the water. This is the way of the disciple. We bow before the mystery of life and say with Mary, "Let it be with me according to your word" (Luke 1:38). We surrender to the present moment and pray, "Thy kingdom come."

This selfless, loving abandonment rooted in the confident belief of God as a loving Abba is enshrined in the famous prayer of Charles de Foucauld. Assassinated in 1916 at the doors of his hermitage in the Algerian Sahara, Charles is the inspiration behind the religious community called the Little Brothers and Little Sisters of Jesus:

> Father, I abandon myself into your hands;
> do with me what you will.
> Whatever you may do, I thank you:
> I am ready for all, I accept all.
> Let only your will be done in me,
> and in all Your creatures—
> I wish no more than this, O Lord.
> Into your hands I commend my soul;
> I offer it to you with all the love of my heart,
> for I love you, Lord,
> and so need to give myself,

to surrender myself into your hands,
without reserve,
and with boundless confidence,
for you are my Father.

Peace and joy. The amazing thing about keepers of the kingdom is that they are unflappable. In the midst of the most intense and destructive storms, they still manage to maintain inner peace and calm. Saint Bonaventure considers this tranquility to be the sixth and highest stage of one's progress in the love of God. He describes the person "as if in Noah's Ark where tempests cannot reach."

Father Medard was a perfect example of this fourth kingdom characteristic. Though he grew old gracefully and died peacefully at age eighty-eight, more than half his life was riddled with both physical and psychological suffering. A bout with tuberculosis, an operation removing half his lung, and fifteen other operations, including one on his heart, left him with a frail physical presence. Surprisingly, though, he had more ministerial energy than most of the other friars with whom he lived, including me.

Medard was never elected to a position among the friars. Frankly, one could say his own religious community ostracized him for many years. Why? During the turbulent time of change in the Roman Catholic Church after Vatican II, Medard was the rector of the Franciscan theology school. The older priests and the faculty of the theology school thought Medard was too progressive, and the students thought he was too conservative. Stuck in the middle and totally misunderstood, he had no friends or confidants in his own Franciscan community.

Such physical trials coupled with his community's lack of appreciation and understanding would have turned many people bitter, angry and resentful. But not Medard. He had no guile, no axes to grind. Everyone who knew Medard remembers him as a friar of deep, abiding peace and joy.

I once asked Medard how he survived the physical pains and emotional downs of his life. "Albert," he said, "there came a point in my life when I discovered that, no matter how terrible the storm raging around me may be, by the grace of God, I'm still in the boat and my Father is at the helm."

Kingdom people like Father Medard are not naïve, irresponsible or living on another planet. They still experience disappointment and sorrow. However, they do not so identify with these feelings that they are consumed or destroyed by them. Theirs is the optimistic conviction of the apostle Paul: "We know that all things work together for good for those who love God, who are called according to his purpose" (Romans 8:28). Or, as the fourteenth-century English mystic Julian of Norwich wrote, "All will be well, and every manner of thing will be well."

Keepers of the kingdom live with the awareness that God is in the driver's seat. "My Father is at the helm," or, as the old song says, "He's got the whole world in His hands." Aware of Abba's selfless, sacrificial love that surrounds them like the air they breathe, they love others in a way appropriate to their lifestyle. They surrender to the present moment while joyfully abandoning themselves to the providence of God, who is as close as a father to his children. Such a manner of life, even in the slightest of circumstances, not only shows how to live the words "Thy kingdom come" but also promotes God's intention for the world.

REFLECTION QUESTIONS

1. How do I promote God's kingdom of peace, love and justice in my own life? How do my words and actions show I am oriented toward the kingdom of God?

2. When did I most recently experience God's love not as an abstraction but as *the* reality of life?

3. Who are the most difficult people in my life to respect? To love?

4. How do I experience and celebrate God's love in and through the single life, celibacy or marriage?

5. When do I struggle to surrender to the present moment? How can I abandon myself more and more into the hands of God?

6. What helps me to maintain deep-seated peace and joy even in the midst of storms?

Gospel Passages for Meditation and Prayer: Luke 4:16-22; 7:18-23

Thy Will Be Done on Earth as It Is in Heaven

Making Faith-Based Decisions

Doing the will of God is allowing our baptismal commitment to influence every decision. Such faith-based decisions are made with awareness, assessment and action.

RON IS AN EXECUTIVE MANAGER for a successful company. He is five years away from retirement. He is also a committed Christian and an ordained deacon in his church.

One day during his monthly spiritual direction session, he told me about an interesting offer he had received from his parish priest. "Father Jones knows how much I have enjoyed focusing my parish ministry as a deacon on religious education. I teach third-grade religion every Saturday morning and help design weeknight adult-education programs as well. He told me two weeks ago that our director of Religious Education is retiring. He would like me to consider taking over the position.

"I'm actually tempted to do it. I would have to resign from my current job and take a substantial cut in salary. But I talked to my wife, and she is willing to support me in the change. There's just one question that keeps coming up."

"What's that?" I asked.

Ron replied, "How do I know if God wants me to do this?"

That is probably the most frequently asked question I hear in my ministry as a spiritual director. "What is God's will for me?" usually arises when we are confronted with the possibility of a job change, the call to church ministry or a critical moment in our lives like marriage, having a child or uprooting the family to another city or country. Indeed, one of the recurring issues in spiritual formation is the discernment of God's will.

JESUS AND THE WILL OF GOD

The full realization of the kingdom of God and doing his Abba's will were virtually synonymous for Jesus. In the Gospel of John, Jesus proclaims, "My food is to do the will of him who sent me and to complete his work" (John 4:34). He made reference to God's will when teaching his disciples to pray, when talking about the nature of discipleship, when encouraging disciples to seek out those who had strayed and when confronting the reality of his imminent death on the Mount of Olives (see Matthew 6:10; 7:21; 18:14; Luke 22:42). Clearly, his daily spiritual nourishment and ministerial momentum came precisely from knowing that the will of God was being accomplished in his life and ministry.

According to Jesus, those who did the will of God formed a new family—one that, surprisingly, had blood ties to Jesus. When told that his family was outside and wanted to speak with him, Jesus told his listeners, "Whoever does the will of God is my brother and sister and mother" (Mark 3:35). Kinship in the kingdom is determined by making the will of Jesus' Abba come true.

And the members of this new family were sometimes a source of surprise even for Jesus. When he saw that the inhabitants of

Chorazin, Bethsaida and Capernaum were not responding to the gift of the kingdom and God's will, Jesus burst into prayer: "I thank you, Father, Lord of heaven and earth, because you have hidden these things from the wise and the intelligent and have revealed them to infants; yes, Father, for such was your gracious will" (Matthew 11:25-26).

This suggests that the "gracious will" of Abba was not always what Jesus had expected. On at least two occasions, the other being on the Mount of Olives, he himself was caught unawares and taken aback by it (see Luke 22:42).

The early church saw its mission rooted in the will of God. And, like Jesus, the church too was sometimes surprised by it. A case in point is found in the twenty-first chapter of the Acts of the Apostles. After spending seven days in Tyre, where the disciples told Paul not to go on to Jerusalem, Paul arrived at Ptolemais. While there, a prophet named Agabus came down from Judea and prophesied that the Jews in Jerusalem would bind Paul and hand him over to the authorities. Those who heard this prophecy urged Paul not to continue to Jerusalem. But he would hear none of it. The response of the listeners to his refusal is telling: "Since [Paul] would not be persuaded, we remained silent except to say, 'The Lord's will be done'" (Acts 21:14).

GOD'S WILL FOR TWENTY-FIRST-CENTURY CHRISTIANS

Praying for the coming of the kingdom implies that we, like Jesus and the early church, are committed to doing the will of God. And so we pray, "Thy will be done on earth as it is in heaven."

But to do the will of God implies we already know what it is. Do we? As Ron asked, "How do I know if God wants me to do this?" Or, even more basically, *can* we ever know the mind of God, "for who has known the mind of the Lord" (Romans 11:34)?

Paul suggested to the church at Rome that God's will consists of three characteristics: "what is good and acceptable and perfect" (Romans 12:2). However, I must admit, Paul doesn't give us too much help in knowing God's will, because what is good, acceptable and perfect is not always clearly evident in every situation. For example, for Ron to maintain his current full-time job and continue his part-time ministry of teaching in the church is certainly good, acceptable and perfect. Yet for him to make the financial sacrifice and begin full-time ministry as the director of religious education also seems good, acceptable and perfect.

One contemporary writer offers a surprising definition of the will of God:

> To understand what Jesus meant by God's will, we might best translate it as "the common good." The common good is whatever is best for the whole human family or the whole community of living beings or the whole universe in its grand unfolding. We are not isolated individuals. We are parts of a greater whole and it is the whole that determines the very existence of the parts. A part exists for the good of the whole because the identity of the part is precisely to be a part of this whole.

I initially balked at such a facile explanation. "The common good" is often just as elusive as "what is good and acceptable and perfect." However, the more I reflect on it, the more I think defining God's will as the common good is wiser than it initially appears. Indeed, it goes to the very heart of God's intention for all creation. It speaks of *Ubuntu,* that we discover who we are in relationship to others and in dedicating our lives for the enrichment of others'. It suggests the interdependence of relationships that was a reality in the Garden of Eden. It implies peace, love and

The will of God . . . means humility in behavior, constancy in faith, modesty in conversation, justice in deeds, mercy in judgments, discipline in morals. We should be incapable of doing wrong to anyone but able to bear patiently wrongs done to us. It requires that we live at peace with our brothers and sisters, loving God with our whole heart: loving him as our Father.

CYPRIAN

justice. It also shows the importance of moving beyond the agenda of the ego with its selfish concerns.

DISCERNMENT

The Christian tradition uses the word *discernment* in reference to the discovery of God's will. From the Latin *discernere*, meaning to "distinguish, separate away, sift off," it points to the challenge of knowing what is and what is not of God. The word is used in a wide variety of ways: discernment of "the signs of the times," of groups and ecclesial movements, of charismatic phenomena, of the true sense of the church, of community decisions, of a person's particular vocation in life.

My experience with discernment—both in my personal life as I have discerned my vocation as a Franciscan, a priest and later as a missionary to mainland China as well as in the lives of my spiritual directees—is that it is, in actual fact, making a faith-based decision rather than "figuring out the will of God."

The fact is, we cannot know the mind of God in every situation. With the exception of the most obvious examples where the commandments are violated or love, forgiveness and mercy are not extended to others, the will of God appears mysterious and incomprehensible. "For my thoughts are not your thoughts, nor are your ways my ways, says the LORD" (Isaiah 55:8).

But discernment is not an exact science in which we try to "pick God's brain." Rather, authentic discernment is allowing the understanding of God's intention as it has come down to us through Christian tradition to inform any decision that we need to make in our lives. It is the concerted effort to think beyond the selfish narcissism of the ego and decide in favor of the common good. It is the desire to do what is good and acceptable and perfect so that the web of relationships in which we are enmeshed continues to be fostered and strengthened. It is allowing our baptismal commitment to be keepers of the kingdom to influence this particular decision so we can be the people God calls us to be, namely, little Christs.

FAITH-BASED DECISION MAKING

AWARENESS	ASSESSMENT	ACTION
• *Distance from the ego* • *Commitments* • *The world "within"*	• *Integrity* • *Scripture* • *Dialogue* • *Energy and passion*	• *Importance of timing* • *The blessing of God*

Figure 6.1. The three movements of discernment

Faith-based decision making, which is my understanding of discernment, is not a scientific procedure that guarantees the same result time and time again. There is no chef's recipe or architect's blueprint for doing it. In fact, in my ministry as a spiritual director, I've noticed that everyone does it differently. One spiritual directee, for example, is very meticulous and methodical as he ponders the next stage of his life. He likes to "think through" a decision. I, on the other hand, have a knack for trusting my gut feelings, which has led me to do what I felt was the will of God. So I tend to "feel my way" through a decision.

Though the actual method for making a faith-based decision differs from person to person and is closely tied to our personalities and temperaments, there seem to be three overarching "movements" that can be identified as an opportunity presents itself and a decision simmers in our minds and hearts. These movements are not necessarily step-by-step procedures. For many people they seem to be more fluid. We move in and out of them as we "test" the wisdom or feelings they elicit (see 1 Thessalonians 5:21). This is exactly where the discerning—"distinguishing, separating away, sifting off"—is most evident as we decide what is good and acceptable and perfect for the common good.

AWARENESS

The first movement occurs when we become aware that a critical juncture in our life is approaching or we have reached a crossroad. We are suddenly conscious that we must make a decision that might lead us beyond the horizon to a brand-new vista. This moment stands apart from the ordinary experience of time and calls for reflection and response.

New Testament Greek has two words for time, *chronos* and *kairos,* which, though not strictly distinguishable, do suggest two different experiences of time.

Chronos is used when time is thought of as a quantity (for example, see John 7:33; 1 Corinthians 7:39). This is our typical experience of the present gradually drifting off into the past and being transformed into the future.

Kairos, on the other hand, is time thought of in terms of quality—as "time for" something (for example, see Mark 1:15; Luke 4:13; 22:53; John 7:8; Romans 13:11). It is sacred time, transformative time, time that calls for a decision or response.

Kairos occurs in our personal lives as we are challenged to make decisions that will have major implications for our lives:

the choice of careers or ministries or spouses, having one's own children or adopting, buying a house or becoming a missionary. *Kairos* also occurs in the life of the world as we confront major issues such as global warming, human trafficking of children, the sweat shops of Asia, the inequality of the American educational system, ethnic cleansing among warring tribes in Africa, the cries for help by those whose lives have been devastated by tsunamis and hurricanes.

Distance from the ego. When we become aware of a *kairos* moment and begin the process of making a faith-based decision, the first challenge we face is to distance ourselves from our obsession with self-concern, self-image, self-preservation and self-gratification.

That is not an easy task. This self-centered agenda is more insidious than we often give it credit, and we are more deeply mired in its quicksand than we realize. The mere fact that we struggle to pull ourselves up and be free from our subjective passions, compulsions and fears alerts us to our slavery. The opportunity to choose, to make a free, deliberate faith-based decision, can begin only with the effort to be objective and not to give in to the promotion and protection of the ego's selfish demands.

Self-concern, self-image, self-preservation and self-gratification, of course, are not bad in themselves. In a healthy adult, they point to a wise, mature sense of boundaries and a realistic understanding of humility. However, they easily take on a life of their own when we become overly invested in them, are obsessed with them and equate them with the trappings of success and happiness. When centered on self, life is viewed through a flawed mirror that distorts reality in a narcissistic way. Hence, during this first movement, we are challenged to step back, get an unbiased perspective on the present landscape of our lives and create a place to freely respond— not simply react—to this sacred moment of transformation.

Commitments. During this initial movement of awareness, as we try to create a place of inner freedom to make a decision, we need to call to mind and also become objective about the important commitments we have already made, specifically those relating to God, others and ourselves. What is good and acceptable and perfect for the common good would rarely violate or trivialize previous commitments made in good faith. Vows to God, commitments to family and friends, and promises to self need to be recalled, reviewed and respected. This, of course, can be "slippery," since some past commitments, upon recall and reflection, might have been made under the influence of an addiction or the pressure of others, in a moment of psychological ill health or with immaturity or dishonesty. Such commitments, therefore, were not freely made. And so, sometimes, previous commitments might have to be renegotiated, not because of infidelity or lack of resolution, but precisely because fidelity to who God calls us to be, a clearer understanding of God's kingdom and a deeper commitment to being a little Christ require it.

The world "within." In the movement of awareness, as we create a place of freedom and objectivity to discern a faith-based decision, it is important to be sensitive to the level of the intellect. Thomas Aquinas reminds us that the sense world, giving delight to what is more visible, more tangible and more readily apparent, easily draws us to that which is "without." We can easily become distracted and preoccupied with the superficial trivialities of life if we always follow down that path. Consequently, we need to make a concerted effort to attend to the less perceptible world "within." The interior level of the intellect has a balanced wisdom that readily facilitates coming to a faith-based decision. Indeed, some decisions just make "plain old good sense."

ASSESSMENT

Having established a sense of freedom and objectivity and with an ear inclined to our interior wisdom, we begin the second movement of discernment, which is assessment. Assessment consists of prayerfully deliberating, reflecting and thinking through a decision. This is where the actual discerning—"distinguishing, separating away, sifting out"—properly occurs.

Integrity. Assessment requires honest self-reflection as we raise the issue of integrity. Integrity first deals with the fundamental direction of our lives. Are we in the habit of making deliberate choices for God, the kingdom and our vocation as little Christs, or do we opt for the ego with its self-centered agenda?

The sixteenth-century spiritual guide and founder of the Society of Jesus ("Jesuits"), Ignatius of Loyola, confronted this most basic issue of integrity with the first two rules of discernment. These rules deal with the different kinds of spiritual stirrings in our hearts. They are worth citing in full:

> *First Rule.* The first rule: in persons who are going from mortal sin to mortal sin, the enemy is ordinarily accustomed to propose apparent pleasures to them, leading them to imagine sensual delights and pleasures in order to hold them more and make them grow in their vices and sins. In these persons the good spirit uses a contrary method, stinging and biting their consciences through their rational power of moral judgement.
>
> *Second Rule.* The second: in persons who are going on intensely purifying their sins and rising from good to better in the service of God our Lord, the method is contrary to that in the first rule. For then it is proper to the evil spirit to bite, sadden, and place obstacles, disquieting with false reasons, so that the person may not go forward. And it is proper to the

good spirit to give courage and strength, consolations, tears, inspirations, and quiet, easing and taking away all obstacles, so that the person may go forward in doing good.

Ignatius's wisdom in these first two rules is striking. Though he is bound to theological images prevalent in the sixteenth century, he makes evident that if our fundamental stance in life is narcissistic ("going from mortal sin to mortal sin," in his words), we will constantly be focused on the candy ("sensual delights and pleasures") offered to us by the powers of evil. Indeed, aspects of our personalities are often aligned with and in allegiance to what Scripture refers to as the "adversary" (1 Peter 5:8), the "tempter" (Matthew 4:3) and the "liar and the father of lies" (John 8:44). However, if we are listening on the interior level of the intellect, our conscience will expose the ruse. In many ways, as Ignatius notes, the powers of evil tend to work in our imagination and fantasies while the Spirit of God works in our conscience through the rational power of moral judgment. Consequently, a guilty conscience can sometimes be a wise guide in waking us up to our truest identity.

If, however, our fundamental option in life is to be faithful to being keepers of the kingdom ("rising from good to better in the service of God our Lord," to quote Ignatius), we might experience the powers of evil trying to rattle our cage with external obstacles, second-guessing or doubts that have no basis in reality. Even in the midst of this, as Ignatius's second rule suggests, we are emboldened and all the more confident in our resolve to do what is good and acceptable and perfect for the common good.

Assessing integrity also includes asking ourselves if the option or options presented during this moment of *kairos* are consistent with our personal history. Which possibility or option is more consistent with the Christian values of our education and upbringing? Does one option more naturally fit the direction in which our life has been moving? For which option have we been better educated and prepared? A sudden change in the direction or a flip-flop of values needs to be seriously scrutinized.

As we reflect on our past life from the vantage point of the present moment, we can all trace themes and threads that God has consistently woven in the fabric of our historical existence. Such themes and threads could include an ongoing use of a God-given talent or a repackaging of a talent to express it differently; the desire to push ourselves beyond complacency; the commitment to serve the poor, marginalized or disadvantaged; the hope of providing a sense of security and safety for our family or friends; the pledge to be informed by and to respond to global issues; the discipline of living a simple lifestyle and not being seduced by consumerism. A wise faith-based decision is often the bow tied around our life as it has been lived up to this moment. Such a decision flows naturally from our past and is a blossom of the present; it is rarely, if ever, grafted onto the present.

As Ron reflected on his past life, he called to mind some of the themes and threads that had emerged: a commitment to education that helped him to make use of his excellent communication skills; his and his wife's desire to raise their children in a home where discussion of their Christian faith was as normal as talking about the headlines in the newspaper; and his decision to apply for diaconal ministry, which had emerged after becoming more and more involved with his church. As he recalled and reviewed all of this, he became aware that full-time ministry as director of Religious Education was certainly not something that would seem out of step with the path he had been walking. In fact, it would seem like the next logical step.

Scripture. During this second movement of assessment, as we continue the process of making a faith-based decision, we submit ourselves and our options to the teachings of Scripture. Which option or options conform to the kingdom characteristics of peace, love and justice as preached by Jesus, and which do not? It is here that we are challenged to explicitly grapple with the ever-elusive trait of what is good and acceptable and perfect for the common good.

Scripture informs the process of making a faith-based decision by reminding us who God calls us to be. It paves the way of the disciple. Though clearly not an exhaustive list, five passages especially are worthy of note and of reflection as we discern—"distinguish, separate away, sift off"—what is and what is not of God in the option or options presented before us.

The first and most obvious Scripture passage that forms behavior is the listing of the Ten Commandments (see Exodus 20:1-17; Deuteronomy 5:6-21). These commandments cause an earthquake in the world of the ego. Though the ego tends to "ease God out" and focus on itself, the Ten Commandments remind it that God and God alone is to be properly worshiped and God's name revered. Furthermore, in the most basic way, the commandments attack our selfish and narcissistic instincts to be insensitive, controlling, vengeful, pleasure seeking, lying and envious. While making a faith-based decision, reflection on the Ten Commandments helps to keep the knee-jerk reactions of the ego in check.

Second, the teachings of Jesus do not negate the Ten Commandments given to Moses but actually fulfill them by addressing the interior attitudes that form the commandments (see Matthew 5:17). This is especially evident in the Sermon on the Mount, which portrays Jesus as a new Moses, as a new lawgiver (see Matthew 5–7). Beginning with the Beatitudes and continuing throughout the entire sermon, Jesus clearly demonstrates that the disciple's response of being meek, justice-oriented, merciful and peaceful is in direct opposition to the ego's reactive obsession with power, acceptance, revenge and hatred. The Sermon on the Mount shows us how to live as keepers of the kingdom in very practical situations such as disagreements, marriage, encounters with the poor and needy, our life of prayer and the anxiety that comes with daily life. In doing this, it actually becomes a practical handbook for transformation into a little Christ.

The explicit expression of the New Commandment that we love one another is the third Scripture passage that informs the process of making a faith-based decision. It reminds us that, as Christians, we are challenged to live beyond our egos and to perform selfless acts of sacrificial love. This is done in direct imitation of the Divine: "Just as I have loved you, you also should love one another" (John 13:34). This attitude of self-forgetfulness is a sure indication that we have disengaged ourselves from the agenda of the ego and are being faithful to our identity as little Christs.

Paul's description of love (see 1 Corinthians 13:1-8) shows us the practical implications of this life of love lived in imitation of the Divine. It is the fourth Scripture passage that helps us make a faith-based decision. Christian love ambushes the natural tendencies of self-centered love. The disciple's love is patient, kind, happy at the success of others, humble and respectful. Most of all, it is expressed in the third characteristic of kingdom people who live lives of trustful surrender: "it bears all things, believes all things, hopes all things, endures all things" (1 Corinthians 13:7). Indeed, the love of the Christian disciple is a stunning witness that Abba can be trusted in the duty and challenges of the present moment.

Finally, as little Christs, we too share in Jesus' mission of bringing good news to the poor, proclaiming release to captives and recovery of sight to the blind, letting the oppressed go free and proclaiming a year of the Lord's favor (see Luke 4:16-21). This mission statement, found in the sixty-first chapter of Isaiah, reminds us that we, like Jesus, are sent on mission. Ours are lives meant to improve the lives of others and, indeed, of all creation. Ours are lives oriented toward the kingdom of God. A disciple without a sense of mission is a stunted Christian.

The Ten Commandments, the Sermon on the Mount, the New Commandment, Paul's description of love and Jesus' declaration of his mission all point us in the direction of what is good and acceptable and perfect. Surprisingly, the way we put these five Scripture passages into action provides great freedom and leeway. That suggests there is not a "predetermined" will of God imposed on us like fate. Rather, as "co-workers for the kingdom of God" (Colossians 4:11), we are encouraged to use our creativity as we choose among the available options in a particular situation.

Dialogue. Of course, any decision we make will naturally have social implications. The common good is a critical factor in making a Christian faith-based decision, and it is often discovered through dialogue. The second movement of assessment includes dialogue with the wider Christian community and the important individuals in our lives.

Consequently, we need to ask ourselves some important questions: Would this activity or option meet a real need in society or the church? What consequences, if any, would it have on the poor, needy and marginalized? How would it positively and negatively affect our relationships with God, others and self? Which option best witnesses to the lordship of Jesus over the world and over our lives?

These questions are best asked and discussed with the people who know us well and who might be affected by our decision. This is precisely what Ron did as he discussed with his wife the financial ramifications of accepting the job as director of Religious Education. It can also be helpful to discuss our options with our spiritual director, our extended family, our support group and, in some cases, those who pastor us in our church.

Discussion with others keeps us honest and can sometimes reveal areas of self-centered attachment of which we are not aware. It also lends an objective ear that can be helpful in sorting out a decision's ramifications and repercussions on commitments we have already made. There is something inherently suspicious when we try to discern alone, without the wisdom and input of others.

Energy and passion. A final element of assessment during a *kairos* moment has to do with our energy and passion. Do we have an internal inclination or impulse for a particular option? Are we stirred to a particular action? Do we emotionally "connect" with one particular option? Do we *want* to do it, and are we capable of carrying out the decision?

Surprisingly, if our hearts are disengaged from the agenda of the ego and we approach a crossroad in life with relative objectivity and an unbiased attitude, our "gut" feelings, desires and passions become a helpful compass in setting the direction for our future. Our passion revs us up and gives us the momentum and courage to take the step into what becomes our future. As someone once said to me, "Trust your gut—but use your head."

ACTION

The third and final movement in making a faith-based decision is the most obvious: following through with what we have discerned during the movements of awareness and assessment. It is the step of action.

Importance of timing. Ignatius of Loyola offers us some time-tested practical advice in regard to action in his fifth rule of discernment:

Fifth Rule. The fifth: in time of desolation never make a change, but be firm and constant in the proposals and determination in which one was the day preceding such desolation, or in the determination in which one was in the preceding consolation. Because, as in consolation the good spirit guides and counsels us more, so in desolation the bad spirit, with whose counsels we cannot find the way to a right decision.

This rule implies an important principle of spiritual formation: timing is everything; hence the scriptural distinction between *chronos* and *kairos*. Indeed, "for everything there is a season, and a time for every matter under heaven" (Ecclesiastes 3:1). Decisions made prematurely sometimes witness to our impatience and a decision-making process that did not adequately respect the movement of assessment. Overdue decisions can miss the transformative grace that distinguishes *kairos* from *chronos*.

More importantly, in his fifth rule, Ignatius offers a specific suggestion: never take action during spiritual desolation. As one Ignatian scholar describes it, "the phrase *spiritual desolation* indicates an affective heaviness (and so 'desolation') directly impacting our faith and pursuit of God's will (and so 'spiritual')." He adds that spiritual desolation can sometimes be occasioned by quite ordinary realities: lack of sufficient nourishment, exercise, rest; being disheartened or depressed; feeling anxious or in relationships that become heavier to sustain.

In other words, it is ill advised to make a faith-based decision when a storm swirls around us or when we are feeling off-balance and not centered. The best decisions are made when our feet are firmly planted on the ground, and we are at an even keel emotionally, not experiencing high and low mood swings. It is then that our "faith and pursuit" are most clearly seen and evidently experienced. Thus, Ignatius speaks of the "good spirit"—the Spirit of God—guiding and counseling us during periods of spiritual consolation, which, according to the Ignatian scholar, are "happy, uplifting movements of the heart (and so, 'consolation') directly impacting our life of faith and following of God's will (and so, 'spiritual')."

There seems to be a misconception among many people that the final step in the process of discernment is a revelation by God. We wait for the skies to open, for thunder to clap and God to speak. Ron's very question, "How do I know if God wants me to do this?" smacks of the belief that God might inform us of the divine will.

As mentioned earlier, I view discernment as making a faith-based decision and not "picking God's brain." Consequently, and in all likelihood, God will not reveal the right decision to us. Rather, the final act of any discernment process—and what makes it precisely a *faith-based* decision—is our own choice and action made in light of the kingdom of God and our baptismal commitment. We take the discerned step cognizant of the fact that "we walk by faith, not by sight" (2 Corinthians 5:7). As an evangelical pastor jokingly remarked to me, "It's really a roll of the dice—but you trust that God, not chance, has the final word."

The blessing of God. And, indeed, God *does* have the final word. God sometimes expresses it by giving us a deep-seated peace or sense that "this is right." That has been my experience.

It was the end of August 2003. I was six hours into the thirteen-hour flight between Chicago and Beijing. For over two months, I had been struggling to discern whether it was time for me to end my missionary life in China. I had come back to the States to discuss the issue with my religious superior. Signs were clearly pointing me home: the security police of Beijing had discovered who I was, what I was doing and where I lived; after eleven years, I was finding it increasingly difficult to live my Franciscan life alone; I was struggling with bouts of depression. And yet, my ego kept telling me that I would be perceived as a "failure" if I returned to the States. As a result, I was determined to doggedly find a way around the police and my feelings. In the middle of this particular flight to the Far East, however, something "clicked" inside me. I heard myself say in a gentle yet definitive way, "It's time to turn around and go back home."

The moment I gave myself permission to say that, I was overwhelmed with a feeling of peace. In that very instant, I felt freed, filled with light and that a burden had been taken off my shoulders. Indeed, a burden was: my ego. Though niggling doubts about what people would say behind my back and legitimate concerns about what would happen to the Roman Catholic community of Beijing remained and confounded me, I experienced a quiet sense that it was time to return home for good. I like to believe that was God's blessing on my decision. In the weeks that ensued, as I further discerned my decision, that peace only deepened.

Faith-based decisions, when respecting the movements of awareness and assessment and then acted on in a timely manner with sincerity and integrity, are often blessed by God. However, that should not be a prerequisite for action. In fact, the feeling of peace or the sense that a decision is "right"—the blessing of God—sometimes only comes *after* the decision has been made. It's a gift in hindsight and not foresight.

THE QUARTERLY REVIEW OF LIFE

- Check-in
- Call of the kingdom
- Scriptural foundation
- Reading, reflecting and listening
- Response
- Faith-based decision for change

Four times a year, two spiritual friends take a day off together. They usually go to the local zoo, arboretum or a public park. Once there, they talk through the Quarterly Review of Life. It is a process of discernment that not only sensitizes the participants to *kairos* moments but also fulfills the need for ongoing discernment and faith-based decision making.

The first step of the Quarterly Review of Life is the *check-in*. In this initial step, we simply step back and gain a perspective on our life since the last Quarterly Review of Life. Without judgment or criticism, we take an honest and loving look at what is currently going on in our personal and professional life and share it with our spiritual friend. What have been the most recent experiences of joy and happiness? What have been the most recent experiences of disappointment, sadness and sorrow? In what situations do we find tension, stress and anxiety raising their heads? Have we been spending an inordinate amount of time pursuing the agenda of the ego? Have we been faithful to our commitments to God (prayer and worship), others (committed relationships and friendships, concern for global issues and their effects on the lives of the poor and marginalized) and ourselves (rest, relaxation, exercise)? This first step in the Quarterly Review of Life is presenting an overview of the most recent events in our lives.

The second step is the *call of the kingdom*. Here we recall and reflect on our responsibility to be keepers of the kingdom and how we have measured up to that baptismal commitment. The questions we ask ourselves include the following: How have we succeeded and how have we failed in deliberately bringing the kingdom characteristics of peace, love and justice to the situations in which we have recently found ourselves? What actions and attitudes have been helpful in keeping God's intention for the world alive and which have been harmful? In this second step, we assess how God's intention and Jesus' ministry have had an impact and informed our everyday lives.

The Quarterly Review of Life continues with a *scriptural foun-*

dation. Is there a story, Gospel parable or Scripture passage that reflects or speaks to our current situation discussed in the second step? Here we approach the Scriptures as our own story and search for an illuminating or thought-provoking analogy. For example, if we are in the process of moving to a new home or uprooting our family to another city, perhaps we need to reflect on the call of Abraham and Sarah (see Genesis 12:1-9). If we are feeling discouragement with the choices our loved ones are making, we can reflect on Jesus' lament over Jerusalem (see Luke 13:31-35). If we feel overwhelmed by the apparent insensitivity to those left behind by society or perhaps if we feel we have been left behind in the ditch, we can turn to the parable of the good Samaritan (see Luke 10:25-37). If we are burdened with worries and anxieties, we can turn to Luke 12:22-34. If we find ourselves struggling or amazed by life, we can reflect on Romans 8:18-30. If we find ourselves struggling with some shameful sin or embarrassing situation, we can turn to the story of the women caught in adultery (see John 8:2-11).

The fourth step of the Quarterly Review of Life is *reading, reflecting and listening.* Having found a Scripture that speaks to our situation, we now mine it for its wisdom. We open our hearts to what God is saying specifically to us in this Scripture. What attitude or action does this Scripture challenge me to adopt or reject? For Gospel stories and parables, it is helpful to imagine ourselves in the scene and play the role of each individual person. For example, if I choose the story of the woman caught in adultery as the scriptural foundation for my life since the last Quarterly Review of Life, my spiritual friend and I initially imagine ourselves as the woman. We ask ourselves, how do we feel as we are publicly shamed? We then imagine ourselves as a person in the crowd and ask ourselves how often and in what recent situations have we self-righteously condemned others? Finally, we place ourselves in Jesus' shoes and ask why would we forgive her, why are we seemingly harsher with the crowd than with the woman caught in adultery? This fourth step can sometimes take as long as one hour as we dialogue and discuss the scene and the characters in it.

As with all scriptural reflection, this step leads to a *response* to what we have reflected on and heard. How can we respond to the message God is speaking to us in our chosen scriptural foundation? In what practical ways can we put flesh and bones on the attitudes and actions that the Scripture challenges forth? In other words, what strategies can we adopt to avoid putting ourselves in a particular sinful situation? How can we show acceptance and forgiveness to the person who betrayed us? What one habit or action can we actively seek to change to show a renewed confidence in the providence of God? We brainstorm about specific attitudes and actions in this step.

The Quarterly Review of Life concludes with the sixth step. We make a *faith-based decision for change*. After we have discerned what is good and acceptable and perfect for the common good in the preceding steps, we now commit to a specific action. In making this commitment and fulfilling it in the next quarter of the year, we believe that we are doing God's will here on earth.

This technique can be done between two or three spiritual friends. It can also provide the format for a monthly meeting with a spiritual director.

Discernment is a process that we use on a regular basis in our lives. Through awareness, assessment and action, it helps us to be keepers of the kingdom when we stand at an important crossroad in our lives. It also helps us to live reflective lives with the Quarterly Review of Life. To pray, "Thy will be done on earth as it is in heaven," is to commit to making faith-based decisions and thus become the brother and sister and mother of Jesus.

REFLECTION QUESTIONS

1. In what ways do I see myself as "brother and sister and mother" to Jesus?

2. When was my last experience of time as *kairos?* How did I know it? How did I respond?

3. In my opinion, what are the essential factors for making a faith-based decision?

4. How do I know if the fundamental option of my life is toward God or my ego?

5. In what ways can I make use of the Quarterly Review of Life for my own spiritual formation? Who would make a good spiritual friend?

Gospel Passages for Meditation and Prayer: Mark 3:31-35; Luke 22:39-46

Give Us This Day Our Daily Bread

Becoming What We Receive

To pray for daily bread is to follow the way of spiritual childhood. It is also to commit to becoming the bread of life for the hungry of the world.

IMAGES OF DEPENDENCY AND NEED can be found almost anywhere: an infant crying to be fed; a hitchhiker along the road; a beggar on the street; an outstretched hand of apology; a child struggling with the multiplication tables; a lonely widow in a nursing home. All of them, and so many more, are daily reminders that we are not independent, self-sufficient beings. We come into the world, live and die as people who are dependent and in need.

In our relationship with God especially, we are all infants, hitchhikers waiting for grace, beggars in need of a handout. To be human is to be in need. To pray, "Give us this day our daily bread," is to recognize our absolute dependency and existential poverty before God.

A story from the desert tradition of Christianity highlights how even the most spiritually mature person can easily forget how weakness and deficiency are part and parcel of the human condition:

> There was a desert father who each day ate just three biscuits. A brother came to him and when they sat down to eat the old man set three biscuits before the brother. The old man saw that the brother needed more food and brought him three more biscuits. After they had their fill and got up, the old man condemned the brother and said to him, "It is not right, brother, to serve the flesh." The brother asked pardon and left.
>
> The next time the old man ate, he placed before himself three biscuits, as was his custom. He ate them and was still hungry although he restrained himself. Again the next day he withstood his hunger. The old man began to weaken and he knew that God had abandoned him. Prostrating himself before God with tears, he begged that he not be abandoned. Then he saw an angel who said to him, "Because you condemned the brother, this has happened to you. Know therefore that the ability to deny the flesh or to do any good work is not within your power; rather, it is the goodness of God which strengthens you."

Everything is a gift. We can claim nothing as our own. We proclaim everything as a grace: looks, personality, friends, talents, our ability to perform acts of penance and devotion. This is the essence of humility. Through the selfless, sacrificial love of Jesus, Abba, the divine Almsgiver, transforms our poverty and dependency into the experience of life in abundance (see 2 Corinthians 8:9).

That spiritual insight gave birth to the voluntary poverty of Francis of Assisi. His poverty was not an expression of self-denial and mortification as it was in the monastic tradition. It was a radical affirmation that God alone is the source of everything that is good. God is the one who clothes us, feeds us, provides for our every need. Voluntary poverty is a living witness to the divine Almsgiver.

In the final days of his life, prompted by the different questions swirling around his simple vision of the gospel lifestyle, Francis wrote his famous "Testament." In this short document of forty-one verses, he summed up the major events of his life and their consequences for himself and his followers. Interestingly, no less than four sentences start with the expression "The Lord gave me . . . " The "Testament" actually begins with this expression as Francis indicates that God was the one who initiated his conversion. He continues by saying that God gave him faith, especially in churches and priests. God also gave him brothers and revealed the life according to the pattern of the gospel. As one scholar has written of the "Testament," Francis "describes a world that is strange to us, a world in which God is the starting point for everything."

And yet the ego wants to "ease God out" and take the credit that belongs to God. Sunday-morning television programs often provide real-life examples of this.

I admire evangelists who have the ability and financial resources to use television and radio in their ministry. Both means of communication take the gospel message beyond a Zip Code and, in some cases, beyond a continent. However, so often in begging money for a ministry that is typically named after the evangelist, I hear the subtle message "I am a success. I am doing good work. Please help me to expand my ministry." It's rare to explicitly hear God getting credit for the gift of expansion and success.

Francis compares this thievery of the ego to Adam and Eve eating the forbidden fruit: "For that person eats of the tree of the knowledge of good who makes his will his own and, in this way, exalts himself over the good things the Lord says and does in him." Whether it's as simple as giving some spare change to a beggar on the street or as impressive as bringing someone to Jesus, our prayer "Give us this day our daily bread" is to recognize the grace, goodness and generosity of God working in and through our daily lives.

Many of us come to an awareness of God as a faithful and trustworthy almsgiver only through personal tragedy. Suffering can unmask the ego's illusion of self-sufficiency. It can challenge us to return to who we truly are: poor beggars dependent on Abba and whose selfless acts of sacrificial love for others are a response to the divine love experienced in life.

After my father's suicide and burial, we discovered that he had a large debt that was not cancelled with his death. We were forced to sell the family home and automobile. My mother had been a homemaker until that time. She now had to learn a skill and find employment to support three of her five children still at home. There must have been many times when she prayed, "Give us this day our daily bread." And God did. Abba, the divine Almsgiver, provided for us.

Before any adversity or misfortune, we need not worry. When we are forced to admit our need and dependence, we need not be anxious. The way of the disciple is paved with trust in the providence of God the divine Almsgiver.

In teaching us to pray for something as ordinary as bread, Jesus also teaches us that nothing is too trifling or too trivial for Abba's concern. *Nothing* is inappropriate to place before God. If it is a worry or a problem or a concern for us, it is also a worry or a problem or a concern for God. We should not hesitate to bring it before Abba, no matter how small or insignificant it may seem. God's love has no limits; God's grace has no measure; God's concern has no boundary. Literally, we are the beloved of God. And so we pray,

"Give us this day our daily bread," while opening up our hands and trusting that God will provide for all our needs.

Jesus exhorts us, "Therefore I tell you, do not worry about your life, what you will eat or what you will drink, or about your body, what you will wear. Is not life more than food, and the body more than clothing?" (Matthew 6:25). For if Abba can feed the birds, who do not sow or reap, and clothe the wildflowers, which do not work or spin, Abba will certainly provide much more for us. Indeed, worry and anxiety clearly indicate what monopolizes human goals, identity and efforts; namely, the agenda of the ego with its overemotional investment in what we have, what we do and what people think of us.

Jesus reminded us that the divine Almsgiver is invested in our needs. Abba is on our side and wants what is good and acceptable and perfect for the common good. "Is there anyone among you who, if your child asks for bread, will give a stone? Or if the child asks for a fish, will give a snake? If you then, who are evil, know how to give good gifts to your children, how much more will your Father in heaven give good things to those who ask him!" (Matthew 7:9-11).

Though trivial worries or personal tragedies sometimes test our faith in the providence and goodness of God, we nevertheless remain the beloved children of God. Who we are in the eyes of God never changes. Carved into the very palms of the Divine, we can never be forgotten by God (see Isaiah 49:15-16). More than mere intellectual assent, a disciple's faith is living life as the beloved firstborn of a God who is as close as a father to his child.

BECOME LIKE CHILDREN

While a deacon, I became friends with one of our elderly friars, who was approaching his eightieth birthday. We loved to tease one another. Father Harold would jokingly mutter about the radical young friars, and I would complain about the old guys. In the midst of our bantering, I once naively said, "Harold, I will never grow old!" With a twinkle in his eye, he solemnly responded, "Albert, that's because you will never grow up!"

He meant it as a joke. But, one day, while reminiscing at Father Harold's grave, I saw his comment in a different light, and it dawned on me: That's actually the key to holiness! Never to grow up—never to outgrow God. In many respects, that posture is critical in spiritual formation. Hopefully, we never foolishly think that we can make it on our own without God or grace; when we do, the ego has clearly "eased God out" of our lives.

Just look at a child who is lost at the zoo or in the grocery store. The look of terror says it all. Children have no illusions. They know they are helpless and dependent. They know who provides them with toys, food and love. Though they may be unable to verbalize it, children instinctively know they are totally dependent on their parents.

To pray the petition "Give us this day our daily bread" is to be childlike and admit my dependency, helplessness and need. For as Jesus challenges us, "Truly I tell you, unless you change and become like children, you will never enter the kingdom of heaven" (Matthew 18:3). Scripture scholars tell us that Jesus holds up children as a model for the disciples not because of any supposed innocence or simplicity but "because of their complete dependence on, and trust in, their parents. So must the disciples be, in respect to God."

Perhaps no other person in the history of Christian spirituality lived this out in a more profound way than Marie-Françoise-Thérèse Martin, known to many as Saint Thérèse of Lisieux or "the Little Flower of Jesus." She spent the last decade of her life behind the walls of a cloistered Carmelite monastery in northern France. Thérèse died in 1897 of tuberculosis at the age of twenty-four and never wrote a single sentence of theology. Yet, surprisingly, Pope John Paul II on October 19, 1997, conferred on her the special honor given very sparingly in the history of Roman Catholicism and only twice before to women. He declared Thérèse the thirty-third Doctor of the Church. Traditionally, this honorific title attests to a saint's "eminent learning" and "great sanctity."

A portion of the pope's homily on the occasion is worthy of note:

> Thérèse of the Child Jesus and the Holy Face is the youngest of all the "Doctors of the Church," but her ardent spiritual journey shows such maturity, and the insights of faith expressed in her writings are so vast and profound that they deserve a place among the great spiritual masters. . . . She counters a rational culture, so often overcome by practical materialism, with the disarming simplicity of the "little way" which, by returning to the essentials, leads to the secret of all life: the divine Love that surrounds and penetrates every human venture. In a time like ours, so frequently marked by an ephemeral and hedonistic culture, this new Doctor of the Church proves to be remarkably effective in enlightening the mind and heart of those who hunger and thirst for truth and love.

There is an irony in the pope noting "such maturity" in Thérèse's approach to spiritual formation. She herself, when asked about it in the final year of her life, called it "the way of spiritual childhood." And when asked to describe it, Thérèse said,

> It is the way of spiritual childhood, the way of confidence and abandonment to God. I want to teach [people] the little means which have proved so perfectly successful for myself. I want to tell them that there is only one thing for us to do here below: to throw at Jesus' feet the flowers of little sacrifices, to win Him through our caresses. That is the way in

which I have taken hold of Him, and that is why I shall get such a good welcome.

About three weeks later, when asked what it meant to remain a little child, Thérèse said,

> It means that we acknowledge our nothingness; that we expect everything from the good Lord, as a child expects everything from its father; it means to worry about nothing, not to build on fortune; it means to remain little, seeking only to gather flowers, the flowers of sacrifice, and to offer them to the good Lord for His pleasure. It also means not to attribute to ourselves the virtues we practice, not to believe that we are capable of anything, but to acknowledge that it is the good Lord who has placed that treasure in the hand of His little child that He may use it when He needs it, but it remains always God's own treasure. Finally, it means that we must not be discouraged by our faults, for children fall frequently.

Thérèse's description of spiritual childhood points directly to the way of the disciple. It acknowledges the importance of trustful surrender and confident abandonment that is a quality of kingdom people. It requires the "flowers of little sacrifices," namely, selfless acts of sacrificial love for God and others. It is an affirmation that we are poor beggars and that everything is a gift from God the divine Almsgiver. As disciples, we walk the path of life with confidence in the generosity, forgiveness and compassion of Abba. We are also challenged not to get sidetracked with the ego's desire to "build on fortune."

It's a curious footnote in the history of Christian spirituality that Thérèse of Lisieux makes no reference to Jesus' injunction to "become like children" in her description of spiritual childhood. In fact, she initially came to this insight by her reflection on two passages from the Hebrew Scriptures.

In a letter to one of her sisters, Marie, Thérèse told the story about how she discovered her way of spiritual formation. She mentioned she was looking for a "very straight, very short, a completely new little way" to heaven. She continues that with the newly invented elevator, people no longer needed to climb the steps of a staircase. "I would also like to find an elevator to lift me up to Jesus, because I'm too little to climb the rough staircase of perfection."

So she decided to search the Scriptures for her elevator. She found this quote from Eternal Wisdom, who had built herself a house: "You that are simple, turn in here!" (Proverbs 9:4). So, as she continued her search through Scripture, Thérèse asked God what God would do with the simple little one who responded to the divine call of Wisdom.

Her eyes fell on the prophet Isaiah: "As a mother comforts her child, so I will comfort you. . . . You shall nurse and be carried on her arm, and dandled on her knees" (Isaiah 66:13, 12).

Thérèse continued in her letter to Marie:

> Oh! Never have words more tender, more melodious, come to rejoice my soul. The elevator that must lift me up to heaven is Your arms, Jesus! For that I do not need to become big. On the contrary, I have to stay little—may I become little, more and more.

And with that discovery and insight, the way of spiritual formation that would make Thérèse of Lisieux the thirty-third Doctor of the Church had begun to be paved.

SELF-SUFFICIENCY VERSUS SELF-DEFICIENCY

The ego tries to convince us that the really important things in life are based on what we have, what we do and what people think of us. If we buy into that illusion, we begin to take charge. We begin wielding power. We become manipulative and greedy. We insist on things being done our way. We demand what we think is rightfully ours and, like the prodigal son, off we go, only to end up in a pigpen!

This independent, self-sufficient approach to life is the fundamental sin of so many of us. It is the refusal of grace. It is the denial of *Ubuntu,* the denial that we need one another to come to know who we truly are. It ignores the common good. It is the failure to acknowledge Abba as the divine Almsgiver. It is Adam and Eve reaching for forbidden fruit all over again.

But, luckily, self-sufficiency can take us only so far. Sooner or later we run up against a brick wall. We get a sudden glimpse into our existential self-deficiency. We finish eating the apple and discover, a few hours later, that we are hungry again. We spend all our inheritance on fun and games, only to worry about how we will buy tomorrow's bread.

Then we have to face the harsh reality that attacks the agenda of the ego. In the words of the prodigal son, "How many of my father's hired hands have bread enough and to spare, but here I am dying of hunger! I will get up and go to my father" (Luke 15:17-18). In other words, we come to recognize our dependency and the futility of preserving and protecting self-concern, self-image, self-preservation and self-gratification.

Preaching has always come easily to me. Even back in high school, my friends would tease, "Wherever two or three are gathered, there is Albert preaching." I spent the first ten years of my ordained ministry promoting my talent. After doctoral studies and a brief stint on a retreat house staff, I began preaching church retreats and parish missions full time. Booked ahead for two years at a time, I crisscrossed the country—and several continents—three weeks of every month. In just over two years, I had earned

150,000 frequent-flyer miles on United Airlines.

I enjoyed the lifestyle of a jetsetter. I met some wonderful people. I saw places I never dreamt I would see—from the tomb of Saint Francis to the body of Chinese Chairman Mao. And, from the many letters I received, I know I touched lots of people along the way.

So why did I give it all up? Because I gradually came to realize that I was not preaching the gospel; I was preaching myself. I had convinced myself of the very lie that I so desperately tried to convince my listeners of: "You need to listen to me. My words can change your life." I began to feel like a fraud as I "eased God out" of my ministry and pumped more and more hot air into an already inflated ego. Then one day it smacked me right in the face: all my self-promotion had gotten me was life in a pigpen—in business class at 37,000 feet!

That encounter with the illusions of the ego threw me into a tailspin and began a two-year process of discerning my unique way of being a keeper of the kingdom. It rekindled a childhood dream that I had put on the back burner when the fame of a preacher became so seductive and enticing. I rediscovered my passion for the Chinese culture and language. I ended up in China for over eleven years and lived most of the time like a child as I struggled to learn how to speak again.

Giving up "my" preaching ministry was one of the toughest decisions I ever made. Now, in hindsight, however, I wonder why I dallied for two years before leaving for China, since I see it as the action of God's generous grace in my life. The sin of my self-*sufficiency* was transformed into the painful awareness of my self-*deficiency*. Life in the pigpen sooner or later brings us to the awareness that we are far from home. And "where sin increased, grace abounded all the more" (Romans 5:20). Responding to the generous alms of God's grace is the secret to spiritual maturity and is Thérèse of Lisieux's way of spiritual childhood.

Interestingly, and much to my surprise, since returning to the United States from mainland China, I find myself being asked time and again to preach retreats and give workshops on spiritual formation. Now though, I am only too aware that it's not "my" preaching ministry but God's. I can take credit for none of it. And as I travel from venue to venue, I find myself more and more dependent on God. Daily I call on God to provide me with the daily bread of strength and stamina to effectively use the talent that has been graciously given to me.

> *The whole Christian life is a life in which the further a person progresses, the more he has to depend directly on God and it's not the other way around at all. . . . The more we progress, the less we are self-sufficient. The more we progress, the poorer we get so that the man who has progressed most, is totally poor—he has to depend directly on God. He's got nothing left in himself.*
>
> THOMAS MERTON

Growth in the spiritual life is measured by our awareness of our absolute dependence on Abba and our continual petition for daily bread. The disciple is a living incarnation of the petition "Give us this day our daily bread." A great paradox in the spiritual life, indeed: to mature is to become a child, poor, needy, helpless and dependent. This is just another way of saying that everything is a gift.

ACTIVE AND CONTEMPLATIVE SPIRITUALITY

Thomas Merton once distinguished between two ways of spiritual formation. The first way, based on the first three Gospels, is characterized by active faith: We "do" things in response to God's gifts and graces. We are in control, take charge and equate spiritual formation with external actions. We go to church. We read Scripture and say our prayers. We fast. We share our time, treasures and talents with those in need. In some respects, this can be characterized as the masculine approach to spiritual formation.

Merton said the second—more contemplative, more mature and more childlike—is based on the words of Jesus in John's Gospel: "I am the way" (John 14:6). In this second approach, the person stops "floundering around and thrashing around and doing this and that." One is content simply to wait for the Lord, expect the Lord and then abide in the Lord.

This second way requires a person to develop a more receptive stance toward the Divine, traditionally a characteristic of the feminine approach to spiritual formation. Perhaps this is why Teresa of Avila refers to Franciscan Peter of Alcantara's statement that women make much more progress along the spiritual path than men.

The active approach of the first way can take us only so far. To advance further along the spiritual path, sooner or later we must surrender control, become receptive and have the humility to be led. In the words of Jesus to Peter, "Very truly, I tell you, when you were younger, you used to fasten your own belt and to go wherever you wished. But when you grow old, you will stretch out your hands, and someone else will fasten a belt around you and take you where you do not wish to go" (John 21:18). The willingness to be led by God shows the maturity and humility of the way of spiritual childhood.

BECOME WHAT YOU RECEIVE

But to pray, "Give us this day our daily bread," is not simply an act of humility and childlike faith in God's providence. It is also an adult commitment to become daily bread for others.

The Gospels indicate that Jesus enjoyed eating and drinking, so much so, that he was accused of being "a glutton and a drunkard" (see Matthew 11:18-19). Furthermore, Jesus often broke bread and drank with the outcasts and public sinners of his day (see Mark 2:15-17). Such meals were a source of scandal for the Pharisees and a topic of their gossip: "This fellow welcomes sinners and eats with them" (Luke 15:2). For in that act Jesus was becoming the bread of Abba's unconditional love and forgiveness for those who had been ostracized and condemned by institutional religion. In his table fellowship, Jesus was making present the heavenly banquet of God's kingdom, where people are invited for who they are, the beloved, and not excluded for what they have done.

Almost immediately after Jesus' death and resurrection, the community of believers experienced Jesus' continuing presence and ministry around the table of fellowship. They told his story again; they received instruction and encouragement; and in the breaking of bread, they discovered not only the Lord but also their own identity and ministry (see Acts 2:42; Luke 24:30, 35).

While preaching in Cameroon, West Africa, I heard the story of a young Christian in his twenties who had come to the village of Shisong with hopes of getting medical treatment at the small hospital staffed by Franciscan sisters. He had the rare disease elephantiasis, in which a person's extremities get exceptionally large, swollen and appear quite grotesque. In the case of this young man, it affected his right arm.

When he came to the village, no one would sell him any food. Villagers were deathly afraid of making any contact with him and wrongly feared that if they touched him or his money, they themselves would catch the disease. So they kept him at a distance from the hospital compound and the market. For two days he could not make his need for medicine known. He also had nothing to eat.

A Muslim in the village heard of this Christian's plight. He went to the open village market and bought mangoes, peanuts and bananas and brought them to the young man. The Muslim did this every day in his very traditional culture, where interreligious exchange on any level is still virtually taboo. One day, the young Christian said to the kind Muslim, "Sir, for the past few days, you have been my daily bread."

The bread we pray for is the same bread we are challenged to become for one another. The Muslim of Shisong intuitively understood this better than the Christians who prayed mere words at the Eucharist. They had forgotten to become what they had themselves received. To receive the Bread of Life is to make the commitment to become the Bread of Life for others. It has profound social consequences. It is truly a "comm-union," from the Latin meaning a "union with."

One night while traveling in mainland China, I was writing letters in the hotel room when there was a knock at the door. It was the hotel's young assistant manager who, like many Chinese, wanted to practice his English. The small Mass book and Mass kit left on the dresser must have given him the clue, for he addressed me as *Shenfu,* the Chinese word for "Father."

The assistant manager cautiously accepted my invitation to come in and sit down. Raising the volume on the television set so no one could overhear our conversation if the room was bugged, he began telling me about the underground Catholic Church. He detailed how he and other Chinese who remain faithful to the Vatican still endured blatant forms of persecution.

Realizing that we had won each other's confidence, I asked him about the student protests for democracy in Tiananmen Square in 1989. With a whisper that contained more pride than fear, he told me how this particular hotel had secretly sent vegetables and tea to help feed the protesters in Beijing.

In astonishment I asked, "Wasn't that a terrible risk for this hotel?"

"Shenfu, Jesus would have commanded it" was his matter-of-fact answer.

In China, in late May and early June of 1989, the Eucharist was not housed in gold tabernacles as it is in Catholic churches throughout the world, but was carried in trucks to Tiananmen Square under the appearance of vegetables and tea.

There are so many hungry people in this world, and their hunger is more than physical. Children are starving for affection. The elderly are groaning out of loneliness. People in our families and circle of friends are craving our time and attention. The poor and the sick yearn for attention and care. The wealthy hunger for meaning. Our challenge as eucharistic people is to become the Bread of Life for others. Like that Muslim and like that Chinese hotel manager, we must become the bread that feeds the hungry people around us. We are called to feed others with selfless acts of sacrificial love. This is communion, the way of the disciple.

That is precisely what we commit ourselves to at each Eucharist. The Communion distributor addresses this challenge to us personally and to the whole community: "Body of Christ," "Blood of Christ." When we say our "Amen," we accept that challenge and discover our truest identity as little Christs.

Saint Augustine once preached,

> "You, however, are the Body of Christ and His members." If, therefore, you are the Body of Christ and His members, your mystery is presented at the table of the Lord, you receive your mystery. To that which you are, you answer: "Amen"; and by answering, you subscribe to it. For you hear: "The Body of Christ!" and you answer: "Amen!" Be a member of Christ's Body, so that your "Amen" may be the truth.

And so our "Amen" translates into "Yes! I am called to break my body and pour out my blood for everybody. Yes! I am daily bread for the hungry people I know and those I don't know."

That "Amen" has profound social consequences. We should

think twice before we say it and receive the Eucharist. It goes to the very heart of our identity as little Christs.

BARRACKS 26 OF DACHAU

Some years ago, on a Wednesday afternoon in June, I walked the grounds of Dachau concentration camp with many other pilgrims from all over the world. I found myself almost paralyzed with grief and sorrow as I walked in stunned silence, trying to understand the satanic horror of Nazi Germany. I remember pausing to pray at the spot where Barracks 26 once stood. It was the prison dormitory that housed so many Roman Catholics—including Gen.

I had met Gen a few years earlier at a suburban church in Chicago. Her experience while imprisoned in Barracks 26 speaks volumes about the meaning of the Eucharist.

Every day Catholic prisoners of Dachau got one meal: a chunk of bread the size of a dinner roll and a cup of watered-down soup. But each day, one Catholic prisoner would voluntarily sacrifice his or her meager bread ration for the celebration of the Eucharist. That chunk of bread would be consecrated by a priest and then secretly passed around as communion for the prisoners.

That daily Eucharist in Barracks 26 of Dachau was never reduced to a pious, sentimental devotion. It was quite literally about dying to one's hunger so that others could be fed. It was about giving so that others could receive. It was, as Merton suggests, "the Sacrament of charity—that charity by which we dedicate our freedom to God and to one another." Indeed, it was the sacrament of *Ubuntu,* humanity for others.

In another Nazi concentration camp, Auschwitz, Franciscan Maximilian Kolbe offered to exchange his life for that of a condemned sergeant, Francis Gajowniczek, whose wife and children were still alive. Kolbe's "eucharistic" death gives stunning witness to the words of his spiritual father, Saint Francis: "The great Almsgiver will accuse me of theft if I do not give what I have to some-one in greater need." To receive the Eucharist is to make the com-mitment to become the Eucharist—for whoever needs it.

BROKEN BREAD AS CHALLENGE AND MIRROR

Francis of Assisi challenged his followers to imitate the eucharis-tic action in the way they live their lives:

> Are we not moved by piety at these things when the pious Lord puts Himself into our hands and we touch Him and receive Him daily with our mouth? Do we refuse to recog-nize that we must come into His hands?

As Jesus has emptied himself into the hands of men and women, so we, as little Christs, are called to empty ourselves without counting the cost. As God in Jesus has given himself totally to us in selfless, sacrificial love, so we are called to give ourselves to-tally to one another.

When we do not intend to become the Eucharist for others, when we do not intend to become daily bread for another person, when we have no intention of giving ourselves totally and break-ing our bodies and pouring out our blood for the salvation of this world, then the Eucharist is reduced to a mere sentimental, empty action. The Bread of Life becomes the appetizer for apathy.

Indeed, if we do not intend to become what we receive, we would do well to absent ourselves from communion. "For all who eat and drink without discerning the body," Paul warned the Cor-inthians, "eat and drink judgment against themselves" (1 Corin-thians 11:29).

In John's Gospel, the humble, selfless act of foot washing replaces the Eucharist. In a sense, it is a vivid reminder that for at least the first hundred years of Christianity, the Eucharist was considered first and foremost an action, not an object. Jesus challenges us with these words, "So if I, your Lord and Teacher, have washed your feet, you also ought to wash one another's feet. For I have set you an example, that you also should do as I have done to you" (John 13:14-15). By virtue of our baptism, we are the body of Christ on earth. And every day, in some way, shape or form, we are challenged to forget ourselves in selfless acts of sacrificial love.

In the breaking of the daily eucharistic bread as well as the humble act of foot washing, we recognize the Lord and the example he has set for us. We should also recognize ourselves and the many times our own hearts have been broken out of love and compassion, the times when we have performed selfless acts of sacrificial love. The broken bread and dirty towel are not simply windows into the life of Jesus. They are also mirrors of our truest identity.

Clare of Assisi is credited with giving birth to the feminine expression of Francis's spirituality. She sees the image of the crucified Christ as a mirror of the disciple. Indeed, in the final year of her life, in her fourth letter to Agnes of Prague, she explicitly refers to the crucified Christ as "that Mirror, suspended on the wood of the Cross." Clare encouraged Agnes to gaze on that mirror each day and to continually study her own face—a little Christ—in it. She writes to Agnes of Prague:

Indeed,
in that mirror [of the crucified Christ],
blessed poverty,
holy humility,
and inexpressible charity shine forth . . .

To gaze on the Crucified is to gaze into a mirror where we see the childlike characteristics of the disciple: poverty and dependency, humility and the awareness that all is gift, charity expressed in selfless acts of sacrificial love for others. Such contemplation also leads us to rediscover who we already are: the body of

Christ called to be broken for the salvation of the world.

When we pray, "Give us this day our daily bread," we are asking for the daily sustenance we need to survive. We call to mind that Abba is the divine Almsgiver who provides for all of our needs. We also call to mind and commit to becoming our truest selves, little Christs, called to be the daily bread for the hungry of the world.

REFLECTION QUESTIONS

1. In what practical ways do I witness to the fact that everything is a grace and gift from God?

2. When did I most recently experience God as the divine Almsgiver?

3. Which of Merton's two ways of spiritual formation is most dominant in my life: the active faith of the first three Gospels or the contemplative childlikeness of John's Gospel?

4. Is my life truly eucharistic? How? When? Is the Eucharist a devotion or a challenge for me?

5. In what ways and what situations am I challenged to wash the feet of others? How do I know if I am washing feet selfishly or selflessly?

Gospel Passages for Meditation and Prayer: Matthew 18:1-4; John 13:1-17

Forgive Us Our Trespasses

Running into a Father's Open Arms

Praying for forgiveness is a vivid reminder that God frees us from debilitating guilt and forgets our past. No sin is written with indelible ink.

MARIE WAS IN HER LATE SIXTIES. I used to refer to her as the "guardian angel" of St. Raymond's Church in the Bronx. She attended daily Mass and would read or be eucharistic minister at a moment's notice. She often unlocked the church on the mornings when I overslept. Her life as a retiree also gave her the opportunity to set up and attend every funeral. Monday mornings found her counting the previous day's collection. Whenever I would thank her for her kindnesses and dedication, Marie would smile, always with a touch of sadness in her eyes, and say, "It's a way to make up for lost time."

It wasn't until a year later that I discovered that her availability at the church was, in fact, a penance she had imposed on herself for what she believed to be "an unforgivable sin": having an abortion as a poor and pregnant seventeen-year-old in a small Midwestern town.

DEBILITATING GUILT AND HEALTHY GUILT

The obsession we sometimes have with our past sins is one of the worst afflictions of the soul and a major obstacle in spiritual formation. We "ease God out" of our lives and allow the ego to become judge and prison guard. As it did in Marie's case, the ego finds us guilty and imprisons us behind the prison bars of shame in the dark, dank cell of our memories. Constantly reminding us of our sin, the ego then condemns us to forced labor in a cemetery where we are repeatedly exhuming skeletons, only to bury them and exhume them again. This is the death camp of the ego. Focused on "me," the ego can be excruciatingly more demanding than God as it demands nothing less than perfect contrition evidenced in external behavior that never quite measures up.

This obsession blankets the soul with a devastating and debilitating guilt. Such guilt puts the heart in a straightjacket that constricts and controls all its movements. Shackled by shame and paralyzed by remorse, we are virtually incapable of repentance. In effect, we become like the living dead, counting off the days remaining on death row.

However, there is another way to approach our sinfulness that instills a guilt that inspires rather than incapacitates. Looking on our sinfulness as our weakness and vulnerability to the self-centered agenda of the ego gives rise to a healthy guilt. Healthy guilt is a wise teacher and trusted companion in spiritual formation. It runs a halfway house of compassion where we are taught to honestly admit our sins, examine their roots and causes, learn from them and move on. Such guilt challenges us never to forget that God has the final word. That's why it is such a trusted companion.

In Marie's case, healthy guilt would have called her to break free from the obsession with self-concern and self-image. It would have helped her to place a thirty-year-old sin within the context of a poor, frightened young teenager whose boyfriend had abandoned her. This understanding, far from justifying her action, would have inspired her to humbly confess her sin with the full knowledge that the open, merciful arms of God had been waiting for her all along. Instead of constricting and imprisoning her as debilitating guilt did, healthy guilt would have freed and impelled her to confession, repentance and celebration. Healthy guilt is only too aware that God is patient with our sinfulness and lavish with divine forgiveness.

A contemporary of Isaiah of Jerusalem, the prophet Micah had an insight into the extravagance of God's forgiveness. Stunned by its reality and filled with awe, he exclaimed:

> Who is a God like you, pardoning iniquity
>   and passing over the transgression
>   of the remnant of your possession?
> He does not retain his anger forever,
>   because he delights in showing clemency.
> He will again have compassion on us;
>   he will tread our iniquities under foot.
> You will cast all our sins
>   into the depths of the sea. (Micah 7:18-19)

Micah's God "delights" in taking the sins of our past and throwing them into the deepest ocean imaginable. They are gone forever. Then God places a sign over that ocean, which reads, "No fishing allowed." When God forgives, God forgets.

In the Hebrew Scriptures, the primary verb *salah*, "to forgive," is used only of God; forgiveness is therefore a divine prerogative reserved exclusively to God. A synonym for this verb, *nasa*, means "to bear, to remove, or to carry away." And so, when God forgives, God "carries away" the sin. And not only that: divine mercy also "removes" the straightjacket of debilitating guilt that the ego forces us to wear.

The divine prerogative of forgiveness throws the ego's case against us out of court. Hence we are to be as merciful and forgiving with ourselves as Abba is. The attitude of Abba sets the standard for our own treatment of ourselves: "Be merciful, just as your Father is merciful" (Luke 6:36). No matter how often we find ourselves knocking on the door of forgiveness, Abba's open arms are always waiting to carry us over the threshold. No matter how often we find ourselves knocking on the door of forgiveness, we offer ourselves mercy and compassion, knowing full well that the Father has "rescued us from the power of darkness and transferred us into the kingdom of his beloved Son, in whom we have redemption, the forgiveness of sins" (Colossians 1:13-14).

THE DIVINE INITIATIVE

Jesus reveals the forgiveness of God in parables that imply that forgiveness is as natural to his Abba as it is to a loving father, an anxious woman and a worried shepherd. He tells us that our saving God is like the loving father of the prodigal son, who waits at home for his beloved child to return; and when he sees his child on the road, the father joyfully runs out and welcomes him back with open arms. The father does not even give his wayward son a chance to apologize. No wonder this parable is sometimes called the parable of the loving or lavish father (see Luke 15:11-32). Such a name change shifts our attention to the exact point Jesus was trying to make in the parable: The father is overly generous with his mercy and understanding.

Our saving God, Jesus says, is like that anxious woman who lights a lamp and very carefully sweeps the floor in hopes of finding the one lost coin. Her anxious desire to find it is more pressing than any other immediate duty or daily obligation before her (see Luke 15:8-10). Indeed, it is *the* duty and obligation of the present moment.

Our saving God is like that worried shepherd who leaves the ninety-nine sheep and frantically goes in search of the one lost sheep. The fact that the shepherd is willing to risk the entire flock for the sake of one betrays an investment and concern that is second to none (see Luke 15:1-7). Such an attitude certainly challenges the obsession with the size of a congregation found so often in contemporary priests and pastors.

God takes the initiative, runs down the road, lights a lamp and leaves the others in order to enter our sinful world with the alms of mercy and forgiveness. All we need do is accept what we are freely offered, to allow ourselves to be found. Indeed, the first question ever addressed to a sinful human being is the very question addressed to us: "Where are you?" (Genesis 3:9). So much of spiritual formation is about coming out of hiding and standing in the light, about moving from remorse to repentance. Debilitating guilt convinces us to cower in embarrassment and shame; healthy guilt convinces us to come forward, bask in divine forgiveness and try again to "sin no more," as Jesus once said (see John 8:11). That is truly the essence of repentance: to be transparent before God about our sinfulness, accept God's forgiveness and recommit to being our truest self, a little Christ.

We have no legal right to God's mercy. We cannot earn it as the ego would have us believe. We do not deserve it. Like all the things that really matter in the spiritual life, forgiveness comes as a pure gift from God, as generous alms from the divine Almsgiver.

Perhaps no other person in the history of Christian spirituality had a greater experience and appreciation for this insight than Martin Luther. His experience of God's unconditional forgiveness set Luther free from his struggles with scrupulosity; his appreciation for it gave birth to a whole new expression of Christianity founded on the divine initiative. Luther used a term from Paul's letter to the church at Rome and called this insight "justification."

When asked to write a summary of his doctrines in 1537, he gave it the place of prominence in what has become known as the Smalcald Articles:

> The first and chief article is this: Jesus Christ, our God and Lord, died for our sins and was raised again for our justification (Romans 3:24-25). He alone is the Lamb of God who takes away the sins of the world (John 1:29), and God has laid on Him the iniquity of us all (Isaiah 53:6). All have sinned and are justified freely, without their own works and merits, by His grace, through the redemption that is in Christ Jesus, in His blood (Romans 3:23-25). This is necessary to believe. This cannot be otherwise acquired or grasped by any work, law, or merit. Therefore, it is clear and certain that this faith alone justifies us. . . . Nothing of this article can be yielded or surrendered, even though heaven and earth and everything else falls (Mark 13:31).

This article makes it clear that for Luther, justification is an action initiated totally by God in Jesus Christ on our behalf. It clearly cannot be "acquired or grasped" by anything the ego would have us do. We receive it as a gift through faith in the suffering of Christ.

JUDAS AND PETER

A story from the fourth-century desert tradition of early monasticism suggests that God not only takes the initiative but also is actively invested in showing mercy and forgiveness:

> An elder was asked by a certain soldier if God would forgive a sinner. And he said to him: Tell me, beloved, if your cloak is torn, will you throw it away? The soldier replied and said: No. I will mend it and put it back on. The elder said to him:

If you take care of your cloak, will God not be merciful to
His own image?

There is never reason to despair or doubt the forgiveness of
God, no matter how hideous, heinous or hateful the sin may be.
Despite the spurious doubts raised by the ego, God would never
withhold mercy from anyone made in the divine image. Indeed, it
is the will of the Father that no one be lost (see Matthew 18:14).

Thomas Merton told a group of religious men and women in
the Far East, "*Don't* set limits to the mercy of God. *Don't* imagine
that because you are not pleasing to yourself, you're not pleasing
to God." Indeed, God loves us not because we are good but because God is good. According to Saint Bonaventure, this is where
Judas made his ultimate mistake. Instead of returning to the foun-
tain of mercy out of hope for forgiveness,
the disciple became terrified by the enor-
mity of his crime and so despaired. I can
only wonder if a single act of despair in a
moment of profound remorse cancelled
all the good that Judas had done in his
life. The Abba revealed by Jesus leads me
to think otherwise.

> *Every soul that stands*
> *under condemnation with*
> *nothing to say for itself*
> *has the power to turn and*
> *discover it can yet breathe*
> *the fresh air of God's*
> *pardon and mercy.*
>
> BERNARD OF CLAIRVAUX

Judas's tragedy can be contrasted with
the experience of Peter. At the charcoal
fire where Peter was warming himself,
we see his obsession with self-image and
self-preservation. Fearing damage to his reputation and maybe
even his life, Peter denied Jesus three times (see John 18:15-27).

It is after the resurrection around another fire that Peter reaf-
firms his commitment to the way of the disciple (see John 21:9). As
he had denied Jesus three times, he is given three opportunities to
respond to the risen Lord's question, "Simon son of John, do you

love me more than these?" And with each affirmation, mercy and forgiveness are granted as he is sent on mission: "Feed my lambs. . . . Tend my sheep. . . . Feed my sheep" (see vv. 15-19).

Peter's experience demonstrates that Abba never tires in presenting us opportunities to show our deepest desires, our truest self. We are never condemned to the finality of a single action. We need only to come out of hiding, to allow ourselves to be found and to be embraced by the father who comes running down the road toward us. Before we have the opportunity to blurt out, "Forgive us our trespasses," we are reunited, robed, ringed and regaled at a homecoming party. There is never a reason to despair of our salvation when everything speaks of mercy and forgiveness. As the beloved of Abba, we are only a heart's request away from forgiveness.

THE TRANSFORMATIVE POWER OF DIVINE FORGIVENESS

Young Francis of Assisi must have been a man steeped in shame and guilt. According to the first biography of the newly canonized saint, the evidence suggests a very sinful past from which Francis needed to repent. And he did.

He sought out a place of prayer one day at Poggio Bustone and reflected on all the good things God was doing through him and all the gifts God had given to him.

While reflecting on these alms with the gratitude of adoration, Francis simultaneously was aware of the abomination of his sins. He started praying, "Lord, be merciful to me, a sinner." As he prayed that prayer, the biographer writes,

Certainty of the forgiveness of all his sins poured in,
    and the assurance of being revived in grace was
        given to him.

At that moment, Francis experienced the alms of God's merciful forgiveness in a way he never before had experienced. He accepted what was given him from the throne of grace: the awareness that God took the initiative, entered into his sinfulness and opened up the arms of salvation to a wayward son. All had been forgiven and forgotten. There no longer was need to brood over his past. The biographer concludes the narration of this event with a telling remark:

> renewed in spirit,
> he now seemed to be changed into another man.

A similar experience would occur in the eighteenth century. John Wesley was one of three people who had tried to revitalize a very rationalistic Anglican Church. Having worked as a minister and missionary, Wesley had a conversion experience that would shape his belief that believers should experience Christ personally. He writes of his experience:

> In the evening [of Wednesday, May 24, 1738] I went very unwillingly to a society in Aldersgate-Street, where one was reading Luther's preface to the *Epistle to the Romans*. About a quarter before nine, while he was describing the change which God works in the heart through faith in Christ, I felt my heart strangely warmed. I felt that I did trust in Christ, Christ alone for salvation; and an assurance was given me, that He had taken away *my* sins, even *mine,* and saved *me* from the law of sin and death.

The mercy of God sets us free from any self-imposed death sentence and entices us to turn around and return to the open arms of our forgiving Abba. Francis of Assisi and John Wesley both testify to the renewal and transformation that occur when we do that. Asking for pardon and experiencing the extraordinary gift of divine mercy is realizing what Judas forgot and Peter remembered: sin is never written with indelible ink. God's lavish forgiveness breaks the shackles of debilitating guilt and paralyzing remorse.

A SIN FORGIVEN

Marie's abortion was an albatross around her neck. Her years of self-inflicted penance simply fed her shame. Her entire spiritual life and personal piety were anchored in the guilt of her sin and an image of God as a judge demanding her to grovel on her knees. She often told me that she was afraid God was going to throw it in her face on Judgment Day. "God cannot forgive something so terrible. I'll have to answer for it and I won't know what to say."

On many occasions Marie and I talked about the Abba of Jesus and how this God forgives and forgets. I tried to take different approaches, yet each time I would run up against the brick wall of Marie's guilt. No argument, no matter its craft or ingenuity, could break through the prison bars Marie's ego had slammed and locked around her soul.

One Saturday afternoon before the vigil Mass, I noticed Marie sitting in her favorite location: the pew before the side altar dedicated to the Sacred Heart of Jesus. That statue of Jesus, with his wounded heart exposed and suggesting divine compassion, had been a source of intellectual comfort for Marie for as long as I had known her. I went up to greet her and ask her to "whisper a prayer for me" as I always did. She looked up and smiled. But something was different. There was no sadness in her eyes. She did not even give her usual response, "And you do the same for me." Instead, she replied, "I'd be delighted to, Father!"

I was the celebrant for the six o'clock Mass the following morning—and I overslept. I got to the sacristy about fifteen minutes before Mass, only to discover that, for the first time since I had been at St. Raymond's, Marie had not unlocked the church.

Over the following weeks, Marie continued to attend daily Mass, but she suddenly asked not to do the first reading at Mass anymore. She said it made her nervous. She still helped out with funeral preparations, but she stopped counting the collection on Mondays. "A retired woman my age should be enjoying the morning talk shows on television," she said.

Something happened between the Sacred Heart of Jesus and Marie on that Saturday afternoon. She once hinted at it but never volunteered the details. Perhaps what she knew intellectually about the meaning of the Sacred Heart had finally commuted her self-imposed death sentence. I suspect she had an experience of God's merciful, loving arms wrapped around her as she sat in her prison cell and obsessed over her past. That was all it took to have her sin carried away and dumped into the ocean.

THE SACRED HEART OF JESUS

For many centuries, the Sacred Heart of Jesus, which so touched Marie that Saturday afternoon, has been the iconographic image for the loving mercy of Christ. Unbeknown to many, the historical roots for devotion to the Sacred Heart lie in the earliest days of Christianity. The scriptural basis for its devotion is found in the Gospel of John: "Instead, one of the soldiers pierced his side with a spear, and at once blood and water came out" (John 19:34). Tradition said that the spear went through Jesus' side and pierced his heart. Hence the side wound was quickly associated with the heart of Christ and the greatest gifts God wanted to bestow on us.

Reflecting allegorically on Scripture, the early fathers of the church saw the origin of the church in the heart of God. Ambrose stated that as Eve had come forth from the side of Adam, so the church was born from the pierced heart of Christ. Augustine wrote that the side wound was "the door of life" thrown open, from which flowed the sacramental life of the church.

In the twelfth century, the side wound was associated with imagery from the Hebrew Scriptures' Song of Solomon: it was the cleft in the rock, the opened portal through which the beloved entered the bridal chamber of divine love, the heart and the nest of the dove. This laid the groundwork for a "mysticism of the heart," a prayerful union of our hearts with the heart of Christ, or in the case of Catherine of Siena in the fourteenth century, a mystical exchange of her heart for the heart of Christ.

During the medieval period, prayers to the wounded Christ often spoke of his heart. The *Summi Regis Cor* ("Heart of the Supreme King"), composed sometime in the twelfth or thirteenth century, is typical:

> Let us live so, Heart to heart,
> Wounded, Jesus, as Thou art.
> If through my heart Thou wilt but strike
> With shame's arrow, sharp and dire.
> Put my heart within thine own,
> Hold me, leave me not alone.
> Here my heart shall live and die,
> To Thee ever drawing nigh;
> Strongly would it thirst for thee,
> Jesus, say not no to me,
> That it may rest in Thee content.

The seventeenth century marked a watershed in devotion to the Sacred Heart of Jesus. In his *Treatise on the Love of God*, Francis de Sales states that the divine love contained in Christ's heart peers through the side wound on our hearts. De Sales makes clear that Christ would be willing to suffer and die again for our sins. The Sacred Heart clearly represents the divine initiative and investment in our lives.

Though devotion to the Sacred Heart would find its first theological and liturgical foundations with John Eudes, it would reach its contemporary expression with Margaret Mary Alacoque in the Visitation Convent at Paray-le-Monial, France, during the French Revolution. She is credited with the traditional iconography of a flaming heart shining with divine light, pierced by the lance wound, surrounded by a crown of thorns, and bleeding.

Pope Pius IX established the devotion to the Sacred Heart as a universal practice within the Roman Catholic tradition in 1856. A little over a century later, it began to wane in practice and popularity with the reforms of Vatican II.

DIVINE MERCY

Closely resembling the meaning of the Sacred Heart devotion is the twentieth-century devotion to God's Divine Mercy practiced and promoted by St. Maria Faustina Kowalska, a Sister of Our Lady of Mercy, in what is now west-central Poland. Before she died of tuberculosis at age thirty-three in 1938, she had mystical experiences that led her to write that Christ did not wish people to despair about the possibility of having their sins forgiven. "I do not want to punish aching mankind," Christ told St. Maria Faustina, "but I desire to heal it, pressing it to my merciful heart."

Devotion to the Divine Mercy, like that to the Sacred Heart of Jesus, can be practiced in a variety of ways: we can reflect on the parables of forgiveness taught by Jesus or scenes from Jesus' life in which he celebrated his Abba's abundant arms of mercy and compassion; we can meditate on the apostle Paul's succinct statement that "God proves his love for us in that while we still were sinners Christ died for us" (Romans 5:8); or we can gaze on the traditional image of Jesus with his heart exposed and note what thoughts and feelings arise within us. In whatever way it might be expressed or experienced in the life of the disciple, this devotion is a vivid reminder that God is anxious, ready and eager to forgive. It calls to mind the divine initiative that Martin Luther experienced. It recalls God's investment in our lives as a forgiving Abba who is as close as a father to his children.

THE OPEN BOSOM OF DIVINE MERCY

Saint Bonaventure used the vivid image of a bosom to describe the mercy of God: "The Good Shepherd extended fatherly affection to the repentant, showing the open bosom of Divine mercy."

Bosom—it can mean a mother's breasts, the very place an infant finds life-giving milk and nourishment. It can also connote the very center of a man's chest, symbolizing strength, security and the heart. Bonaventure's image hints at both the masculine and the feminine dimensions of the mercy of God.

As proof of the divine mercy of the Good Shepherd, Bonaventure calls on four witnesses from the Gospels: Matthew, Zacchaeus, the sinful woman who washed the feet of Jesus with her tears and the woman caught in adultery. Each of these witnesses saw and took nourishment from the open bosom of divine mercy. And each, like Francis of Assisi, Martin Luther, John Wesley and Marie, was changed into another person.

Matthew was collecting taxes when he encountered the Good Shepherd (see Matthew 9:9-13). He must have been stunned by Jesus' simple invitation, "Follow me." This meticulous tax collector, whose preoccupation centered around adding up debits, was standing before Jesus, the shepherd of forgiveness who only knew subtraction. Matthew could respond in only one way: "He got up and followed [Jesus]" (v. 9). His life changed drastically. So did the lives of so many of the poor for whom Matthew's calling meant a cancellation of their tax debts. In touching one person, God's mercy is supposed to affect others.

This is precisely the point of the parable of the unforgiving servant (see Matthew 18:23-35). God's forgiveness sets the standard for the actions of the disciple. A refusal to forgive demonstrates, from Jesus' perspective, an unbelievable ingratitude to God, who has been so merciful and compassionate. One scholar has suggested that this parable be titled "Don't Forgive—and See What Happens!"

Zacchaeus's small stature was symbolic of his self-respect and self-image. The embarrassment of being a tax collector, and therefore a man to be mistrusted, sent him scampering up a sycamore tree (see Luke 19:1-10). The Good Shepherd was not content to let Zacchaeus hide. So Jesus took the initiative and called Zacchaeus to stand tall and bask in the light of divine mercy. He issued an invitation: "Hurry and come down" (v. 5).

Zacchaeus was as stunned as the crowd, which grumbled at the Master going to the house of a sinner. But Zacchaeus also saw a ray of light guiding him out of his past criminal extortions, and he responded to Jesus with the promise of amends. He then shared his daily bread with the Good Shepherd. Sometimes we know what we want; we just need someone to give us the practical encouragement and added push.

The sinful woman of Luke's Gospel (see 7:36-50) was so aware of the abomination of her sinfulness before the open bosom of divine mercy that she wept at the feet of Jesus. Her ego demanded that she prove the depths of her heart's contrition. But her past life had taught her only one way to relate to men.

So she touched the Lord, washing his feet with her tears, her kisses and her costly ointment.

The touch itself was enough. With staggering sensitivity and compassion, Jesus understood. The Good Shepherd said to her, "Your sins are forgiven. Your faith has saved you; go in peace" (vv. 48, 50).

The woman caught in adultery (see John 8:3-11)—we can only imagine her fear and shame as her sin was paraded before the entire town. The Mosaic law stated her sentence clearly: death (see Leviticus 20:10).

There was no need for a judge in this case. However, the scribes and Pharisees brought the woman before Jesus not to have her sentence of death confirmed but to test Jesus. Indeed, despite their self-righteous pretense of being in compliance with the law, they, in fact, lacked an important requirement: they had no witnesses to this act of adultery (see Deuteronomy 17:6).

And what does the Good Shepherd do? Rather than further humiliate the woman who has been turned into a courtroom pawn, he does not hesitate to demonstrate that no sin is written with indelible ink: "Neither do I condemn you. Go your way, and from now on do not sin again." These words, as one scholar suggests, "urge that the freely given acquittal become the beginning of a new life." Indeed, divine mercy transforms the sinner into a saint.

Bonaventure concludes his reflection on the mercy and forgiveness of the Good Shepherd with an exhortation that summarizes the attitudes of these four Gospel witnesses who experienced the compassionate affection of Jesus and his open bosom of divine mercy. He writes,

> Like Matthew, therefore
> follow this most devoted shepherd;
> like Zacchaeus
> receive him with hospitality;
> like the sinful woman
> anoint him with ointment
> and wash his feet with your tears,
> wipe them with your hair
> and caress them with your kisses,
> so that finally,
> with the woman presented to him for judgment,
> you may deserve to hear

the sentence of forgiveness:

"Has no one condemned you? Neither will I condemn you.
Go, and sin no more."

When we pray, "Forgive us our trespasses," in the Lord's Prayer,
we stand in line with Matthew, Zacchaeus, the sinful woman and
the woman caught in adultery. With these great Gospel witnesses,
we too experience the power of divine forgiveness. Abba throws
our sins into the ocean, forgets the past and welcomes us home
with wide-opened merciful arms.

REFLECTION QUESTIONS

1. Over what sins of my past do I continue to obsess? Why? Why
   do I struggle to believe in God's forgiveness?

2. How do I set limits on the mercy of God in my life and in the
   life of others?

3. In my opinion, how did Abba respond to Judas's act of
   despair?

4. How could meditation on the Sacred Heart of Jesus foster awareness of God's loving mercy in my life?

5. Of Bonaventure's four Gospel witnesses to the Good Shepherd's
   forgiveness, with whom do I identify the most? Why?

Gospel Passages for Meditation and Prayer: Mark 2:13-17; Luke
15:1-32

As We Forgive Those Who Trespass Against Us

Seeing with the Eyes of Compassion

God's forgiveness of our sins impels us to forgive others with mercy and compassion. A process of inner healing can sometimes help facilitate our offer of forgiveness.

THE LIFE AND SPIRIT OF THE AMISH COMMUNITY of Nickel Mines in Bart Township of Lancaster County, Pennsylvania, was radically tested on October 2, 2006. On that particular Monday morning, at approximately 10:30 a.m., Charles Carl Roberts IV, a thirty-two-year-old milk tank truck driver, entered the one-room Amish schoolhouse with a 9mm handgun. Within minutes, he ordered the schoolgirls, ages ranging from six to thirteen, to line up against the chalkboard. He started binding the arms and legs of his young hostages with plastic ties. Thirty minutes later, ten children were shot execution-style. The tragedy came to an end when Roberts turned the gun on himself. Three of the girls died instantly, two more died early the next morning. Five more were left in critical condition.

The nation was shocked that such a violent tragedy should befall a God-fearing community known for its irreproachable life of simplicity and Christian living. However, in the days that followed, the nation was even more stunned to learn the response of the Amish community.

On the very day of the shooting, the grandfather of one of the murdered girls said, "We must not think evil of this man." A member of the Brethren community living near the Amish, explained: "I don't think there's anybody here that wants to do anything but forgive and not only reach out to those who have suffered a loss in that way but to reach out to the family of the man who committed these acts."

And reach out and forgive was precisely the Amish response. An Amish neighbor comforted the Roberts family hours after the tragedy and extended forgiveness to them. One Amish man is reported to have held Roberts's sobbing father in his arms for as long as an hour. Some thirty members of the Amish community attended Roberts's funeral, and his widow was one of the few outsiders invited to the funeral of one of the murdered children.

Scholars of the Amish community have noted that these acts of forgiveness were not isolated decisions by godly individuals but rather the community's countercultural practice rooted in its three-hundred-year history and in the teachings of the New Testament.

THE REVOLUTION OF FORGIVENESS

Of all the teachings of Jesus, it was his teaching on forgiving one's neighbor that could be rightly deemed countercultural. Traditional Judaism saw revenge, as long as it respected the law of equivalence, as a way of ensuring that justice was done: "life for life, eye for eye, tooth for tooth, hand for hand, foot for foot, burn for burn, wound for wound, stripe for stripe" (Exodus 21:23-25).

Indeed, the Hebrew Scriptures describe justice as an equitable revenge with no greater harm being exacted.

Jesus challenged this traditional approval and endorsement of revenge—and caused a revolution in the thinking about forgiveness. Though his teaching was so important that it is the one and only human activity mentioned in the Lord's Prayer, the evangelists remember its exact formulation in different ways.

The earliest Gospel clearly states that forgiveness of our neighbor is the precondition for God's forgiveness: "Whenever you stand praying, forgive, if you have anything against anyone; so that your Father in heaven may also forgive you your trespasses" (Mark 11:25).

Luke's version of the Lord's Prayer nuances Jesus' teaching found in Mark by having us petition for divine forgiveness precisely because "we ourselves forgive everyone indebted to us" (Luke 11:4). Earlier in Luke's Gospel, Jesus made a direct connection between the forgiveness of our neighbor and God's forgiveness: "Forgive, and you will be forgiven . . . for the measure you give will be the measure you get back" (Luke 6:37-38).

Matthew's version of the Lord's Prayer implies that our forgiveness of others is a "paradigm" for God's forgiveness (see Matthew 6:12). However, in the commentary that follows the Lord's Prayer, Matthew returns to Mark's idea of the precondition and emphasizes it using both positive and negative language: "For if you forgive others their trespasses, your heavenly Father will also forgive you; but if you do not forgive others, neither will your Father forgive your trespasses" (Matthew 6:14-15). More so, in the parable of the unforgiving servant, Jesus states that withholding forgiveness is a hypocritical form of injustice that makes us loan sharks liable for punishment (see Matthew 18:23-35).

Jesus' novel teaching seems evident: authentic forgiveness is not a business deal, a tit for tat, as the Hebrew Scriptures would like us to think. Jesus is remembered as saying that justice is served not by getting revenge and balancing the ledger but by generously sharing with others what we ourselves have experienced in the alms of God. Indeed, forgiving our neighbor and performing selfless acts of sacrificial love is our response to God's forgiveness (see Luke 7:47).

The disciple is so sensitive to the generous alms of divine forgiveness and so eager to preserve the common good that he or she does not hesitate to take the first step toward reconciliation. Whenever a disciple discovers anything that separates himself or herself from another, even the slightest harm or inadvertent hurt, it is the disciple who immediately starts walking the path toward forgiveness. This is the precondition for worship of a God who is Abba:

> So when you are offering your gift at the altar, if you remember that your brother or sister has something against you, leave your gift there before the altar and go; first be reconciled to your brother or sister, and then come and offer your gift. (Matthew 5:23-24)

Indeed, the ritualized worship of God who is Abba is only authentic when there are peace and reconciliation among the members of the family; when *Ubuntu*, the awareness of our lives offered for the common good, is present and preserved; when we share with others what God has given to us. The memory and personal experience of a God as close as a father to his child, running down the road with arms outstretched in mercy, compassion and forgiveness, get us up and running toward our sister or brother. Again, the action of Abba sets the benchmark for the way of the disciple.

NOT MERELY AN ACTION BUT AN ATTITUDE

We are all sinners (see Romans 5:12-21). And "if we say that we have no sin, we deceive ourselves, and the truth is not in us" (1

John 1:8). This awareness shapes our willingness and readiness to forgive others. It also shapes the humble, nonjudgmental attitude with which we approach others.

The ego makes us conveniently forget our own sinfulness. Due to its emotional need to protect and promote self-concern, self-image, self-preservation and self-gratification, it insists on "easing God out" and enthroning itself on the seat of judgment. From that lofty position, it self-righteously pounds its fists with outlandish criticism of others or pontificates with an air of superiority.

In direct opposition to this attitude and aware of the sinfulness of all, Jesus challenges those "without sin" to cast the first stone at the woman caught in adultery (see John 8:2-11). He also challenges the self-righteous attitude of Simon the Pharisee (see Luke 7:36-50). In Matthew's Gospel, he not only forbids any kind of judgmental attitude but also highlights its hypocrisy: "Do not judge, so that you may not be judged. . . . Why do you see the speck in your neighbor's eye, but do not notice the log in your own eye?" (Matthew 7:1, 3). Disciples, rooted in authentic humility, are only too aware of their own fragility, weakness and sinfulness.

An attitude of acceptance and respect for the other permeates any act of forgiveness. This attitude develops as we put God back where God belongs, recognize how we ourselves have enjoyed the free gift of God's forgiveness and make the decision to renounce any arrogance and self-righteousness. When a disciple asked his master for instructions in how to forgive others, the master replied, "If you never condemned, you would never need to forgive."

This humble attitude of acceptance and respect, arising from the disciple's realization of his or her own sinfulness, is one of the consistent teachings from the fourth-century desert fathers:

A brother who had sinned was turned out of the church by

the priest; Abba Bessarion got up and went with him, saying, "I, too, am a sinner."

One day Abba Isaac went to a monastery. He saw a brother committing a sin and he condemned him. When he returned to the desert, an angel of the Lord came and stood in front of the door of his cell, and said, "I will not let you enter." But he persisted saying, "What is the matter?" And the angel replied, "God has sent me to ask you where you want to throw the guilty brother whom you have condemned." Immediately he repented and said, "I have sinned, forgive me." Then the angel said, "Get up, God has forgiven you. But from now on, be careful not to judge someone before God has done so."

A brother at Scetis committed a fault. A council was called to which Abba Moses was invited, but he refused to go to it. Then the priest sent someone to say to him, "Come, for everyone is waiting for you." So he got up and went. He took a leaking jug, filled it with water and carried it with him. The other monks came out to meet him and said to him, "What is this, Father?" The old man said to them, "My sins run out behind me, and I do not see them, and today I am coming to judge the errors of another." When they heard that, they said no more to the brother but forgave him.

The teaching is clear: disciples live with an awareness of their own sinfulness. They do so not to be tied into the straightjacket of debilitating guilt but to keep their feet on the ground and to overcome the temptation to self-righteously judge and condemn others.

This attitude goes beyond simply biting our tongue. Indeed, Jesus' stunning words of forgiveness from the cross certainly gives us cause to pause: "Father, forgive them; for they do not know what they are doing" (Luke 23:34). In imitation of Christ, a little Christ's first inclination is to try to understand and justify the betrayer's action rather than to condemn. This presumes the willingness to discover the motivation that produces the action and preserves a nonjudgmental attitude.

THE MECHANICS OF FORGIVENESS

Along with an international group of Franciscans traveling in mainland China in the early 1990s, I went to meet a Chinese bishop and fellow Franciscan. A member of the Franciscan Order before the Communist takeover, this bishop was arrested in the late 1940s. He was sentenced to make umbrella handles in one of his own churches, which had been turned into a factory for the People's Republic of China. His treatment was less than humane.

With Deng Xiaoping and the changing political winds in China in the late 1980s, this bishop was released and restored to his diocese under the direction and supervision of the government-sponsored Chinese Catholic Patriotic Association which, at that time, did not permit him any ties whatsoever with the Vatican.

By the time of our visit, the Chinese government suspected the Vatican had secretly approved this elderly man as the local bishop, and so he was being continually harassed and interrogated. Two months before our visit, he had been awakened in the middle of the night, brought to a local police station and questioned intensely for some ten hours.

When he was led into the parlor by his government-appointed "assistant," he greeted us with the traditional Franciscan salutation in Latin, "Pax et bonum!" ("Peace and goodness!"). Though small in stature, he exuded a bold yet self-effacing spirit. His large, round eyes radiated an inner peace and contentment.

We spoke through a translator. I could tell the bishop took an instant liking to me, perhaps because I dropped all episcopal etiquette and called him by the religious name he held in the Franciscan Order.

I asked him directly, "Brother Bernardine, are you angry at what has happened to you?"

"Fratre Alberte," he said, "to dwell on the many times people have slapped me on the cheek is simply to prolong the pain of my—" He hesitated for the word. He looked at the government translator out of the corner of his eyes, and then continued, "the pain of my *hospitalization*. I have decided not to give my *doctors* that much enjoyment."

Brother Bernardine refused to let his history of forced labor scar him for life and fill him with rancor. He renounced the ego's temptation to let the anger and bitterness stick. Had he done otherwise, he would have remained psychologically imprisoned. Instead, he offered forgiveness, which became a wise, healthy choice for himself. Consequently, he was filled with the very "peace and goodness" with which he greeted us.

Brother Bernardine had decided to let the hurt go. And in doing that, he opted out of the cycle of violence and was set free from the prison of the past.

Before leaving for missionary activity in mainland China, I had the opportunity to attend a five-day retreat by a very dynamic, national speaker and writer. He had an incredible gift for making insightful comments. However, the overzealous energy he exuded and the sweat that rolled down his face after five minutes of speaking left me emotionally drained and wondering about the intensity of his emotions. Was there something more going on inside him than a deep feeling of conviction about what he was saying? As perceptive as his message was, it also seemed somewhat caustic and cynical.

Some fifteen years later, I heard him again. But his speaking style was qualitatively different. In a question-and-answer period, he publicly admitted that he had been an angry man steeped in bitterness. He mentioned that he would be completely wiped out emotionally and psychologically after giving even a short fifteen-minute talk or presentation. He was angry at God, the world and himself. He said that life became so difficult that he finally decided to get help for what he described as an infatuation with anger, hatred and grudges.

It takes a lot of emotional and psychological energy to keep a wound open, to keep a grudge alive. And the more we work to keep it alive, the more emotionally drained we become as the grudge saps us of our strength. The longer we allow a wound to fester, or the longer we keep picking its scab, the more bitterness, anger and self-pity poison our blood and eat at our hearts.

The ego has a "Velcro personality" to which all hurts stick: "Five years, four months and two days ago, so-and-so did this to me!" Treasured emotional wounds and scars become like fish bones stuck in the throat. Even the smallest bone can be excruciating—and the more we struggle to dislodge it, the more it hurts.

The disciple is challenged to develop a "Teflon personality," which lets all hurts slide right off. The "Teflon" is the result of a *decision* to let the hurt go, as Brother Bernardine reminds us. Disciples might not forget, but they *choose* to forgive. They choose to stop picking the scab. They dump the hurt into the ocean of the past, just as Abba does. Indeed, the attitude and action of God become the measure and standard of action for the disciple.

FORGIVING WITH OUR EYES

Eyes shed a lot of light on the condition of a person's heart. Jesus himself called our eyes "the lamp of the body" (see Matthew 6:22). They can blaze with anger; they can be as peaceful as an evening sunset; they can dance with excitement and passion; they can soothe with the balm of mercy and kindness.

In a letter written to an anonymous regional leader of the Franciscan Order, Saint Francis offered some advice on how to deal with friars who sin publicly and said they should discover mercy "in your eyes." In effect, he suggests our very eyes should offer mercy and pardon to those desperate people who, like the sinful woman of Luke's Gospel (see 7:36-50), crave forgiveness but never learned the social grace of asking for it. Practically speaking, that means our eyes and body language do not avert from the sinner. Rather, we maintain a compassionate eye contact while becoming a refuge of acceptance for the other person.

Francis adds that even if the other does not ask for forgiveness, we are challenged to take the initiative and with tender kindness ask the person if he or she would like it. Sometimes this can best be done without explicitly broaching the topic. Simple questions such as "How are you doing?" or "Is everything okay with you?" are often all it takes. Keeping the lines of communication open is a tried-and-true method for conveying forgiveness. Such a personal connection preserves familial bonds with the other. What an abundant alms it is to preserve the dignity of the person by offering forgiveness, whether requested or not, with our eyes when life, for whatever reason, has robbed the other person of the ability to ask for it with words.

I wish to know in this way if you love the Lord and me, His servant and yours: that there is not any brother in the world who has sinned—however much he could have sinned—who, after he has looked into your eyes, would ever depart without your mercy, if he is looking for mercy. And if he were not looking for mercy, you would ask him if he wants mercy. And if he would sin a thousand times before your eyes, love him more than me so that you may draw him to the Lord; and always be merciful with brothers such as these.

SAINT FRANCIS
OF ASSISI

I once had a very unfortunate and painful disagreement with another friar in my community. In hindsight, I now realize the disagreement was rooted in my childhood fear of rejection. Because of the argument, living together on a daily basis became quite a challenge. We were politely civil toward one another, though the tension between us could have been cut with a knife. Unrelated circumstances forced both of us, within a matter of six months, to live in different locations.

A little while later, we happened to find ourselves not only at a Franciscan regional meeting, but also assigned with barbequing the hamburgers on the outdoor grill together. I was uneasy and nervous about having to work with him. I even tried to convince a friar friend to take my place, with no success. Surprisingly, this turned out to be a blessing in disguise. As soon as we had the grill fired up and started flipping burgers, I looked the other friar directly in the eye, and before I could say anything, he gently touched my shoulder and said, "Don't even go there. It's all forgiven. We are first and foremost brothers in the Franciscan Order." And with that, a burden was lifted from my shoulders as I saw pardon in his eyes and heard it in his words.

That friar rightly realized that some of us live *through* the wounds, scars and pain of our past. Charity demands that a disciple try to become aware of the wound out of which the other may be living—even when the other's brokenness inflicts hurts. To be sensitive to the hurt of another's heart is the essence of merciful compassion. It is also to imitate the crucified Jesus, whose first inclination from the cross was to understand and justify rather than condemn.

In trying to understand the hearts of people and accepting others with compassion, we sometimes discover that what we thought was intentional was never intended. But even if the harm was intended, Saint Francis challenges us to offer mercy and forgiveness—and "a thousand times" if need be.

This goes to the very heart of Jesus' revolution about forgiveness. As God's forgiveness is limitless, so we are challenged never to tire sharing with others what we ourselves have enjoyed. We can only imagine Peter's surprise when, while discussing forgiveness with Jesus, he asked with a tone of exaggeration, "As many as seven times?" Jesus replied, "Not seven times, but, I tell you, seventy-seven times" (Matthew 18:21-22). Forgiveness is the gift that we keep on giving—to ourselves and to others. It breaks the stranglehold of debilitating guilt.

THE DYNAMITE OF GRACE

Some hurts strike so deeply that we feel unable to forgive. We begin drowning in resentment, bitterness and anger. Sometimes we truly want to forgive, yet seem unable to find the emotional strength to do so.

What do we do when we want to move beyond the hurt, when we want to forgive, but we just don't know how? An incident in the life of Corrie ten Boom gives us a solution.

Corrie ten Boom lived in Amsterdam during World War II. Because her family was caught sheltering Jews, she and her sister Betsie were sent to the infamous Ravensbrück concentration camp. Only Corrie survived.

After the war, Corrie committed herself to a life of lecturing. She traveled throughout Europe, speaking on the topic of forgiveness and reconciliation.

One day in 1947, after giving a talk in Munich, a man came forward to thank her. Corrie couldn't believe her eyes. He was one of the Nazi guards who had stood duty in the women's shower room in Ravensbrück.

The man reached out to shake Corrie's hand, but she froze. After all her talks on forgiveness, she could not reach out her hand

in friendship. Her physical body remembered too sharply the horror of the camp and the death of her beloved sister. Corrie was
blocked emotionally, stuck in the crippling rut of resentment, bitterness and hatred.

As Corrie stood there, frozen with shock, the battle raged inside of her. She was torn between the seductive desire to balance
the scales of justice with revenge and to heed Jesus' challenge of
forgiveness, which she herself had preached so often. So she
prayed silently to herself, "Jesus, I cannot forgive this man. Give
me your forgiveness."

As she prayed that prayer and as her mind's eye reviewed the
years of brutality, suffering, humiliation and death, something incredible happened. This is how she described the experience:

> The current started in my shoulder, raced down my arm,
> sprang into our joined hands. And then this healing warmth
> seemed to flood my whole being, bringing tears to my eyes.
>   "I forgive you, brother!" I cried. "With all my heart."
>   For a long moment we grasped each other's hands, the
> former guard and the former prisoner. I had never known
> God's love so intensely as I did then.

Corrie ten Boom's experience reminds us that forgiveness is
not simply a matter of making a decision, an act of the will. It is
also a grace from God. We have to be willing to pray for it: "Jesus, I cannot forgive this person. Give me your forgiveness."
Willpower and personal desire are not always enough to break
through the prison walls of resentment and bitterness that the
ego builds around the heart. Sometimes we need the dynamite of
God's grace.

And it will come. It might come like lightning, as in Corrie's
case and that of the Amish in Nickel Mines. It might take years, as
it did with the famous speaker and writer. So we patiently, lov-

ingly and confidently pray for the grace to forgive those who trespass against us.

INNER HEALING

When I meet people in spiritual direction who are stuck in the rut
of bitterness or who seem particularly attached to a certain past
hurt or injustice, I ask them two questions: What are you gaining
by keeping the grudge alive? What need is it satisfying in you?

Our desire for revenge or self-pity and our need to hold on to a
grudge are sometimes the tip of an iceberg that runs deep down
inside us. We have to get below the surface of the self-pity and
emotional need for justice to find the deeper issues manifested in
the grudge or desire for revenge. In other words, some grudges are
actually pointing to deeper aspects of our personality that have
yet to be faced and integrated.

A grudge can be a sturdy prop against which our bruised ego can
lean. It might make us feel vindicated or satisfy the obsession to always be right. Deliberately hanging on to a lingering past hurt sometimes justifies a pity party or the emotional need to be a victim.

What are we gaining by keeping a grudge alive? What need is it
satisfying inside us? Answers to these questions often reveal fundamental wounds out of which many of us live our lives and the very
reason we react to others out of bitterness and malice. The hostility
directed toward others is really a projection of our inner wound.

Lack of self-acceptance, the absence of a loving parent during
the formative years of childhood, the scars of sexual abuse, living
in the shadow of a talented sibling—these wounds never really
heal. Just like the wounds still visible on the risen Christ, some
have so shaped our present identity that they remain with us forever. Yet, also like the wounds on the risen Christ, these *do stop
bleeding*. They no longer drain us of our emotional and psychological energies. They no longer condemn us to our past. By the

grace of God, they become our marks of victory and the very signs of God's healing power in our lives. They paradoxically become proclamations that "death has been swallowed up in victory" (1 Corinthians 15:54).

The wounds of crucifixion stop bleeding and are transformed into the marks of resurrection the moment our desire for revenge is converted into the balm of mercy and forgiveness. That change—or emotional shift—often occurs through the grace of an insight. Sometimes we arrive at that insight through some form of inner healing. Sometimes we arrive at that insight through psychotherapy, prayer, membership in a twelve-step support group or dialogue with a loved one, a trusted friend or spiritual director.

FIVE PRINCIPLES OF INNER HEALING

- The continuing presence of a loving, compassionate Christ
- A review of the past event
- The "step of compassion"
- Calling on the healing ministry of Christ
- The proclamation of new life

I often suggest to my spiritual directees that they develop their own method of inner healing based on five important principles: the continuing presence of a loving, compassionate Christ; a review of the past event; the "step of compassion"; calling on the healing ministry of Christ; and the proclamation of new life.

The continuing presence of a loving, compassionate Christ. The first principle of inner healing is that it is always done in the presence of Jesus the divine Physician. He is the one who heals, comforts and consoles. The Jesus who wept at the news of Lazarus's death is the same compassionate Jesus who ministers to us. He has an investment in our broken hearts. "The LORD is near to the brokenhearted, and saves the crushed in spirit" (Psalm 34:18). "[God] heals the brokenhearted, and binds up their wounds" (Psalm 147:3). We must believe that as we approach any method of inner healing.

A review of the past event. We return to the past event and take another look at it. This is the hardest task of inner healing because we tend to live our lives through our wounds or around our wounds, evading our hurts and skirting our scars. We rarely, if ever, confront them head-on.

Mary has a fine reputation among the religious sisters of her Catholic congregation of nuns. In public, she appears organized, upbeat and fun loving. But the people who live with her see a very different side of Mary: troubled, lethargic, abusing alcohol and constantly drained. Mary has spent most of her life refusing to confront some deep emotional issues that are probably centered around her mother, whom she never talks about. Mary is living her life around her wound.

Our external behaviors often betray the fact that we are running away from something or actively repressing something. Sex, alcohol, workaholic busyness—these are usually not the problems. They are what we are doing *about* the problems. The process of inner healing is delving below the manifestation of the problem to get to its root and cause. We get rid of weeds by pulling them up by their roots. We confront the past head-on.

Many will claim that "dragging up the past" is fruitless and wastes precious time on things that are best forgotten. Nothing could be further from the truth. Emotional wounds are like physical wounds: They do not heal if they are neglected; they only become infected. The hurt must be brought into the light of day, recognized and then treated.

This does not mean, however, that all wounds can—or should—be confronted *now*. We must not violate ourselves and force ourselves to confront issues or events we are not ready to face. To do so can actually subvert the healing process.

Healing is not an achievement; it is a gift. When the time is right, the memory will "float up" to the level of conscious awareness. That is a sign that it is time to begin the healing process. In the meantime, Abba has given us our defense mechanisms precisely so that we can protect ourselves from the very issues or wounds that we are not yet ready to confront. Joan's tragedy offers a vivid example.

At an early age, Joan was sexually abused by an uncle. For twenty-six years, she had repressed its memory. At age thirty, she fell in love with Bill. At times she began to feel "uncomfortable" during their relationships but didn't quite know why. She often projected those "uncomfortable" feelings on Bill. These mixed signals strained their relationship. Then dreams began, and Joan would awaken to feelings of stress and anxiety. Finally conscious flashbacks to the past incident with her uncle arose. The wound was throbbing, and the memory had floated up to the level of conscious awareness. It was calling for attention and healing. It was time to face the past abuse. It was time for Joan to stop living her life through her wound, unconscious as it had been.

Healing begins with the journey to the past event—but in the presence of the risen Christ. We must allow ourselves to enter again into the darkness of the betrayal, the abuse, the hurt, the wound. We expose the entire incident to the light shining through the wounds of the risen Christ. We recall the details of the experience and the feelings it raised inside of us. At this point, verbalizing the experience to a caring friend or someone in the helping professions can be of utmost value.

The "step of compassion." The third step of inner healing is the "step of compassion," when we momentarily step through our pain, anger and hurt to place our feet in the shoes of the betrayer, to understand the heart of the betrayer. This is exactly what Jesus did as he hung on the cross and asked God's forgiveness for those who executed him. Understanding leads to compassion, which opens up the choice to forgive and the decision to move beyond the past.

Several questions help in that process of understanding our betrayer: Out of what emotional wound was the betrayer living? What pain filled the heart of the betrayer that would cause a person to react to us or treat us in the way the betrayer did? How emotionally healthy is the betrayer? An insight will sometimes plant itself within our souls as we try to understand the betrayer's heart, as we walk in the shoes of the one who betrayed us, as we enter into the flames of the betrayer's hell.

Only when we understand the weaknesses and imperfections of others can we forgive them with humility and compassion—the two virtues Thomas Merton believes are essential to Christian forgiveness. He writes,

> If we forgive [others] without humility, our forgiveness is a mockery: it presupposes that we are better than they. Jesus descended into the abyss of our degradation in order to forgive us after He had, in a sense, become lower than us all. It is not for us to forgive others from lofty thrones, as if we were gods looking down on them from Heaven. We must forgive them in the flames of their own hell, for Christ, by means of our forgiveness, once again descends to extinguish the avenging flame. He cannot do this if we do not forgive others with His own compassion.

The wound left by my father's suicide began to dry up as I became more and more aware that he was probably doing the best he could on that day. If he could have done better, he probably would have. But on October 22, 1968, that was all he was capable of. And Joan began to be relieved of some of the trauma of her early sexual abuse as she grew in the realization of her uncle's emotional sickness. That awareness certainly did not excuse her uncle's criminal behavior, but it did help Joan come to a place of compassionate forgiveness and find the strength to let go of the past.

Inner healing begins to blossom when we realize that most of the time, most people were doing the best they could. Sadly, the people who shape our broken personalities are broken themselves. Does that brokenness exonerate them from the trauma or injury they inflicted on us? Does that absolve or vindicate those who deliberately betray our trust? No. The "step of compassion" has but a twofold purpose: to forget the ego and to walk in the shoes of the betrayer in order to realize that crippled people cannot walk without a limp. And life being as it is, we are all limping.

Calling on the healing ministry of Christ. After we have lived through the experience again in the presence of the risen Christ and tried to understand the heart of the betrayer, we can then take the next step to inner healing. We turn to Jesus and ask him to minister to us.

The risen Christ is both the physician and the balm. We allow the healing light that shines through his glorified wounds to penetrate the deep recesses and caverns of our broken hearts. The power "flowing from Jesus' resurrection" (see Philippians 3:10) will often burn away the ego's need to crusade, to be vindicated, to be justified, to have revenge. And through Christ's healing touch, light appears where darkness once prevailed. Life comes forth as Jesus calls down the wounds of our past, "Come out!"

Sometimes, even after life is restored, there is work to be done. After raising Lazarus, Jesus said to those standing by, "Unbind him, and let him go" (John 11:44). In restoring life to those areas in our past that have so wounded us or caused us deep emotional pain, Jesus often enlists the help of others to unbind us. Thus, professional counseling, spiritual direction and membership in support groups often accompany inner healing.

The proclamation of new life. Over time and through the continued practice of inner healing, the wounds of the past begin to stop bleeding. They no longer drain us of our emotional energy. The infections of anger, bitterness and self-pity gradually fade from our lives. Though we cannot help but look at the world through the wounds and hurts that have shaped us, we begin to realize that it is not nearly as hostile as we originally suspected.

An emotional shift occurs. We begin to walk on equal ground with other broken people who are sometimes in need of our forgiveness *again*. We also find ourselves reaching through our wound to extend a helping hand of compassion to those suffering the same pain or hurt that we once endured.

The final step of healing comes when we can announce our own new life. When someone asks, "Where is that teenager whose life was shattered by his father's suicide?" or "Where is that bitter, distrusting woman who was sexually violated by the very uncle she so innocently trusted?" or "Where is that person who was so severely scarred by divorce?" or "Where is that man who had no self-respect?" we reply with the angels at the tomb on Easter morning, "Why do you look for the living among the dead? He is not here, but has risen" (Luke 24:5).

When we pray, "As we forgive those who trespass against us," we are actually praying for the grace to share with others what God has already given to us: mercy, compassion and forgiveness. This grace goes far beyond a simple action to a deeper nonjudgmental attitude that seeks to truly understand the betrayer. That understanding helps to set us free from the inflicted wound and leads us to a personal experience of the resurrection.

REFLECTION QUESTIONS

1. Whom do I struggle—or refuse—to forgive? Why? What am I gaining by keeping the grudge alive? What need is it satisfying in me?

2. In a recent act of forgiveness, what did I learn about my betrayer?

3. Which selfless acts of sacrificial love arise from my awareness of being forgiven by God?

4. When did I experience someone forgiving me with their eyes? How did I react to that?

5. How have I experienced the healing power of Christ's resurrection in my own process of inner healing?

Gospel Passages for Meditation and Prayer: Matthew 5:38-48; 18:21-35

Lead Us Not into Temptation

Refusing to Dance with the Devil

We pray against temptation and commit to resisting Satan's eight thoughts, which attack the body, mind and soul. Awareness, mindfulness and vigilance help us in this spiritual discipline.

WE ALL EXPERIENCE TEMPTATION. We're tempted to keep our mouths shut and not tell the lady at the drugstore that she gave us a dollar too much in change. We're tempted sexually. We're tempted to ignore the outstretched hand begging for loose change. We're tempted to tell a little white lie for the sake of our pride or reputation. We're tempted to remain silent before the injustices committed against the poor and powerless. We're tempted to lash out with angry, hurtful words against those closest to us. Temptation wears many hats and comes in different degrees, but by its very nature, it's always enticing and seductive.

Rationalization and justification sometimes build the bridge joining the land of temptation to the desert of evil and sin. "The cashier at the drugstore should be more careful when giving change.

If she wants to give me an extra dollar, I'll take it!" "If that poor fellow went out and got a job like me, he wouldn't have to beg for money on the street corner." "I can't be bothered with writing a letter to my senator about the government's involvement with unjust regimes in Central America. It doesn't concern me." "Visiting this Internet site doesn't do any harm to my spouse or children."

More than mental processes for coming up with an excuse or a more convincing explanation to vindicate ourselves, rationalization and justification can also betray our alliance with the power of evil.

SATAN AS TEMPTER

What is this "power of evil"? The Hebrew noun for "adversary" or "accuser" is often transliterated into English as *Satan*. It is found in only three places in the Hebrew Scriptures, all of them dating to postexilic times (see Job 1–2; 1 Chronicles 21:1; Zechariah 3:1-2). In these passages, the adversary is a member of God's court who accuses human beings before God. The idea that Satan was an enemy of God or the embodiment of evil had not yet developed.

Over time, however, Satan did develop into a celestial ruler of the powers of evil who had an army of demons. He represented the personification of all the influences that tempted Israel from living up to God's intention for herself and all creation. It was also during the late postexilic period that the devil, or Satan, came to be identified with "the serpent" found in the third chapter of Genesis.

At the time of Jesus, Satan was believed to have a kingdom that stood in direct opposition to the kingdom of God that Jesus had come to establish (see Mark 3:23-26). The satanic forces were understood to be the cause of physical and mental sickness as well as natural calamities. Giving in to the temptations of these forces led to human sin and misery.

Appearing often in the New Testament, Satan is known as the

devil, the tempter, the accuser, the prince of demons and the ruler of this world (see Matthew 4:1, 3; Revelation 12:10; Luke 11:15; John 12:31). Though causing havoc now, Satan will inevitably be overthrown by the power of God. The book of Revelation describes Satan's demise as one in which the devil is thrown into a lake of fire and sulfur and tormented for all eternity (see Revelation 20:10). But until then, popularly depicted with a tail, horns and a pitchfork, Satan tries to tempt, entice and seduce us away from the path of the disciple.

"HORSING AROUND" WITH EVIL

Thomas Merton told the young monks of Gethsemani Abbey that he doubted if the devil had a tail or horns, or carried a pitchfork. But he added, "Behind the attractions and the surface of things in the world, there is a force at work to deceive people—a force of deception." Language is inadequate to describe this force, yet Merton stated bluntly, "Something's cooking. . . . And look out! . . . If you stay out of the way of this force—whatever it is—you are better off. And if you go horsing around with it, you are in trouble."

Concocting fanciful excuses and far-fetched explanations to rationalize a morally questionable decision or justify a sinful action are ways of "horsing around" with the devil. They clearly reveal that there is a side of us that is attracted to and enticed by Satan's agenda.

The process of thinking promoted by the power of evil is sometimes coldly logical and cruelly detached from emotion—and disruptive of any sense of *Ubuntu*. Merton once wrote that the decision to fire nuclear weapons will be made by "sane people" who "have *perfectly good reasons,* logical, well-adjusted reasons, for firing the shot. They will be obeying sane orders that have come sanely down the chain of command. . . . When the missiles take off, *it will be no mistake.*"

How often do we find ourselves splitting hairs to come up with a rational explanation for doing something we know in our hearts is wrong? How often do we perform mental gymnastics to justify something—"sane" as it may be—that is steeped in our obsession with self-concern, self-image, self-preservation and self-gratification? Whenever we do, the music has started playing and the slow dance of temptation has begun. "Lead us not into temptation . . . "

I must confess that I am more embarrassed by my temptations than by my sins. To sin takes a split second. It is the heart's dive into the pool of a deliberate, willed decision. Unfortunately, though, I usually spend a lot more time planning the dive, "horsing around" with the temptation and seeing just how far and just how long I can go before backing down and deciding not to act on it. Sadly, the longer I fiddle with a temptation, the more difficult it is to walk away.

The way we tinker with our temptations and tweak our reasons for acting on them are indications that we actually enjoy dancing the tango with the devil. The way we abruptly pause and then grab the temptation by the waist reveals our continuing obsession and infatuation with the swaggering excitement of Satan's agenda.

THE EIGHT THOUGHTS

While the Roman Empire was collapsing during the fourth century, John Cassian traveled to the Egyptian desert, where he spent many years with the desert fathers and mothers, who were living radical Christian lives of prayer and work. What he learned during his time in the desert has come down to us in two of his works, the *Institutes*, dealing with the organization of monastic communities, and the *Conferences*, dealing with spiritual practices and teachings.

In both works, Cassian describes eight thoughts Satan confronts us with in the spiritual life. Awareness of, wrestling with and overcoming these thoughts are basic spiritual disciplines. Mastering them is crucial since these tempting thoughts are the seeds that sprout into desires and passions that can ultimately lead to sinful actions. These eight thoughts are about food, sex, things, anger, dejection, acedia, vainglory and pride. Cassian's order of the thoughts is insightful since it moves from the most external dealing with the body (food, sex, things) through the mind (anger, dejection) to the most internal dealing with matters of the soul (acedia, vainglory, pride).

TEMPTING THOUGHTS, SAVING VIRTUES

Despite their ancient roots in the fourth-century desert, the eight thoughts are uncannily contemporary. They point directly to our temptations toward and obsession with self-concern, self-image, self-preservation and self-gratification. Though each thought will express itself in each one of our lives in a variety of ways and for

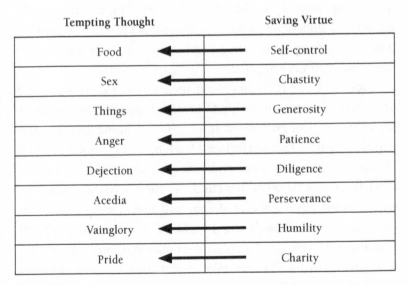

Figure 10.1.

a variety of reasons, a cursory overview of each might prove helpful. After all, we need to be able to recognize them as we pray,
"Lead us not into temptation."

And yet, overcoming the eight tempting thoughts is not simply
a question of being able to recognize them. We also need to be
proactive against these temptations by living a life of virtue. And
specifically, that means making a daily and weekly commitment
to practicing the eight virtues that step on the feet of the eight
temptations.

Food and self-control. Thoughts about food can fuel a compulsion toward gluttony. These temptations could be rooted in the
fear of facing certain emotions. Rather than addressing psychological issues through stress management or anger resolution with
their resulting change in lifestyle, we seek gratification in "comfort food." What we don't realize is that our comfort food often
disguises displeasure and sometimes discomfort. By gorging ourselves, we repress uncomfortable or painful emotions and refuse
them an opportunity for healthy expression. When acted on, ob-
sessive thoughts about food thus become a form of self-medication. This is precisely how many addictions—not just with food—
begin and are later triggered.

Sometimes our thoughts about food reveal a more basic and
unduly preoccupation with self-preservation. Ever stock up on
something at the grocery store only to get home and discover
you already have four of the item? Such hoarding points to a lack
of trust in the providence and care of a loving God who is as
close to us as a father to his child. "Is there anyone among you
who, if your child asks for bread, will give a stone? Or if the
child asks for a fish, will give a snake? If you then, who are evil,
know how to give good gifts to your children, how much more
will your Father in heaven give good things to those who ask
him!" (Matthew 7:9-11).

Daily struggle though it is, a friend makes a concerted effort to watch what she eats. Though her struggles with thoughts of food seem to be never-ending, she is well aware that self-control helps her to get in touch with childhood feelings and memories that she often tries to ignore. Indeed, whether it's with thoughts of food, as in her case, or any other compulsive thoughts that attempt to strangle us with an addiction, the temperance and restraint of self-control are ways that keep us honest about a healthy desire for self-preservation.

Sex and chastity. Thoughts about sex can easily ignite the passion of lust and conjure up a world even more far-fetched than the afternoon soap operas on television. Such temptations, rooted in self-gratification, will sometimes cause us to confuse sex with love as we end up saying more with our bodies than we feel in our hearts.

When acted on, sexual temptations entice us to make what can only be considered incredibly selfish, stupid—and sometimes tragic—decisions. It was exactly this temptation that caused the beheading of John the Baptist (see Matthew 14:1-12). Herod's affair with Herodias, his niece and wife of his half-brother Philip, was incestuous (see Leviticus 18:16; 20:21) and opposed by John. In a birthday party dominated by the presence of males, the dancing of Herodias's daughter was an overtly sexual act. It excited Herod so much that it led to the granting of Herodias's wish for the head of John. The point is obvious: if acted on, sexual thoughts can destroy relationships and lead to devastating consequences.

Chastity stands up to temptations about sex. However, it is not simply being faithful to our sexual commitments in the single life, marriage or a religious community; that kind of physical fidelity to ourselves, our spouse or our community speaks only of a rightful expression of celibacy. Chastity is much more than the appropriate physical control of our sexual desires. Incorporating a celibacy that respects our chosen lifestyle, chastity is the deliberate decision to promote and protect a loving attitude toward our own bodies as well as the bodies of others. It reverences certain physical boundaries as well as attitudes and topics of conversation. It chooses not to discuss with others over coffee what is sacred and confidential between lovers. In a sex-crazed, boundaryless world that is saturated with Internet pornography, sexual innuendos and the sexual exploitation of children, chastity is a countercultural virtue that proclaims that our physical bodies with their sexual desires are first and foremost temples of the Holy Spirit (see 1 Corinthians 6:19). Consequently, we treat them with the reverence afforded all things holy.

Things and generosity. Cassian's third thought, about things, can become temptations toward greed. When such thoughts are fueled and fostered, we become obsessed with certain possessions we think we desperately need in order to be happy. And unfortunately, enough is never enough as we buy and hoard for an illusory future. And illusory future it is: think of Jesus' parable about the man who compulsively filled his barns with food only to have his life suddenly taken away (see Luke 12:16-21).

Lives bloated with knickknacks, trinkets and superficial possessions betray a deep spiritual hunger that is being improperly nourished with "junk food." As Jesus warns, "Be on your guard against all kinds of greed; for one's life does not consist in the abundance of possessions" (Luke 12:15).

My friend Joseph is a perfect example of how generosity counteracts thoughts of things and the greed that sometimes arises as a result. Incredibly successful in an accounting firm, Joseph knows only too well the temptation to hoard his financial assets and possessions. Yet he makes a deliberate effort to donate money to worthwhile charities as well as to share his vacation home in Florida with others. Using the words of the marketplace in which he works, he once confided to me, "Every act of charity is a divinely inspired deposit we make in our spiritual bank accounts. I hope on Judgment Day, when God closes my account, I will have enough to enjoy an everlasting retirement." Joseph combats notions of an illusory earthly future with the hope of an eternal heavenly reward.

Anger and patience. Anger is the fourth tempting thought. It is often our knee-jerk reaction to unfulfilled desires or unmet expectations. Awareness of what is triggering angry thoughts can easily unmask the agenda of self-concern in our lives. When we choose to stoke the fires of anger, we lose our inner peace and expend so much of our emotional energy. Angry thoughts prompted by a bruised ego become the devil's furnace if we insist on immediately reacting to them. "A fool gives full vent to anger, but the wise quietly holds it back" (Proverbs 29:11).

And yet disciples committed to peace, social justice and the integrity of creation remind us that not all angry thoughts lead directly to the devil's furnace. Anger can also be the prophet's fire as it compels people to work for the humane treatment of prisoners in our jail system, for a responsible resolution to the issue of illegal immigration, for the protection of earth's natural resources and the end to unjust wars. Angry thoughts can challenge us to help bring about a fuller manifestation of the kingdom of God. This was the very nature of Jesus' anger in the temple (see John 2:13-17). These thoughts can urge us to stand up for what is right, preserve a sense of *Ubuntu* and promote the awareness of the family of creation. Indeed, angry thoughts are not always a temptation that can potentially lead to sin; they can also be the stimulus and force for bringing about a peaceful, loving and just world.

In a fast-paced culture that thrives on ease, expediency, convenience and self-gratification, patience is an intentional choice disciples make when they are irritated, frustrated, find their nerves tested or are tempted to strike out with anger and hostility. In opposition to the selfish, controlling demands of the ego, patience is the deliberate, measured response of an accepting heart that allows a situation to unfold in its own way. It is the blossom of trustful surrender to the present moment, one of the four characteristics of keepers of the kingdom.

Dejection and diligence. Sometimes I turn my angry thoughts inward. That leads to sadness. And my sad thoughts sometimes lead to dejection. When I totally identify with thoughts of dejection, I become depressed, and my thinking and reasoning are blurred. I lose my zest and zeal for life. As the proverb says, the attempt of others to lift me up emotionally only feels like a burden: "Like vinegar on a wound is one who sings songs to a heavy heart. Like a moth in clothing or a worm in wood, sorrow gnaws at the human heart" (Proverbs 25:20). When I am dejected, I find myself tempted to choose one of a multitude of unhealthy behaviors to distract me from the self-pity and heaviness of my mood: cruel inner monologues that are critical of myself or others, loitering around inappropriate Internet sites, excessive gossiping or reaching for unhealthy forms of self-medication, such as food or drink.

Over a course of a few months, my spiritual director became aware of my tendency toward self-absorption in depressing thoughts and feelings that can darken my day. He suggested that I practice the virtue of diligence on a regular basis. Diligence sometimes is an antidote to feelings of dejection and is a good virtue to have in my back pocket when the clouds of dejection roll in. Simply put, diligence is doing a particular task, such as washing the dishes or folding the laundry, with full attention and deliberateness; nothing else matters nor am I thinking about anything else but the task at hand. The spiritual discipline of diligence pulls my awareness and attention away from myself and focuses them on the sacrament of the present moment and the present duty before me. In effect, this practice lifts me above the dark clouds and thus saves me from being trapped in internal sadness and thoughts of dejection.

Acedia and perseverance. Cassian's sixth thought, acedia, is often identified as spiritual laziness or sloth. But that is a misinterpretation of this temptation. These thoughts attempt to throw the cold water of lethargy and indifference on our spiritual formation and make us feel spiritually weary. They can be prompted by the ego's insistence that spiritual progress is easy and noticeably measurable within weeks of beginning a full regimen of spiritual formation practices. When we don't see the desired immediate results, we not only become discouraged but also are tempted to discontinue. This was a frequent temptation for novice monks as they began their life in the fourth-century desert. Beginning with zeal and enthusiasm in the early dawn, they became bored and listless by noon. No wonder acedia was referred to as the "noonday devil."

When we give in to the temptation of the noonday devil and believe ourselves to be spiritual failures, we throw in the towel and reject anything dealing with spiritual formation. Acedia's thoughts serve cocktails of spiritual dislike and divine disgust and entice us to abandon our commitments to God in marriage, ministry and the marketplace. They promote half-hearted lives that are sluggish and slow and stagnant. We could also refer to this temptation as the "midlife devil," since we are especially tempted to renege on lifelong promises and important responsibilities as we journey through our forties and fifties.

Perseverance is the virtue that challenges the temptation toward acedia. It is rooted in the awareness that spiritual formation is a lifelong, ongoing process. Perseverance is the persistent openness to God's grace and the spirit of endurance that never ceases to respond. Indeed, there is no "spiritual microwave oven" that guarantees instant holiness; holiness occurs in the slow cooker of daily fidelity. Our daily fidelity to God and neighbor, no matter the external circumstances in which we find ourselves, is a stunning witness to the commitment to spiritual formation.

Vainglory and humility. I have a spiritual directee who does not wrestle with the noonday devil. His tempting thoughts attack on a different front. He gives himself a slap on the back when he thinks about what he has managed to accomplish in his personal, professional and spiritual lives. This is the temptation of vainglory, which promotes a belief in self-sufficiency and the self-satisfaction of a bloated self-image. We praise ourselves for being so kind, so generous and so prayerful. It is the opposite of dejection as we raise ourselves up and wave the flag of rugged independence, self-determination and self-made success. We have little need of God or grace as we come into the divine presence and smugly say with the Pharisee, "God, I thank you that I am not like other people: thieves, rogues, adulterers, or even like this tax collector. I fast twice a week; I give a tenth of all my income" (Luke 18:11-12).

Paul is a highly articulate, charismatic and talented pastor of a large church. Many members of his congregation travel a considerable distance on Sundays to listen to his consoling, insightful and sometimes challenging sermons. Of course, Paul is only too aware that his is a God-given speaking talent, not something he has cultivated by himself or for himself. The virtue of humility dissolves vainglory with its heresy that we are all self-made, self-sufficient individuals. Indeed, humility keeps our feet on the ground as we recognize God as the divine Almsgiver of everything we have in life.

Pride and charity. Vainglory tries to seduce us into thinking we can accomplish anything or everything on our own. Pride, on the other hand, tempts us to go one step further and actually believe we have made it. It tries to coax us into thinking we are better

than others. It offers justifications for a pompous attitude of superiority and rationalizes away a hundred special requirements that
should be met in the light of our magnificence. It is often the motivation behind the emotional need for being treated like a VIP.
The temptation toward pride is the afterglow left behind by
vainglory.

To the surprise of many, charity is the virtue that has traditionally kept thoughts of pride in check. Pride is the arrogance that
puts us on a pedestal above everyone else; it is the self-absorption
of the narcissistic megalomaniac who perpetually stares in the
mirror. Charity, on the other hand, takes the focus off self and
breaks the mirror. It looks toward others and tries as best as it can
to respond to the needs of the marginalized and the less fortunate.
It is what drove the good Samaritan to action. Indeed, charity is
the virtue that puts us right where we belong and where God intends us to be: at the service of others with selfless acts of sacrificial love as we willingly share our time, talent and treasures.

MAY I HAVE THIS DANCE?

Cassian's eight thoughts are rooted in our fixation with self-
concern, self-image, self-preservation and self-gratification. As
such, they are the most basic of temptations used by the devil and,
like an adolescent infatuation at a high-school prom, can easily
sweep us off our feet if we insist on horsing around or tinkering
with them. In other words, temptation is the tap on the shoulder
that asks "May I have this dance?" Our "yes" begins the process of
rationalization and justification that could lead to a sinful act.

Though our practice of the virtues promotes habits and dispo-
sitions that are antithetical to the eight thoughts, we still must
wrestle with and resist these temptations when they arise. Practically speaking, that means promptly refusing them as soon as we
become aware of them. If given undue or sympathetic attention,

these thoughts become infused with a seductive energy that can explode in sinful consequences and implode by strengthening the ego's self-centered agenda in our lives.

This is precisely the lesson taught in two accounts of Jesus' temptation in the desert (see Matthew 4:1-11; Luke 4:1-13). Jesus' temptations are not toward sinful actions; rather, they are toward a preoccupation with self-preservation (changing a stone into bread), self-image (receiving the power and glory of the kingdoms of the world) and self-gratification (presuming angelic support in a precarious situation). In each of the three instances, Jesus chooses not to fiddle or fuss with the suggestions of the devil. Rather, he immediately unmasks their lies and confronts them with the truth of reality.

The music of temptation's tango begins when we find ourselves in a situation that either consciously or unconsciously elicits one of the eight thoughts inside us. That is the ritual of temptation in a nutshell. We see an image on the television or in a magazine that gives rise to a sexual thought. Someone treats us disrespectfully and an angry inner monologue begins inside us. We receive disappointing news and begin to feel down on ourselves. We walk into a situation that triggers a painful childhood memory and our immediate reaction is to seek out some form of self-medication. We try to pray, but soon abandon prayer because we are riddled with distractions. We complete a task successfully and instantly want to give ourselves a pat on the back or think ourselves better than others.

Simple awareness that the music has begun is critical and crucial in not giving the tempting thought more attention than it deserves. Once the music has started, we now have to decide whether or not we want to accept the devil's hand and start the dance. The dance begins when we start fantasizing how and why we should respond to the sexual temptation. We horse around with the temptation by planning different forms of revenge or justifying how to punish ourselves for a failure. In a single instant, we think of a reason we should refuse the request for spare change or lash out in anger toward the colleague. We begin to think that catching up on today's news would be more productive and a better use of our time than trying to pray. The more we fiddle with reasons for acting on the thought, the closer we come to committing a sinful action.

Our refusal to act on any one of the eight thoughts is emboldened by three facts that we sometimes forget in the heat of the moment. First and foremost, we are not our superficial thoughts and the resulting desires they sometimes open up inside of us. This is often forgotten. To totally identify ourselves with our thoughts and their desires is to dance cheek-to-cheek with the power of evil and become its partner. Such identification pushes us dangerously close to acting on any of the eight temptations. This can potentially put our names on the dance card of compulsive behavior as we mistakenly believe we are unable to disengage from our thoughts and have no choice but to act on what we think or feel.

Second, John Cassian's eight thoughts and the feelings they give rise to are lonely, desperate dancers who have no sense of fidelity or commitment. Like the devil trying to entice and coax Jesus with three different suggestions, these thoughts and feelings come and go, walking around the dance floor of our present circumstances, touching our shoulder and asking the perennial question "May I have this dance?"

Third, these thoughts and desires disappear and move on if we choose not to dance with them. This is clearly evident in Luke's account of Jesus' temptation, which concludes, "When the devil had finished every test, he departed from him until an opportune time" (Luke 4:13). In fact, the devil's agenda, if ignored, shows its true colors as being no more lasting than bubbles blown through a plastic wand. Should we decide to grab its hand and waist, we run the risk of leaving the dance hall with it once the music has stopped. And that is what sin is all about: the decision to act on the thought or feeling.

REFUSING TO DANCE WITH THE DEVIL

Refusing to dance with the devil is as simple as it is challenging. It presupposes that we live with an awareness of what is going on inside of us. Within the Eastern Orthodox tradition of Christianity, this is called *nepsis,* the practice of mindfulness and vigilance to what is going on in the mind and heart.

Mind	*LET GO* of thoughts that come down the stream of consciousness
Heart	*SCRUTINIZE* motivations behind feelings and desires
Situations ⟶ Thoughts and Feelings ⟵ AWARENESS	

Figure 10.2. The practice of *nepsis*

When practicing the discipline of *nepsis,* we make a concerted effort to let go of every thought that sails down the stream of consciousness. As the thought comes down the stream, it will be fishing for our attention and interest. We refuse the bait. We allow the tempting thought to continue downstream. We do not actively "fight against" the thought, since that becomes a form of engagement with it. Rather, we simply let it go. This simple exercise, practiced while waiting at a stoplight or during a period of prayer when our attention is focused on the divine presence, helps to build up resistance to the seduction of tempting thoughts.

We also make a concerted effort to be vigilant toward the impulses, desires and passions of the heart. We pay careful attention to every feeling and scrutinize its motivation. This reflection on the throbbing of the heart (feelings and desires) and what is pumping the emotional blood (motivation) helps to short-circuit the natural tendency to respond to any feeling of self-concern, self-image, self-preservation and self-gratification willy-nilly.

In some respects, *nepsis* is the very first step of spiritual formation. Without awareness, mindfulness and vigilance, we easily become dance partners with every single whim and wish of the devil. We find ourselves saying and doing things that are selfish, cruel, arrogant and disruptive of the family of creation.

With awareness, mindfulness and vigilance, however, we are in a position to unmask and confront the most deceptive and capricious temptations offered by the devil. The minute we find ourselves obsessing with thoughts and feelings swirling around self-concern, self-image, self-preservation and self-gratification, we make the deliberate choice not to feed them and not to give them any attention whatsoever. We turn our backs on them (the Greek word for conversion, *metanoia*, literally means "turning around") and focus our attention elsewhere. When we do that, the tempting thought usually goes up in smoke. Should it momentarily return, we simply brush it off again.

Once this simple practice of mindfulness and awareness of what is going on in our minds and hearts has become a regular

> *There is a vast difference between being tempted and yielding to it. And yet, if I know in advance that certain places will tempt me and I go there anyway, I am guilty of each temptation that comes my way.*
>
> *The way to deal with temptations is to look away from them and at the Lord. If you are still subject to them, continue to resist. There is no sin as long as you say no.*
>
> FRANCIS DE SALES

part of our spiritual practice, we can then begin practicing a deeper form of *nepsis*. This is learning to be aware of what situations elicit what thoughts and feelings. Each one of us is vulnerable to certain situations that can trigger a particular tempting thought and its resulting feeling or desire. I know, for example, that I am prone to anger when I am around people whom I perceive to be arrogant or self-centered. I am also tempted to vainglory when I feel defensive and have to justify myself or my priestly ministry. Being sensitive to the situations in which we are vulnerable and actually avoiding them when possible go a long way in getting us out of Satan's dance hall and in protecting us from the advance of other and more powerful temptations (see Matthew 12:43-45).

SPIRITUAL COMBAT

It is important to remember that the eight thoughts are just that, thoughts. They are temptations. They are the devil's taps on the shoulder. Some of them come naturally, depending on the situation in which we find ourselves or place ourselves. We should not become discouraged when we are tempted, for that instantly gets the devil's band warming up with tunes of dejection and acedia.

The fact is, we never outgrow temptation. And so we pray daily, "Lead us not into temptation." This is inherent in Luke's reference to the devil waiting for "an opportune time" to tempt Jesus again at the conclusion of the temptation in the desert (Luke 4:13). Indeed, Scripture says that ours is a "struggle . . . against the rulers, against the authorities, against the cosmic powers of this present darkness, against the spiritual forces of evil in the heavenly places" (Ephesians 6:12). That struggle never comes to an end in this life.

The sixteenth-century spiritual classic *Spiritual Combat*, written by Lawrence Scupoli, attained great success and notoriety. Francis de Sales always kept a copy of it in his pocket and encouraged all his spiritual directees to read it. The text promoted the idea that spiritual perfection can be attained by means of a constant, courageous struggle against our evil human nature. In Scupoli's words,

> Since, therefore, you seek the highest degree of perfection, you must wage continual warfare against yourself and employ your entire strength in demolishing each vicious inclination, however trivial. Consequently, in preparing for the combat you must summon up all your resolution and courage. No one shall be rewarded with a crown who has not fought courageously.
>
> But remember that as no war can be carried on with greater fierceness, the forces, no other than ourselves, being equal on both sides, so the victory when gained is most pleasing to God and most glorious to the conqueror. For whoever has the courage to conquer his passions, to subdue his appetites, and repulse even the least motions of his own will, performs an action more meritorious in the sight of God than if, without this, he should tear his flesh with the sharpest disciplines, fast with greater austerity than the ancient Fathers of the Desert, or convert multitudes of sinners.

Spiritual Combat is clearly a product of its own time. It promotes a practice of spiritual formation that was typical in Roman Catholic circles in the sixteenth and seventeenth centuries. Many contemporary Christians are uncomfortable with the text's emphasis on works and self-sufficiency. Furthermore, many people cannot relate to the book's militaristic language of warfare. But, that being said, the text offers us a valid reminder: spiritual formation is an ongoing challenge to refuse temptations and to say no to the obsession with self-concern, self-image, self-preservation and self-gratification.

Figure 10.3. The practice of *nepsis*

Though we never outgrow temptations, we do grow in the ability to say no to the devil's dance request with awareness, mindfulness and vigilance. As our ability to refuse the dance strengthens and becomes second nature to us, we approach the state of *apatheia*. Often confused with the English word *apathy* and misinterpreted as being passionless and without emotion, spiritual *apatheia* is actually "a state of self-mastery and attention from which one cannot be dislodged by distractions or by the kinds of outbursts of spiritual energy that expresses itself in anger and resentment." In other words, we are in control. We are focused and self-possessed. We are not swayed by the devil's insistent taps on the shoulder or the whims and egotistical desires of the heart. Our priorities indicate that our decision to be faithful to our vocation as little Christs has taken hold. This is the realization of God's intention for us. This is the way of the disciple.

To pray, "Lead us not into temptation," is to confront the power of evil, which stands in direct opposition to God. It is a commitment to become aware of the eight tempting thoughts in our lives and to resist them. It also implies a dedication to living a life of virtue that helps to transform us into the people God created us to be.

REFLECTION QUESTIONS

1. What has been my experience with evil? Have I ever experienced it as a personal force against God called "Satan"? If so, when?

2. What are the signs that point to the fact that I am rationalizing or justifying some action I know in my heart is sinful?

3. Which of the eight thoughts am I most prone to act on? What situations make me especially prone to thinking and acting on them?

4. Which of the eight virtues come naturally to me? Which ones do I need to begin making an intentional effort to practice?

Gospel Passages for Meditation and Prayer: Matthew 12:43-45; 25:1-13

11

Deliver Us from Evil

Embracing the Cross

Spiritual darkness purifies us from the ego and can help transform us into little Christs. As a cross, it challenges us to surrender to God with trust.

WATCHING THE EVENING NEWS OR READING the headlines of today's newspaper reveals a world seemingly pervaded with evil: hate crimes, prejudice, the sexual exploitation of children, unjust wars, sweat shops, the denial of human rights, deliberate deception, ethnic genocide, personal and national apathy toward victims of natural disasters. The list is endless.

Tragically, as Scripture suggests, so much evil in the world—perhaps *all* evil in the world—originates in the human heart (see Genesis 6:5; 1 Samuel 24:13; Mark 7:20-23). The human heart seems so susceptible and weak before the temptations of the devil. In fact, whenever we give in to the temptation to "ease God out" of a situation and promote our own agenda to the detriment of God's will and kingdom, evil has arisen. Such rebellion against God has tragic consequences for the family of creation.

Matthew's version of the Lord's Prayer concludes with a petition for deliverance from such evil. However, as every disciple knows, we will never be delivered from this evil until our egos are willing to put God back where God belongs and take a backseat to God's will and kingdom. Until then, our prayer, "Deliver us from evil," is a plea to be set free from our obsession with self-concern, self-image, self-preservation and self-gratification.

THE TRIAL AS A TEST OF FAITH

There is an alternate translation of Matthew's final petition that raises an important issue in spiritual formation. Slightly different from the petition "Deliver us from evil," which we actually pray, it is typically rendered, "And do not bring us to the time of trial, but rescue us from the evil one" (Matthew 6:13).

According to Jewish belief in the end of the world, the time of trial would be the time of Satan's final assault (see Revelation 3:10). There would be a final confrontation between believers and the power of evil. This time of trial would be so challenging, devastating and destructive that many people would fall away, give up the faith and lose all hope. Believing that God had lost interest and abandoned them, they would despair.

Jesus proclaimed the beginning of God's kingdom, where Satan no longer has any power or dominion: "But if it is by the finger of God that I cast out demons, then the kingdom of God has come to you" (Luke 11:20). And to his followers, Jesus bequeathed this power and authority to defeat the prince of evil: "I watched Satan fall from heaven like a flash of lightning. See, I have given you authority to tread on snakes and scorpions, and over all the power of the enemy; and nothing will hurt you" (Luke 10:18).

With the advent of Jesus' kingdom, a new springtime of invincible faith, hope and love had arrived. There would now never be reason to give in to evil's illusion that Abba is disinterested or unapproachable. Indeed, Jesus taught us that Abba is as close and approachable as a father to his children. Never would a trial warrant giving into the evil one's temptation toward hopelessness and despair. As Jesus had reminded his disciples at their last meal together, "In the world you face persecution. But take courage; I have conquered the world!" (John 16:33).

And yet we still experience trials and tribulations that challenge both our belief in God as a loving Abba and our ability to cope. One thinks of Abraham, who experienced the agony of God calling him to sacrifice his own son (see Genesis 22:1-19). One thinks of the crucified Jesus as he prayed the words of the psalmist in a last cry of desperation, "My God, my God, why have you forsaken me?" (Mark 15:34).

Like Abraham, we too have felt challenged to let go of someone or something very dear and precious to us: a job in which we invested so much of our time and energy; a loved one in death; friends and familiar surroundings when we move to another city. Like Jesus, most of us have experienced at least one trial or tragedy in life when we asked, "Where are you, God? Have you forgotten me?"

THE DARK NIGHT

Some famous people in the history of Christian spirituality have had such experiences, traditionally called the dark night. Occasionally, their experiences have lasted for years. Jane Frances de Chantal experienced the feeling of abandonment by God for three decades. Paul of the Cross's spiritual trial was even lengthier, but he was granted relief toward the end of his life. The final eighteen months of Thérèse of Lisieux's short life were consumed with physical, emotional and spiritual suffering. But perhaps the longest documented experience of feeling abandoned by God was in the life of Agnes Gonxha Bojaxhiu, known to the world as Mother Teresa of Calcutta.

On September 10, 1946, while traveling by train from Calcutta to a retreat house in Darjeeling, Mother Teresa had a mystical experience of Jesus that would ultimately lead her to leave the convent of the Sisters of Loretto to which she belonged and begin a new religious congregation that ministered to the destitute and dying of Calcutta's streets. For the next year or so, she experienced a deep union with Jesus. And then, suddenly, it all came to a grinding halt. A profound spiritual darkness and feeling of being abandoned by God came over her. A letter she wrote to her spiritual director in April 1961 gives us an inkling of her pain:

> Now Father—since 49 or 50 this terrible sense of loss—this untold darkness—this loneliness—this continual longing for God—which gives me that pain deep down in my heart.— Darkness is such that I really do not see—neither with my mind nor with my reason.—The place of God in my soul is blank.—There is no God in me.—When the pain of longing is so great—I just long & long for God—and then it is that I feel—He does not want me—He is not there.—Heaven— souls—why these are just words—which mean nothing to me.—My very life seems so contradictory. I help souls—to go where?—Why all this? Where is the soul in my very being? God does not want me.—Sometimes—I just hear my own heart cry out—"My God" and nothing else comes.— The torture and pain I can't explain.—From my childhood I have had a most tender love for Jesus in the Blessed Sacrament—but this too has gone.—I feel nothing before Jesus— and yet I would not miss Holy Com. [Communion] for anything.

Mother Teresa of Calcutta's dark night would continue for the next fifty years until her death. Before she died, she made peace with the darkness. She wrote to her spiritual director:

For the first time in this 11 years—I have come to love the darkness.—For I believe now that it is a part, a very, very small part of Jesus' darkness & pain on earth. You have taught me to accept it [as] a "spiritual side of 'your work'" as you wrote.

The experience of the dark night reminds us of an important principle of spiritual formation: Feelings are not a trustworthy guide in the spiritual life; they can be misleading and deceptive. Feelings of desolation—of sadness, grief and disappointment—can falsely indicate that the God who is as close to us as a father to his children has abandoned us. The two disciples on the road to Emmaus were wrapped up in their sadness, yet the risen Lord was actually walking alongside them (see Luke 24:13-35). Mary of Magdala was consumed with grief even as the resurrected Lord stood before her (see John 20:11-18). Indeed, our feelings say nothing about the absence of God.

The opposite is also true. Feelings of consolation—of peacefulness, joy, contentment and happiness—are no sure indication that God is closer to us than God is to others or that our spiritual life is more seasoned and developed than others'. Granted, such feelings can have a profound positive effect on us, as we saw in the lives of Francis of Assisi and John Wesley; nevertheless, we need to heed Paul's warning: "Even Satan disguises himself as an angel of light" (2 Corinthians 11:14). Lest we be tricked, we need to be discriminating and discerning; that's why it's wise to "test everything" (1 Thessalonians 5:21).

In fact, in times of desolation as well as times of consolation, God is still like the air we breathe. Abba remains as close to us as a father to his children.

When we mistakenly allow feelings to become the barometer of our souls, we risk the possibility of our spiritual life devolving into a self-centered narcissism focused on "me" and not on "Thee."

The goal of spiritual formation, instead of being transformation into little Christs, suddenly becomes an emotional high or a "feel good" devotion. This reeks of the ego's obsession with self-gratification. We learn an important principle from the "saint of darkness," as Mother Teresa once referred to herself: just because we believe we are doing the will of God does not guarantee feelings of consolation nor insulate us from feelings of abandonment. Clearly, feelings are an unreliable and undependable gauge of what is going on in God's relationship with us.

PURIFICATION AND TRANSFORMATION

But human beings that we are, we do need to make some sense of our trials and feelings of abandonment, lest we lose hope and despair. It's clear that Mother Teresa only came to "love the darkness" once she came to understand her dark night as "a very, very small part of Jesus' darkness & pain on earth," as the "spiritual side of '[her] work.'"

The letter to the Hebrews gives us another way of interpreting the tribulations and sufferings that come our way. The writer says,

Endure trials for the sake of discipline. God is treating you as children; for what child is there whom a parent does not discipline? If you do not have that discipline in which all children share, then you are illegitimate and not his children. Moreover, we had human parents to discipline us, and we respected them. Should we not be even more willing to be subject to the Father of spirits and live? For they disciplined us for a short time as seemed best to them, but he disciplines us for our good, in order that we may share his holiness. Now, discipline always seems painful rather than pleasant at the time, but later it yields the peaceful fruit of righteousness to those who have been trained by it. (Hebrews 12:7-11)

And so, one way of understanding dark nights and spiritual trials—in whatever way they come to us—is that they are forms of purification, of "discipline." They often attack the life-support system of the ego with its self-centered concern with what we have, what we do and what people think of us. The more we are invested in the obsession with self-concern, self-image, self-preservation and self-gratification, the more painful will be our experience of the trial.

But the flip side of purification, of "discipline," according to the letter to the Hebrews, is transformation into the "holiness" of God. That's the good news. Trials can help us become who we are called to be, namely, little Christs: "Although he was a Son, he learned obedience through what he suffered; and having been made perfect, he became the source of eternal salvation for all who obey him" (Hebrews 5:8-9). Trials and testings wean us away from the ego and teach us "obedience" (from the Latin word *audire*, "to listen") to the call of God and the way of the disciple. As one contemporary Scripture scholar has written:

> What we suffer in our lives, if we can perceive and accept such suffering in faith, enables God to shape Jesus' own "sonship" in us. Ancient Greeks had the maxim *mathein pathein*, "to learn it is necessary to suffer." Being educated as children of God requires a painful transformation, for the goal is the holy God (Hebrews 12:10).

That simply means suffering allows God to take possession of us and perform the purifying transformation that only God's grace can accomplish. As Paul reminded the church at Corinth,

> So we do not lose heart. Even though our outer nature is wasting away, our inner nature is being renewed day by day. For this slight momentary affliction is preparing us for an

eternal weight of glory beyond all measure, because we look not at what can be seen but at what cannot be seen; for what can be seen is temporary, but what cannot be seen is eternal. (2 Corinthians 4:16-18)

The first letter of Peter, written to the church in Asia Minor during a time of persecution, states the same idea by comparing trials to the fire that tests gold:

Even if now for a little while you have had to suffer various trials, so that the genuineness of your faith—being more precious than gold that, though perishable, is tested by fire—may be found to result in praise and glory and honor when Jesus Christ is revealed. (1 Peter 1:6-7)

BLIND FAITH

On two occasions, I had the opportunity to travel to Cameroon, West Africa, to preach a retreat to some Franciscan sisters in the small village of Shisong. Over a few weeks, I developed a friendship with an African named John who was blind from birth. He and I spent an hour every day talking about God, the spiritual life and spiritual formation. On one occasion, the topic of disabilities came up. I remember somewhat naively asking him, "John, what's it like being blind?"

Without missing a beat, he replied, "Father, don't you know? After all, when it comes to living our faith, we all walk as blind people."

Though it is tested and challenged by our very sufferings and tribulations, blind faith is the torch we carry as we walk through the dark night. Paul says it best: "For we walk by faith, not by sight" (2 Corinthians 5:7). The very essence of faith is a radical trust that sometimes can only fumble and stumble through the darkness.

Jesus shows us the practical implications of living out blind faith in the midst of our trials and tribulations. As he struggled to pray on the Mount of Olives, "not my will but yours be done" (Luke 22:42). And as he said from the cross, "Father, into your hands I commend my spirit" (Luke 23:46). Indeed, the feeling of abandonment *by* God is a challenge to make an act of abandonment *to* God. That's putting blind faith into action.

All four Gospels agree that once Judas and the crowd arrived in the Garden of Gethsemane, Jesus did nothing to defend himself, vindicate himself or save his life. On the contrary, with shocking deliberateness, Jesus bowed before the mystery of suffering and gave himself into the hands of his executioners. He accepted, surrendered and embraced the cross. In that gracious surrender to the way of the cross, in that deliberate acceptance of the *via dolorosa,* in that act of self-abandonment to Abba, Jesus showed us how to turn pain into praise and suffering into the song of salvation.

TRUE AND PERFECT JOY

Saint Francis once made the same point to his close friend, Brother Leo. Francis began by telling Leo explicitly what true joy does *not* consist in: the brotherhood attracting scholars, bishops and kings; the friars converting all the nonbelievers to the Christian faith; the presence of a certain friar with the special grace to heal the sick or perform miracles.

When Brother Leo, somewhat puzzled, asked, "Then what is true joy?" Francis replied,

> I return from Perugia and arrive here in the dead of night. It's winter time, muddy, and so cold that icicles have formed on the edges of my habit and keep striking my legs and blood flows from such wounds. Freezing, covered with mud and

ice, I come to the gate and, after I've knocked and called for some time, a brother comes and asks: "Who are you?" "Brother Francis," I answer. "Go away!" he says. "This is not a decent hour to be wandering about! You may not come in!" When I insist, he replies: "Go away! You are simple and stupid! Don't come back to us again! There are many of us here like you—we don't need you!" I stand again at the door and say: "For the love of God, take me in tonight!" And he replies: "I will not! Go to the Crosiers' place and ask there!"

I tell you this: If I had patience and did not become upset, true joy, as well as true virtue and the salvation of my soul, would consist in this.

In a startling reversal of values, Saint Francis says true and perfect joy is found in our acceptance of the trial of betrayal, in our surrender to the tribulation of rejection.

The ego is easily threatened and considers its reputation at stake in every situation. Rather than surrender to a test or trial with trust in God, the ego has the emotional need to take a stand and fight. It immediately draws the battle lines. It would view the porter who answers the door as the enemy to be defeated. Anger and revenge are its weapons as it seeks to defend itself. In fact, the ego has a knee-jerk reaction to any person or situation that challenges its self-concern, self-image, self-preservation and self-gratification. Consequently, it goes through life banging its fists on the table and barking like an angry dog.

The alternate translation of Matthew's concluding petition, "Do not bring us to the time of trial, but rescue us from the evil one," is a prayer to renounce the kind of egocentric self-assertion, violent reaction and obsession with self-preservation that are the sources of so much evil in this world. And so this petition is a prayer to be delivered from the evil that we ourselves impose on the world. It is also a prayer for the grace of blind faith: to learn how to accept and surrender with trust—and thus respond as a little Christ.

As Jesus shows us, disciples do not have an emotional need to react, take a stand, justify and defend themselves. In fact, the more and more we are formed into our identity as little Christs, the less we have to prove, protect and preserve. As little Christs, knowing full well that God has the final word, we simply submit and surrender. As Christ did on the cross, we stop the cycle of violent self-assertion and absorb the trial or others' evil within ourselves.

Once, while preaching a weeklong retreat, I met an elderly nun. She had been retired for a number of years and, when the weather permitted, spent her days gardening and, when the weather did not, visiting the bedridden nuns in the infirmary. Sadly, however, two years before I met her, this nun had been accused of sexually abusing one of her students some four decades before. She told me she was stunned by the accusation and that a terrible emotional darkness came over her. Her religious community enlisted the help of a lawyer for her case. After a year and a half, it became apparent that the accuser was mentally unstable. The nun was totally exonerated of the charge.

As she told me her story, I couldn't help but think that this nun must have felt rightfully angry and bitter toward the accuser. I certainly would have. I asked her if she had pursued any legal means to have the accuser punished and her reputation restored. Her reply challenged me: "Absolutely not. I want the damage to stop with me." To quote the words of Jesus, "Do not resist an evil-doer. But if anyone strikes you on the right cheek, turn the other also" (Matthew 5:39).

As I reflected on that conversation later, I realized the hundreds of times I have sought to continue the cycle of violence and egocentric self-assertion. I am embarrassed to admit that my emotional crusades are about petty disagreements regarding decisions in the community, how a party should be planned and who is going to cook the weekend meal. These crusades all pale in the light of that nun's experience.

Many of us might consider that nun's attitude absurd. We criticize it as passive, as becoming a doormat. We look on such a response as the most basic form of weakness and giving the devil free reign to unleash all the evil in human hearts.

The way of the disciple, on the other hand, knows only too well that some truths speak for themselves and have no need of justification. It actively seeks to preserve *Ubuntu,* the reality that we discover who we are in relationship to others and are called to live our lives in selfless acts of sacrificial love for others. It is quite content to absorb the evil of another.

Some forms of frustration and emotional suffering—like those we experience as a result of our need to control and manipulate the situations we find ourselves in—are the price we pay to keep the ego alive and thriving. But other forms of suffering—like the trials and tribulations of the dark night, when we feel as if God has abandoned us—confront the agenda of the ego head-on, unmask its illusions and attempt to purify us of its lies. Our ultimate attachment to the agenda of the ego or the way of the disciple often appears in times of trial and tribulation. When we surrender to a test or trial with trust in the fidelity of God, we are renouncing the ego's agenda. We are choosing to accept, validate and live in the present moment and to allow it to unfold in its own way. This, according to the Franciscan tradition, is the meaning of true and perfect joy and the salvation of the soul.

In his gracious surrender to the way of the cross, in his deliberate acceptance of the *via dolorosa,* in the act of self-abandonment to Abba, Jesus showed us how to turn pain into praise and suffering into the song of salvation. Indeed, the thick, ominous clouds of the dark night crackle with the lightning of spiritual transformation. Surrender with trust, or to use Mother Teresa of Calcutta's words, "to love the darkness," is the only response that robs any test or trial of its power to destroy us.

SUFFERING AS SONG: THE "CANTICLE OF CREATURES"

The last two years of Saint Francis's life are very well documented in the memories of some of his closest companions, who cared for the saint in his final years. According to one text, Francis spent more than fifty days in a small hut adjacent to the church of San Damiano. The hut was infested with mice. These mice tormented the now blind and frail saint during his prayer and during his meals. The early companions tell us that Francis went into a depression and started feeling sorry for himself. He prayed for hope and patient endurance in the face of this dark night. Francis heard these words in response from God, "Brother, be glad and rejoice in your illnesses and troubles, because as of now, you are as secure as if you were already in my kingdom."

Hearing these words, Francis cast aside his self-pity and stopped fighting against the sickness, his blindness and the mice. Like Jesus, whom he constantly tried to imitate, Francis accepted the cross of the present moment and trusted that God would keep the divine promise and remain as close to him as a father to his child.

Rooted in that moment, Francis renounced the temptation to control and change the situation. From that stance, he suddenly became aware of the divine presence that surrounded him like the air he breathed. The blind saint saw creation in all its ordinariness and sacramentality. It became a ladder leading him to God. It was on this very day that Saint Francis composed the "Canticle of Creatures," which begins,

Praised be You, my Lord, with all Your creatures,
Especially Sir Brother Sun,
Who is the day and through whom You give us light.
And he is beautiful and radiant with great splendor;
And bears a likeness of You, Most High One.

In a most profound way, the blind saint's inner eyes were opened. The sun was the bringer of the light of day—and a reflection of God! He recognized the family of creation—"Sister Moon," "Brother Wind," "Sister Water," "Brother Fire," "Sister Mother Earth"—as he composed this great hymn of praise. He again experienced God as the divine Almsgiver and himself as a beggar: "Through every kind of weather . . . You give sustenance to Your creatures." He gave praise to Sister Death, whom he no longer feared; he referred to her as "the second death," the first, no doubt, being the moment when he began to renounce the agenda of the ego before the bishop and citizens of Assisi. And, in this tremendous moment of spiritual enlightenment, Francis became more deeply rooted in his truest identity as he rediscovered who he already was and who he was called to be: as a little Christ, he was a humble servant of God's will. "Praise and bless my Lord and give Him thanks and serve Him with great humility."

The "Canticle of the Creatures" is Saint Francis's resurrection song in the face of his own Calvary. In the saint's gracious surrender to the cross and his act of fervent trust in God, agony became adoration, pain became praise and suffering quite literally became song.

TAKE UP YOUR CROSS

"If any want to become my followers, let them deny themselves and take up their cross and follow me" (Matthew 16:24). That is a requirement Jesus places on anyone who wishes to follow the way of the disciple. It is direct and unequivocal, and the Gospel tradition repeats it five times (see Matthew 10:38; 16:24; Mark 8:34; Luke 9:23; 14:27).

Jesus does not simply encourage us to passively accept and surrender to the cross of the present moment. He commands us to actively embrace it.

What is it about actively embracing the crosses of our trials that makes them so important—even the prerequisite—for Christian discipleship?

Tim taught me the answer.

Tim's medical doctor suggested that he might want to make his peace with God, since his aggressive cancer left little chance for remission. Tim sought me out for spiritual direction. I was privileged—I use that adjective deliberately—to know him for a short eight months. Talking with dying Tim taught me so much about how to live.

In many of our twice-monthly sessions, he stressed over and over how, in the face of his sickness, all he had left was his simple trust in God. "At this point, Father, I just put my life in God's hands. It's God's call when and how my life continues."

Tim didn't doubt that his life would continue. He just left it up to God to decide how. He said those words in our third session together. And when he said them, it dawned on me that the cross of trials and tribulations has a unique ability to bring the reality of our faith to the fore. Tim's faith seemingly blossomed with his medical death sentence. Maybe that's why Jesus made the cross the prerequisite for discipleship. It tests the "genuineness of [our] faith," as the first letter of Peter suggests (1 Peter 1:7).

During the eight months that Tim and I met for spiritual direction, I was going through a particularly difficult time in community life. I once shared my struggles with Tim. Much to my surprise, even when he was too sick to come to my office for spiritual direction, he would call, and the first question would always be, "And, Father, how are *you* doing? I've been praying for you and thinking of you."

Despite his own grieving process, Tim's first concern was me and my situation. In a conversation with one of his colleagues after hearing of his death, I discovered this was "typical Tim." In the final months of his life, he was more concerned about others than himself. In other words, the cross of cancer had become his channel to compassion.

Unfortunately, I was preaching in Beijing when news of Tim's death reached me. It was Holy Week, the holiest days before Easter Sunday. During the Good Friday evening service, with Roman Catholics around the world, I approached and venerated a large wooden cross. As I kissed the cross, I thought of Tim, and then it dawned on me: this cross does not simply represent the cross on which Christ died; it represents every cross that has found its way into my life. I *need* a cross for faith and love. Without a cross, my faith would be shallow; without a cross, my compassion would be superficial.

When we actively embrace the cross and allow it to try our faith like gold tested in fire; when we allow its pain and sorrow to move us beyond self-pity to sensitivity for the sufferings of others, we are transformed into our truest selves, little Christs. We develop an unshakable faith in Abba, along with a love and compassion for other people. We are then able to grasp an insight and an appreciation for the curious words of the apostle Paul:

> May I never boast of anything except the cross of our Lord Jesus Christ, by which the world has been crucified to me, and I to the world. For neither circumcision nor uncircumcision is anything; but a new creation is everything! . . . Let no one make trouble for me; for I carry the marks of Jesus branded on my body. (Galatians 6:14-15, 17)

Paul was only too aware that many viewed the cross as "foolishness" and a "stumbling block" (1 Corinthians 1:23). Indeed, the self-centered ego could not think otherwise. However, from Paul's perspective, the cross is God's chosen birth canal to our truest identity and thus to a "new creation." When we actively embrace it, we are set free from the ego and begin to live as little Christs: "I have been crucified with Christ; and it is no longer I who live, but it is Christ who lives in me" (Galatians 2:19-20). Or, in the famous words written by the apostle to the church at Rome:

> Do you not know that all of us who have been baptized into Christ Jesus were baptized into his death? Therefore we have been buried with him by baptism into death, so that, just as Christ was raised from the dead by the glory of the Father, so we too might walk in newness of life.
>
> For if we have been united with him in a death like his, we will certainly be united with him in a resurrection like his. We know that our old self was crucified with him so that the body of sin might be destroyed, and we might no longer be enslaved to sin. (Romans 6:3-6)

The embrace of the cross, as it did with Tim, thrusts us out of the "body of sin," the agenda of the ego, and brings us into a "newness of life," namely, who we are called to be.

LIVING HOPE

The knowledge that we are in the birth canal leading to a new life during our trials and tribulations, gives us a "living hope" (1 Peter 1:3). And so we actively embrace the cross of the present moment, knowing full well that, despite the deception of our feelings, Abba is as close to us as a father to his children. Indeed, acceptance and surrender without hope can lead to despair. Acceptance and surrender without hope is fatalism.

Our trials and experiences of the dark night are not simply times of purification and transformation. As our Judeo-Christian tradition has shown time and time again, times of trial are also times when God once again proclaims that we have not been forgotten or abandoned.

This living hope is based on the central symbol of Christianity. And despite what we find in most churches today, it is not the cross—but an empty tomb! As Paul reminded the Corinthians, "if Christ has not been raised, then our proclamation has been in vain and your faith has been in vain" (1 Corinthians 15:14).

When we find ourselves falling over the edge in times of testing or tragedy, we pray, "And do not bring us to the time of trial, but rescue us from the evil one." And God provides us, the beloved, with trust and hope. "Can a woman forget her nursing child, or show no compassion for the child of her womb? Even these may forget, yet I will not forget you" (Isaiah 49:15).

God's covenant with us is eternal and unconditional. God will always be present to us as Savior and Deliverer, even when our senses do not apprehend God's presence. Abba is on our side. Abba will never forget, abandon or forsake the beloved. That is the deepest meaning of grace. When everything falls apart and our world comes caving in, God enters and manifests the divine presence. Indeed, the hand of God transforms testings, trials and tragedies into moments of amazing grace. That is the story of Easter resurrection. Despite what Jesus felt as he hung on the cross, Abba did not abandon his beloved

For perfect hope is achieved on the brink of despair when, instead of falling over the edge, we find ourselves walking on the air. Hope is always just about to turn into despair, but never does so, for at the moment of supreme crisis God's power is suddenly made perfect in our infirmity.

THOMAS MERTON

Son. Abba was there, quietly waiting for the right moment. And suddenly, the tomb was found empty and an angel proclaimed, "Do not be afraid; I know that you are looking for Jesus who was crucified. He is not here; for he has been raised, as he said" (Matthew 28:5-6).

EASTER IN MY BONES

After a few spiritual direction sessions with Linda, I knew something was brewing inside her. And many clues were beginning to suggest deep, unresolved psychological issues based on a childhood trauma. Though I did not want to make her feel further isolated and abandoned, I was also aware that the issues were well beyond my competence. I suggested she pursue counseling, and she soon entered a six-month, inpatient, holistic health program.

In a short Christmas letter, Linda wrote that she was facing many areas of her life that were both frightening and painful. "Between the group sessions, the individual counseling sessions and my spiritual direction appointments, I find myself broken into many pieces that are scattered in different meeting rooms down the hallway. It's hard work. Pray for me."

Around mid-April, I received a lengthy letter, written the Monday before Easter. She only had ten days left in the program and was looking forward to getting back into the rhythm of life. She felt good, vibrant. "I've rediscovered myself." She concluded that letter with words that still bring a smile to my face: "P.S. God surely didn't let me down. Celebrate with me. I feel Easter in my bones."

Andrew's ten years of denying his alcoholism had destroyed his first marriage, wrecked two automobiles and was on the verge of destroying his second marriage. I called him the first night after he was released from a sixty-day program for addiction in a local hospital. When I asked him about his newfound sobriety, all he could say was, "God is good and getting better every day."

Jean Marie was a very active woman and a nurse by profession. At the age of thirty-five, she was diagnosed on the operating table with a rare disease that causes degeneration of the spinal cord. The doctors could not tell her how long she could continue living her active lifestyle before crutches, braces and orthopedic shoes would be her lot.

Jean Marie went into a deep depression. She feared how she would ultimately end up. Since there is currently no cure for the disease, she knew it was just a matter of time before she ended up in a wheelchair or lay bedridden. That was seventeen years ago.

When I met Jean Marie for the first time, she was wearing orthopedic shoes and a stiff neck brace. She had been told to spend at least half her waking hours sitting in a chair. But amazingly, she is totally at peace with her disease and the inconvenience that is now part of her daily routine. She told me that it took nearly one full year to get out of the initial depression and to reconcile herself to the inevitable: the disease was not going to disappear; she would have to accept it. Over twelve months, her pain became praise and her suffering became song as she surrendered to the disease and trusted that God would stay near to her. As she said to me, "God has walked with me this far. I know he won't abandon me now."

Each of these stories illustrates the saving power of God in the midst of a trial, test or human infirmity. Grace brings forth life from suffering and death. Grace gives us the courage to accept what we cannot change. Grace makes the impossible suddenly possible. It appears as a miraculous solution in the throes of a devastating problem. It causes something to shift internally, and life becomes worth living again. God's grace is the foundation of our trust—and, indeed, makes trust possible.

Trust in God's power and grace can never be overdone, since no situation is too complex, too complicated or too convoluted for God. It is never too late for a miracle, because divine power can write straight with crooked lines. Grace is always waiting around the corner for the right moment. Thus, Paul could write unabashedly to the Corinthians,

> We are afflicted in every way, but not crushed; perplexed, but not driven to despair; persecuted, but not forsaken; struck down, but not destroyed; always carrying in the body the death of Jesus, so that the life of Jesus may also be made visible in our bodies. (2 Corinthians 4:8-10)

To proclaim God as Abba in prayer is to proclaim God as the Abba of amazing grace. As absurd, irresponsible and naïve as it may sound, those who walk the way of the disciple will actively embrace and surrender with trust to every cross that comes their way. When they pray, "And do not bring us to the time of trial but rescue us from the evil one," they are filled with unshakable patience and invincible hope. No matter where they are, no matter what situation they find themselves in, they know who they really are. These are the beloved. They have captured the attention of a God who is as close to them as a father to his children. There's nothing more they need. So they remain as little Christs, who surrender with trust to the cross before them.

REFLECTION QUESTIONS

1. What have been the key moments of testing and trial in my life? How did I respond to them? How did I maintain hope?

2. How do I continue to promote the ego's agenda by constantly taking a stand, justifying and defending myself? Why do I have an emotional need to be vindicated?

3. When has pain become praise in my life?

4. How do I express my devotion to the cross? How do I "take up the cross" in my daily life?

5. What have been the important graces and miracles in my life?

Gospel Passages for Meditation and Prayer: Luke 24:13-35; John 11:1-44

Conclusion

Living the Lord's Prayer

THE LORD'S PRAYER SUMMARIZES the important attitudes and teachings that Jesus lived and preached to his followers. It reminds us that God is an Abba who provides us with everything we have. God lavishes heavenly love on us in creation, enfleshes it in our neighbor and dreams the reality of its fullness in Jesus' kingdom of peace, love and justice. God forgives all our sins with mercy and compassion. And this loving God never abandons us in times of temptation, testing or trial. No matter the situation or circumstance, God is as close to us as a father is to his beloved children.

Such divine lavishness and generosity set the benchmark for a disciple's behavior and response. We live lives of selfless, sacrificial love as we claim everyone as family; we live lives of humility as we claim everything as alms from the divine Almsgiver. We dedicate ourselves to bringing about the fullness of the kingdom by working for peace, love and justice. We allow our baptismal commitment to influence every decision we make, and we forgive those who trespass against us. We resist temptations and live virtuously. Aware of God's abiding and continual presence, we surrender with trust and hope to every cross that comes our way.

Not a method or technique, this prayer is truly "an abridgement of the entire Gospel," as Tertullian said in the late second century. To live the Lord's Prayer is to walk the way of the disciple.

As the days became weeks, the weeks months and the months years, the hermit's skin became like leather as his soul was tried and tested by the rigors of desert life.

His worries about whether or not the sale of mats would be enough to support him soon gave way as he experienced more and more the hand of God providing for all his needs. He stopped worrying about his former life of sin as he grew in the confidence of God's mercy and compassion. And even visitors to the desert who found their way to his hut were no longer viewed as distractions or disturbances but as opportunities to share the loving hospitality that the hermit enjoyed in the divine presence.

One day, as he himself had done years and years ago, a young man stood at the entrance to his hut.

"Father," the young pilgrim said, fingering his prayer beads in one hand and holding the Scriptures in the other, "I have heard of your renown. I have given up everything and wish to follow the way of our divine Master. I come with only the clothes on my back, my beads and the Book. How do I begin the way of a disciple?"

Remembering the words of advice from his own spiritual father, now deceased for decades, the elderly hermit said, "There is only one way to begin praying and living: Our Father, who art in heaven, hallowed be Thy name . . ."

Notes

Preface: Guiding Spiritual Formation

page 13   Jews and Gentiles preparing for: From Didache 8:3, posted on New Advent, <http://www.newadvent.org/fathers/0714.htm>.

page 13   The concluding doxology: Paul J. Achtemeier, gen. ed., *Harper-Collins Bible Dictionary*, rev. ed. (San Francisco: Harper-SanFrancisco, 1996), p. 622.

page 14   "an abridgement of the entire Gospel": Tertullian, "On Prayer," in *Tertullian: Disciplinary, Moral and Ascetical Works*, trans. Rudolf Arbesmann, Sr. Emily Joseph Daly and Edwin Quain, vol. 40 of *The Fathers of the Church* (New York: Fathers of the Church, 1959), p. 159.

page 14   "If somebody said, give me . . . ": Dr. Rowan Williams, "Reflections on the Lord's Prayer," BBC Religion and Ethics—Christianity <http://www.bbc.co.uk/religion/religions/christianity/prayer/lordsprayer_1.shtml>.

Chapter 1: God as Father

page 17   Jesus was not the first: I am indebted to Fr. William Burton, O.F.M., for his scholarly research on this point.

page 18   "nuance of intimacy": Paul N. Evdokimov, *In the World, of the Church: A Paul Evdokimov Reader* (Crestwood, N.Y.: St. Vladimir's Seminary Press, 2000), p. 123.

page 18   Indeed, without the experience of: Edward Schillebeeckx, *Jesus: An Experiment in Christology*, trans. Hubert Hoskins (London: Collins, 1979), pp. 266, 268.

page 27   That's why some scholars have: Daniel J. Harrington, S.J., *The Gospel of Matthew*, Sacra Pagina 1 (Collegeville, Minn.: Liturgical Press, 1991), p. 284.

page 28   Anselm of Canterbury wrote *Cur Deus Homo*: "Anselm (1033-1109): *Cur Deus Homo*," posted on Internet Medieval Sourcebook <http://www.fordham.edu/halsall/basis/anselm-curdeus.html>.

page 29   Two centuries after Anselm, the: For an accurate and easy-to-read description of John Duns Scotus's understanding of the incarnation, see Seamus Mulholland, O.F.M., "Incarnation in Franciscan Spirituality: Duns Scotus and the meaning of love," <http://www.franciscans.org.uk/2001jan-mulholland.html>.

page 29   "the humanly constructed obstacles to achieving": Zachary Hayes, O.F.M., *The Gift of Being* (Collegeville, Minn.: Liturgical Press, 2001), p.105.

page 31   Their term for a woman's womb: George Arthur Buttrick, gen. ed., *Supplementary Volume* of *The Interpreter's Dictionary of the Bible* (Nashville: Abingdon, 1976), pp. 368-69.

page 32   In the second century, Clement: Clement Alexandrinus, *Paidegogos*, ed. O. Stählin (Leipzig, 1905), 1.6.

page 32   In the fourteenth century: M. L. Del Mastro, trans., *Revelations of Divine Love of Juliana of Norwich* (New York: Doubleday, 1977), pp. 187-89.

page 32   Pope John Paul I: Giovanni Paolo I, "Angelus Domini," <http://www.vatican.va/holy_father/john_paul_i/angelus/documents/hf_jp-i_ang_10091978_it.html>. The translation from the Italian is my own.

page 32   All the perfections of created: Thomas Merton, "Hagia Sophia," in *The Collected Poems of Thomas Merton* (New York: New Directions, 1977), p. 367.

page 34   From now on I will: Thomas of Celano, "The Remembrance of the Desire of a Soul," 12, in *The Founder,* vol. 2 of *Francis of Assisi: Early Documents,* ed. Regis J. Armstrong, O.F.M. Cap., J. A. Wayne Hellmann, O.F.M. Conv., and William J. Short, O.F.M., 3 vols. (New York: New City Press, 1999-2001), p. 251.

Chapter 2: "Our" Father

pages 36-37   [Ubuntu] is the essence of: Sonal Panse, "Ubuntu: African Philosophy" (July 22, 2006), posted on Buzzword <http://www.buzzle.com/editorials/7-22-2006-103206.asp>.

page 37   A traveller through our country: "Ubuntu (philosophy)," on Wikipedia <http://en.wikipedia.org/wiki/Ubuntu_%28philosophy%29>.

page 39   This expression has its: As one scholar has written, "The disciples are not 'of the world' *(ek tou kosmou)* as Jesus is not 'of the world' *(ek tou kosmou)* (v. 16; cf. 15:19). This does not mean that the disciples form an otherworldly enclave. The expression *ek tou kosmou* indicates that they do not belong to the prince of this world, to the son of perdition (cf. v. 12), to the power of darkness, to the forces of evil that are lining up against Jesus in order to kill him (e.g., 11:49-50, 57; 12:9-11). Jesus has come to make God known, but 'the world' has rejected him, the one who sent him, and his disciples (v. 14; cf. 15:18-16:3)." See Francis J. Moloney, S.D.B., *The Gospel of John*, Sacra Pagina 4 (Collegeville, Minn.: The Liturgical Press, 1998), p. 468.

page 40   The greatest saints guarded their: Thomas à Kempis, *The Imitation of Christ: A Spiritual Commentary and Reader's Guide*, ed. Dennis J. Billy, C.Ss.R. (Notre Dame, Ind.: Ave Maria Press, 2005), bk. 1:20, p. 54.

page 40   That person is truly blessed: Ibid., bk. 2:7, p. 85.

page 47   Spiritual formation must move beyond: Albert Haase, O.F.M., *Coming Home to Your True Self: Leaving the Emptiness of False Attractions* (Downers Grove, Ill.: InterVarsity Press, 2008), p. 101.

page 47   "The way to salvation is": Jill Haak Adels, *This Wisdom of the Saints: An Anthology* (New York: Barnes and Noble, 1987), p. 137.

page 48   they addressed one another as: Wes Howard-Brook, *The Church Before Christianity* (Maryknoll, N.Y.: Orbis, 2001), p. 72.

page 48   following the custom practiced by: Sara Parvis, "The Open Family: Kinship in the Bible and the Pre-Reformation Church," *The Pastoral Review* 1, no. 3 (2005): 34.

page 50   Some have suggested that the: See Richard Leakey and Roger Lewin, *The Sixth Extinction: Biodiversity and Its Survival* (London: Weidenfeld and Nicholson, 1996).

page 50   In beautiful things [Francis] contuited: Saint Bonaventure, "The Major Legend of Saint Francis," 9:1, in *The Founder*, vol. 2 of *Francis of Assisi: Early Documents*, p. 596. The translator notes on p. 532 that "the Latin word, *contuitus*, is used nine times by Bonaventure in LMj [Major Life], and can be translated as 'concomitant gaze or insight.'" The translator appears to have made up the English word *contuit* to capture the original meaning of the Latin.

page 52   From the first two stages: Saint Bonaventure, *The Soul's Journey into God*, 2:11, in Bonaventure, *The Soul's Journey into God, The Tree of Life, The Life of St. Francis*, trans. Ewert Cousins (New York: Paulist Press, 1978), pp. 75-76.

page 53   Rabbits were busily eating all: Thomas Merton, "A Life Free from Care," *Cistercian Studies* 3, no. 4 (1970), p. 223.

242

<table>
<tr><td>page 53</td><td>In the "Canticle of: Francis of Assisi, "Canticle of Creatures," v. 4, in The Saint, vol. 1 of Francis of Assisi: Early Documents, p. 113.</td></tr>
<tr><td>page 53</td><td>Even Francis mentions in his: Ibid., v. 7, p. 114.</td></tr>
<tr><td>page 54</td><td>Brother Wolf, you do much: "Little Flowers of St. Francis," 21, in The Prophet, vol. 3 of Francis of Assisi: Early Documents, p. 602.</td></tr>
<tr><td>page 55</td><td>Afterwards, that same wolf lived: Ibid., p. 603.</td></tr>
</table>

Chapter 3: Who Art in Heaven

<table>
<tr><td>page 59</td><td>"without beginning and end, is": Earlier Rule, chapter 23:11, in The Saint, vol. 1 of Francis of Assisi: Early Documents, ed. Regis J. Armstrong, O.F.M. Cap., J. A. Wayne Hellmann, O.F.M. Conv., and William J. Short, O.F.M., 3 vols. (New York: New City Press, 1999-2001), p. 86.</td></tr>
<tr><td>page 60</td><td>[Moses] teaches, I think, by: Gregory of Nyssa, The Life of Moses, trans. Abraham J. Malherbe and Everett Ferguson (Mahwah, N.J.: Paulist Press, 1978), no. 46, p. 43.</td></tr>
<tr><td>page 60</td><td>"and there . . . sees God": Ibid., no. 163, p. 95.</td></tr>
<tr><td>page 60</td><td>This is the true knowledge: Ibid., no. 163-64, p. 95.</td></tr>
<tr><td>page 60</td><td>For Gregory of Nyssa: An excellent description of Gregory of Nyssa's understanding of "luminous darkness" can be found at <http://www.monachos.net/library/Gregory_of_Nyssa:_Luminous_Darkness>.</td></tr>
<tr><td>page 62</td><td>You are love, charity: Francis of Assisi, "The Praises of God," v. 4, in The Saint, vol. 1 of Francis of Assisi: Early Documents, p. 109.</td></tr>
<tr><td>page 63</td><td>Meister Eckhart, the fourteenth-century: Cited by Kathleen Fischer, Women at the Well: Feminist Perspectives on Spiritual Direction (Mahwah, N.J.: Paulist Press, 1988), p. 62.</td></tr>
<tr><td>page 64</td><td>"ladder for monks by which": Harvey Egan, ed., An Anthology of Christian Mysticism (Collegeville, Minn.: Liturgical Press, 1991), p. 208.</td></tr>
<tr><td>page 65</td><td>"sprinkled with sweet heavenly dew": Ibid., p. 210.</td></tr>
<tr><td>page 65</td><td>When this happens, Guigo says: Ibid., p. 211.</td></tr>
<tr><td>page 66</td><td>By virtue of our baptism: This theme runs throughout Albert Haase, O.F.M., Instruments of Christ: Reflections on the Peace Prayer of Saint Francis of Assisi (Cincinnati, Ohio: St. Anthony Messenger Press, 2004).</td></tr>
<tr><td>page 66</td><td>"Christ was made sharer of": Psalm CXVII, Sermon XIX, 6, as cited in Catherine of Genoa, Catherine of Genoa: Purgation and</td></tr>
</table>

Purgatory, The Spiritual Dialogue, trans. Serge Hughes (New York: Paulist Press, 1979), p. 30.

page 68   Martin of Tours gave half: Sulpicius Severus, *Life of Martin of Tours,* trans. Alexander Roberts, chap. 3, posted at <http://www.users.csbsju.edu/~eknuth/npnf2-11/sulpitiu/lifeofst.html#3>.

page 68   "Any guest who happens to": *The Benedictine Handbook* (Collegeville, Minn.: Liturgical Press, 2005), p. 74.

page 68   Bonaventure, interpreting Isaiah 53:3: Saint Bonaventure, "The Major Life of Saint Francis," 1:6, in *The Founder,* vol. 2 of *Francis of Assisi: Early Documents,* p. 534.

page 68   "Our faith is given us": Thomas Merton, "The Power and Meaning of Love," in *Disputed Questions* (New York: Farrar, Straus and Giroux, 1960), p. 125.

page 68   "I see God in every": Jonne Johnson Lewis, "Mother Teresa Quotes" posted on About.com: Women's History <http://womenshistory.about.com/od/quotes/a/mother_teresa.htm>.

page 69   "One ought to become": "Talks of Instruction," 22, in Raymond B. Blakney, trans., *Meister Eckhart: A Modern Translation* (New York: Harper & Row, 1941), p. 36.

page 69   Tragically, many of us do not: Thomas Merton, *New Seeds of Contemplation* (New York: New Directions, 1962), p. 106.

page 70   Mental categories and images suddenly: I explored this theme in Albert Haase, O.F.M., *Coming Home to Your True Self: Leaving the Emptiness of False Attractions* (Downers Grove, Ill.: InterVarsity Press, 2008).

page 71   Once [Merton] met a Zen novice: Belden C. Lane, "Merton as Zen Clown," *Theology Today* 46, no. 3 (October 1989), 259-60.

page 72   "You are I and I": Paul Lachance, ed., *Angela of Foligno: The Passionate Mystic of the Double Abyss* (New York: New City Press, 2006), p. 74.

Chapter 4: Hallowed Be Thy Name

page 74   But to the patriarchs God: *HarperCollins Bible Dictionary,* Paul J. Achtemeier, gen. ed. (New York: HarperCollins, 1985), p. 284.

page 75   God revealed to Moses: Ibid., p. 736.

page 75   Thomas Merton considered this text: Thomas Merton, *Seasons of Celebration: Meditations on the Cycle of Liturgical Feasts* (New York: Farrar, Straus and Giroux, 1950), p. 192.

page 75   "succinct expression of this faith": *HarperCollins Bible Dictionary,* pp. 736-37.

page 76   Francis of Assisi sings in: Francis of Assisi, "Canticle of Crea-
             tures," in *The Saint*, vol. 1 of *Francis of Assisi: Early Documents*,
             p. 113.

page 77   "our proud attempts at upward": *Saint Benedict's Rule*, chap. 7 in
             The Benedictine Handbook, ed. Anthony Marett-Crosby (College-
             ville, Minn.: Liturgical Press, 2003), p. 28.

page 77   Benedict says that the ladder: The twelve rungs are (1) living
             with a sense of awe in God's presence; (2) renunciation of our
             own desires; (3) submission of the will to superiors for the love
             of God; (4) patient acceptance of difficult, contrary or even un-
             just conditions; (5) humble confession of evil thoughts and
             deeds; (6) acceptance of the lowest and most menial treatment
             and acknowledgement of being "poor workers" in the given
             task; (7) honest acknowledgement and belief in our inferiority
             when compared to others; (8) doing nothing which goes beyond
             what is approved and encouraged by the monastery's common
             rule and the example of elders; (9) refraining from unnecessary
             speech; (10) stifling empty laughter; (11) speaking appropri-
             ately in a brief and reasonable way; (12) manifesting in action
             the humility of our hearts.

page 78   "mark the decisions we are": *Saint Benedict's Rule*, p. 28.

page 79   "In itself, humility is nothing": James Walsh, S.J., ed., *The Cloud
             of Unknowing* (Mahwah, N.J.: Paulist Press, 1981), p. 148.

page 79   "What a person is before God": Francis of Assisi, Admonition
             19:2, in *The Saint*, vol. 1 of *Francis of Assisi: Early Documents*, p.
             135.

page 81   Let us refer all good: Francis of Assisi, *The Earlier Rule*, chap. 17, v.
             17, in *The Saint*, vol. 1 of *Francis of Assisi: Early Documents*, p. 76.

page 81   "If the only prayer I": Quoted in Albert Nolan, *Jesus Today: A
             Spirituality of Radical Freedom* (Maryknoll, N.Y.: Orbis, 2006),
             p. 114.

page 81   "To be a saint is to": Ronald Rolheiser, *The Holy Longing: The
             Search for a Christian Spirituality* (New York: Doubleday, 1999),
             p. 66.

page 83   "Whenever that glorious name is": From "Second Council of
             Lyons—1297," Constitution 25, posted at <http://www.piar.hu/
             councils/ecum14.htm>.

page 83   "The Jesus Prayer is like": Igumen Chariton of Valamo, *The Art
             of Prayer: An Orthodox Anthology* (London: Faber & Faber,
             1966), p. 99.

page 83   "The Name of our Lord": "Conversation Between a *Starets* and a
            Disciple," in *La Prière de Jésus selon l'évêque Ignace Briantchani-
            noff (1807–1867)*, trans. Emile Simonod (Sisteron: Editions Pres-
            ence, 1976), p. 100.

page 83   "The Name of the Lord is": John Iliytch Sergieff ("Father John"),
            My Life in Christ, trans. E. E. Goulaeff (London: Cassell, 1897),
            pp. 430, 436.

page 85   When I began to pray: Helen Bacovcin, trans., *The Way of the
            Pilgrim* and *The Pilgrim Continues His Way* (Garden City, N.Y.:
            Image Books, 1978), p. 34.

page 85   I spent the rest of: Ibid., pp. 23-24.

page 88   Jesus, Name full of glory: "The Name of Jesus," posted at <http://
            landru.i-link-2.net/shnyves/The_name_of_Power.html>.

Chapter 5: Thy Kingdom Come

page 93   "When you say, 'Thy kingdom": Augustine, Sermon 56.6, cited
            in Arthur A. Just Jr., ed., *Luke*, Ancient Christian Commentary
            on Scripture, New Testament 3 (Downers Grove, Ill.: InterVar-
            sity Press, 2003), p. 187.

page 94   Christ has no body but: Dan Clendenin, comp., "The Journey
            with Jesus: Poems and Prayers," posted on Journeywithjesus.
            net <http://www.journeywithjesus.net/PoemsAndPrayers/
            Teresa_Of_Avila_Christ_Has_No_Body.shtml>.

pages 98-99 "Heaven forbid that any man": Mishnah Yadayim 3:5; see
            "Song of Songs," Wikipedia <http://en.wikipedia.org/wiki/
            Song_of_Solomon>.

page 99   "to the mystical text par excellence": Bernard McGinn, ed., *The
            Essential Writings of Christian Mysticism* (New York: Modern Li-
            brary Classics, 2006), p. 6.

page 99   "You (the soul) are like a": Mechtild of Magdeburg, *Flowing
            Light of the Godhead*, bk. 2.25, as quoted in Saskia Murk Jansen,
            "Bridal Mysticism (Brautmystic)," in *The New Westminster Dic-
            tionary of Christian Spirituality*, ed. Philip Sheldrake (Louisville,
            Ky.: Westminster John Knox Press, 2005), pp.155-56.

page 99   There he taught me a science: John of the Cross, "Spiritual Can-
            ticle" 407, as quoted in ibid., p. 156.

page 99   But when this most wealthy: Teresa of Avila, *Conceptions of the
            Love of God*, as quoted in ibid., p. 156.

page 100   One scholar has noted that: Ibid., p. 156.

page 101   "Love in fact is the": Thomas Merton, *The Wisdom of the Desert:*

| | *Sayings from the Desert Fathers of the Fourth Century* (New York: New Directions, 1961), p. 17. |

page 103   "efficacious signs of grace, instituted": *Catechism of the Catholic Church,* para. 1131 (New York: Image Books, 1995), p. 320.

page 104   "the sacrament of the moment": Jean-Pierre de Caussade, *Abandonment to Divine Providence,* trans. John Beevers (New York: Image Book, 1975), p. 24.

page 105   "is the ready acceptance of all": Ibid., p. 26.

page 105   "What God arranges for us": Ibid., p. 27.

page 105   "There is never a moment": Ibid., p. 36.

page 105   "To sum up: we must": Ibid., p. 79.

page 106   "It is the fulfilling of": Ibid., p. 28.

page 106   "Let [people] realize that all": Ibid., p. 34.

page 106   "There is nothing safer and": Ibid., p. 99.

page 107   "My dear souls, you are": Ibid., pp. 54-55.

page 107   Surprisingly simple and yet profoundly challenging: Cheslyn Jones, Geoffrey Wainwright and Edward Yarnold, S.J., eds., *The Study of Spirituality* (New York: Oxford University Press, 1986), p. 416.

page 108   Father, I abandon myself: Cathy Wright, lsj, *Charles de Foucauld: Journey of the Spirit* (Boston: Pauline Books & Media, 2005), p. 78.

page 109   "as if in Noah's Ark": "The Triple Way," 2:11, in *Mystical Opuscula,* of *The Works of Bonaventure* (Paterson, N.J.: St. Anthony Guild Press, 1960), 1:78.

page 110   "All will be well, and": Julian of Norwich, *Showings,* trans. Edmund Colledge, O.S.A., and James Walsh, S.J. (New York: Paulist Press, 1978), p. 225.

Chapter 6: Thy Will Be Done on Earth as It Is in Heaven

page 115   To understand what Jesus meant: Albert Nolan, *Jesus Today: A Spirituality of Radical Freedom* (Maryknoll, N.Y.: Orbis, 2006), p. 188.

page 116   The will of God . . . means humility: Lorraine Kisly, ed., *Christian Teachings on the Practice of Prayer: From the Early Church to the Present* (Boston: New Seeds, 2006), p. 119.

page 116   The word is used in: Manuel Ruiz Jurado, *El discernimiento espiritual: Teologia, historia, practica* (Madrid: BAC, 1994), pp. 9-11.

page 118   *Kairos,* on the other hand, is . . . : Achtemeier, *HarperCollins Bible Dictionary,* p. 1152.

page 120   Consequently, we need to make: Thomas Aquinas *Summa Theologica* 1-2, q. 2, a.6, reply obj. 2; q. 31; q. 73.

page 121   *First Rule.* The first rule: This translation is found in Timothy M. Gallagher, O.M.V., *The Discernment of Spirits: An Ignatian Guide for Everyday Living* (New York: Crossroad, 2005), p. 7.

page 122   In many ways, as Ignatius notes, the powers: Ibid., p. 36. This is how Gallagher distinguishes the work of Ignatius's "enemy" and "good spirit."

page 123   Such a decision flows naturally: Haase, *Coming Home to Your True Self*, p. 116.

page 127   *Fifth Rule.* The fifth: in time of: Gallagher, *The Discernment of Spirits*, p. 8.

page 128   "the phrase *spiritual desolation*": Ibid., pp. 60-61.

page 128   "happy, uplifting movements": Ibid., p. 49.

page 130   Four times a year, two spiritual: I am indebted to Fr. Gilberto Cavazos-Gonzalez, O.F.M., for introducing me to the Quarterly Review of Life.

Chapter 7: Give Us This Day Our Daily Bread

page 136   There was a desert father: Dom Columba Stewart, trans., *The World of the Desert Fathers: Stories and Sayings from the Anonymous Series of the Apophthegmata Patrum* (Oxford: SLG Press, 1986), p. 22.

page 137   In the final days of: Francis of Assisi, "The Testament," vv. 1, 4, 6, 14, in *The Saint,* vol. 1 of *Fanncis of Assisi: Early Documents,* pp. 124-25.

page 137   "describes a world that is": Regis J. Armstrong, *St. Francis of Assisi: Writings for a Gospel Life* (New York: Crossroad Publishing, 1994), p. 228.

page 137   "For that person eats of": Francis of Assisi, Admonition 2, in *The Saint,* vol. 1 of *Francis of Assisi: Early Documents,* p. 129.

page 139   Indeed, worry and anxiety clearly: *The New Interpreters Study Bible: New Revised Standard Version with the Apocrypha* (Nashville: Abingdon, 2003), p. 1758.

page 140   "because of their complete dependence": Donald Senior and John J. Collins, eds., *The Catholic Study Bible: The New American Bible,* 2nd ed. (New York: Oxford University Press, 2006), p. 1286.

page 141   Traditionally, this honorific title attests: "Doctor of the Church," Wikipedia<http://en.wikipedia.org/wiki/Doctor_of_the_Church>.

page 141   Thérèse of the Child Jesus: As cited in St. Thérèse of Lisieux, *The Story of a Soul. A New Translation*, trans. and ed. Robert J. Edmonson, C.J. (Brewster, Mass.: Paraclete Press, 2006), pp. v-vi.

page 141   It is the way of: Rev. Francois Jamart, O.C.D., *Complete Spiritual Doctrine of St. Thérèse of Lisieux* (New York: Alba House, 1961), p. 15.

page 142   It means that we acknowledge: Ibid., pp.15-16.

page 143   "very straight, very short": As cited in St. Thérèse of Lisieux, *The Story of a Soul*, p. xvi.

page 143   Oh! Never have words more: Ibid., pp. xvi-xvii.

page 146   The whole Christian life is: Thomas Merton, *Monastic Spirituality: Citeaux* (Kansas City, Mo.: National Catholic Reporter Publishing Company, 1994), AA 2083, audiocassette.

page 147   "floundering around and thrashing around": Thomas Merton, *Monastic Spirituality: Part II* (Kansas City, Mo.: National Catholic Reporter Publishing Company, 1994), AA 2084, audiocassette.

page 147   Perhaps this is why Teresa: Teresa of Avila, *Book of Her Life*, chap. 40:8, in *The Collected Works of St. Teresa of Avila*, trans. Kieran Kavanaugh, O.C.D., and Otilio Rodriguez, O.C.D. (Washington, D.C.: ICS Publications, 1976), 1:357.

page 150   "You, however, are the Body": Saint Augustine, *Sermon* 272, ed. J. P. Migne, Patrologiae Cursus Completus, Series Latina (Paris: Migne, 1844–1864), 38:1246-48.

page 151   "the Sacrament of charity": Thomas Merton, *The New Man* (New York: Farrar Straus Giroux, 1961), p. 136.

pages 151-52   "The great Almsgiver will accuse": Bonaventure, "The Major Legend of Saint Francis," 8:5, in *The Founder*, vol. 2 of *Francis of Assisi: Early Documents*, p. 589.

page 152   Are we not moved by: Francis of Assisi, "Exhortations to the Clergy (Earlier Edition)," 8-9, in *The Saint*, vol. 1 of *Francis of Assisi: Early Documents*, p. 53.

page 153   "that Mirror, suspended on the: Clare of Assisi, "The Fourth Letter to Agnes of Prague," v. 24, in Regis J. Armstrong, O.F.M., Cap., trans., *Clare of Assisi: Early Documents, The Lady*, rev. ed. (New York: New City Press, 2006), p. 56.

page 153   Indeed, in that mirror: Ibid., p. 55.

Chapter 8: Forgive Us Our Trespasses

page 157   In the Hebrew Scriptures: Joyce Ann Zimmerman, C.PP.S., et al., *Living Liturgy: Spirituality, Celebration, and Catechesis for*

Sundays and Solemnities, Year A, 2008 (Collegeville, Minn.: Liturgical Press, 2007), p. 101.

page 160   The first and chief article: Martin Luther, "The Smalcald Articles," in *Concordia: The Lutheran Confessions.* (Saint Louis: Concordia, 2005), p. 289, pt. 2, art. 1.

page 160   An elder was asked by: Thomas Merton, *The Wisdom of the Desert* (New York: New Directions, 1960), p. 76.

page 161   "*Don't* set limits": Thomas Merton, *Sanctity* (Kansas City, Mo.: National Catholic Reporter Publishing Company, 1994), AA 2459, audiocassette.

page 161   Instead of returning: Bonaventure, *Tree of Life* 20, in *Bonaventure: The Soul's Journey into God. The Tree of Life. The Life of Saint Francis*, trans. Ewert Cousins (New York: Paulist Press, 1978), p. 143.

page 161   Every soul that stands under: Bernard of Clairvaux, *On the Song of Songs*, cited in Bernard Bangley, comp. and ed., *Nearer to the Heart of God: Daily Readings with the Christian Mystics* (Brewster, Mass.: Paraclete Press, 2005), p. 45.

page 163   renewed in spirit, he now: The entire event is narrated in Thomas of Celano *The Life of Saint Francis* 26, in *The Saint*, vol. 1 of *Francis of Assisi: Early Documents*, p. 205.

page 163   In the evening of Wednesday: John R. Tyson, ed., *Invitation to Chrisitan Spirituality: An Ecumenical Anthology* (New York: Oxford University Press, 1999), p. 320.

page 165   Ambrose stated that as Eve: Saint Ambrose, *In Luc*, J. P. Migne, ed., Patrologiae Cursus Completus, Series Latina (Paris: Migne, 1844-1864), 2, 85-89; PL 15, pp. 1666-1668.

page 165   Augustine wrote that the side: Saint Augustine, *Tractates on the Gospel of John*, trans. J. W. Rettig (Washington, D.C.: Catholic University Press, 1988-1995), tractate 120.2.

page 166   Let us live so: Quoted in Timothy Terrance O'Donnell, *Heart of the Redeemer: An Apologia for the Contemporary and Perennial Value of the Devotion to the Sacred Heart of Jesus* (San Francisco: Ignatius Press, 1992), pp. 96-97.

page 166   The seventeenth century marked a watershed: Ibid., p. 118.

page 167   "I do not want to": Maria Faustina Kowalska, *Diary of Saint Maria Faustina Kowalska: Divine Mercy in My Soul* (Stockbridge, Mass.: Marian Press, 2005), #1588.

page 168   "The Good Shepherd extended": Bonaventure, *Tree of Life*, 13, in *Bonaventure: The Soul's Journey into God. The Tree of Life. The Life of Saint Francis*, p. 136.

page 169   One scholar has suggested that: *The New Interpreter's Study Bible: New Revised Standard Version with the Apocrypha,* p. 1780.

page 170   "urge that the freely given": Ibid., p. 1923.

page 170   Like Matthew, therefore: Bonaventure, *Tree of Life* 13, in *Bonaventure: The Soul's Journey into God. The Tree of Life. The Life of Saint Francis,* p. 137.

Chapter 9: As We Forgive Those Who Trespass Against Us

page 173   "We must not think evil": "Amish grandfather: 'We must not think evil of this man,'" *CNN,* October 5, 2006. As cited in "Amish school shooting," Wikipedia <http://en.wikipedia.org/wiki/Amish_school_shooting>.

page 173   "I don't think there's anybody": Ibid.

page 173   An Amish neighbor comforted: "Amish prepare to bury shooting victims," *Yahoo! News,* October 5, 2007. As cited in "Amish school shooting," Wikipedia <http://en.wikipedia.org/wiki/Amish_school_shooting>.

page 173   One Amish man is reported: Art Carey, "Among the Amish, a grace that endures," *Philadelphia Inquirer,* October 1, 2007. As cited in "Amish school shooting," Wikipedia <http://en.wikipedia.org/wiki/Amish_school_shooting>.

page 173   Some thirty members: Ibid., and "Amish killer's widow thanks families of victims for forgiveness," *The Daily Telegraph,* October 17, 2006. I have followed closely the Amish response to this tragedy as described in "Amish school shooting," Wikipedia <http://en.wikipedia.org/wiki/Amish_school_shooting>.

page 173   Scholars of the Amish community: An understanding of this event and the moving Amish response can be found in Donald B. Kraybill, Steven M. Nolt and David L. Weaver-Zercher, *Amish Grace: How Forgiveness Transcended Tragedy* (San Francisco: Jossey-Bass, 2007).

page 174   Matthew's version of the Lord's: Matthew's Greek *hos* ("as") weakens the Lucan *kai gar autoi* ("for we ourselves also"). See George M. Soares-Prabhu, *The Dharma of Jesus,* ed. Francis Xavier D'Sa (Maryknoll, N.Y.: Orbis, 2003), p. 222.

page 176   When a disciple asked his master: Ibid., p. 226.

page 176   A brother who had sinned: Bessarion no. 7 in Benedicta Ward, S.L.G., trans., *The Sayings of the Desert Fathers: The Alphabetical Collection,* rev. ed. (Kalamazoo, Mich.: Cistercian Publications, 1984), p. 42.

page 177   One day Abba Isaac went: Isaac the Theban no. 1 in ibid., pp. 109-10.

page 177   A brother at Scetis committed: Moses no. 2 in ibid., pp. 138-39.

page 177   In imitation of Christ, a little: Soares-Prabhu, *Dharma of Jesus,* p. 225.

page 181   I wish to know in: Francis of Assisi, "A Letter to a Minister," in *The Saint,* vol. 1 of *Francis of Assisi: Early Documents,* pp. 97-98.

page 184   The current started in my shoulder: Corrie ten Boom, *Clippings from My Notebook* (Nashville: Thomas Nelson, 1982), p. 94.

page 189   If we forgive [others] without: Thomas Merton, *No Man Is an Island* (Garden City, N.Y.: Image Books, 1967), p. 163.

Chapter 10: Lead Us Not into Temptation

page 194   The Hebrew noun for "adversary": Paul J. Achtemeier, gen. ed., *HarperCollins Bible Dictionary* (New York: HarperCollins, 1985), pp. 974-75.

page 194   Over time, however, Satan did: Ibid. See also "Satan" by Regina A. Boisclair in *An Introductory Dictionary of Theology and Religious Studies,* ed. Orlando O. Espin and James B. Nickoloff (Collegeville, Minn.: Liturgical Press, 2007), p. 1226.

page 194   The satanic forces were understood: *HarperCollins Bible Dictionary,* pp. 974-75.

page 195   But until then, popularly depicted: John Milton's *Paradise Lost,* completed in 1667, played a role in our depiction of Satan with a tail, horns and holding a pitchfork. See ibid.

page 195   "Behind the attractions and the": Thomas Merton, *The Patience of Conversion* (Kansas City, Mo.: National Catholic Reporter Publishing Company, 1994), AA 2232, audiocassette.

page 195   "sane people" who "have *perfectly*": Thomas Merton, "A Devout Meditation in Memory of Adolf Eichmann," in *Raids on the Unspeakable* (New York: New Directions, 1964), p. 47.

page 197   Cassian's order of the thoughts: Mary Margaret Funk, O.S.B., *Thoughts Matter: The Practice of the Spiritual Life* (New York: Continuum International Publishing Group, 1998), p. 123. More than one hundred years later, Gregory the Great took Cassian's eight thoughts, deleted vainglory and proposed the famous list of the seven capital sins. Funk had noted earlier that the change in terminology was unfortunate since it distorted Cassian's teaching. Gregory shifted attention away from the earlier *temptation* of the thoughts and placed it on the *sinfulness* of the subsequent action; in doing that, the spiritual discipline of wrestling with the temptation took a backseat to the emphasis on sin. See Mary Margaret Funk, O.S.B., *Thoughts Matter*, p. 21.

page 199   In a birthday party dominated by: *The New Interpreter's Study Bible*, p. 1772.

page 209   There is a vast difference between: Francis de Sales, *Introduction to the Devout Life*, cited in *Nearer to the Heart of God*, comp. and ed. Bernard Bangley (Brewster, Mass.: Paraclete Press, 2005), p. 187.

page 211   "Since, therefore, you seek the": This entire translation of *Spiritual Combat* can be found online at <http://www.catholic tradition.org/Classics/combat.htm#MENU>.

page 212   "a state of self-mastery and attention": Andre Louth, *The Wilderness of God* (Nashville: Abingdon, 1991), p. 64.

Chapter 11: Deliver Us from Evil

page 217   Now Father—since 49 or 50: Brian Kolodiejchuk, M.C., ed., *Mother Teresa, Come Be My Light. The Private Writings of the "Saint of Calcutta"* (New York: Doubleday, 2007), p. 210.

page 218   For the first time in: Ibid., p. 214.

page 219   "saint of darkness": Ibid., p. 230.

page 220   What we suffer in our: Luke Timothy Johnson, "The General Letters and Revelation," *The Catholic Study Bible*, 2nd ed., ed. Donald Senior and John J. Collins (New York: Oxford University Press, 2006), p. 500.

page 222   I return from Perugia and: Francis of Assisi, "True and Perfect Joy," in *The* Saint, vol. 1 of *Francis of Assisi: Early Documents*, pp. 166-67.

page 226   "Brother, be glad and rejoice": The Assisi Compilation 83 in *The Founder*, vol. 2 of *Francis of Assisi: Early Documents*, p. 185.

page 227   Praised be You, my Lord: Francis of Assisi, "Canticle of the Creatures" in *The Saint*, vol. 1 of *Francis of Assisi: Early Documents*, p. 113.

page 227   "Praise and bless my Lord": Ibid., p. 114.

page 231   For perfect hope is achieved: Thomas Merton, *No Man Is an Island* (Garden City, N.Y.: Image Books, 1967), p. 157.

For more information about Albert Haase, O.F.M.,
and his ministry of the Word,
visit his website at <www.AlbertOFM.org>.

formatio
TRADITION. EXPERIENCE.
TRANSFORMATION.

Formatio books from InterVarsity Press follow the rich tradition of the church in the journey of spiritual formation. These books are not merely about being informed, but about being transformed by Christ and conformed to his image. Formatio stands in InterVarsity Press's evangelical publishing tradition by integrating God's Word with spiritual practice and by prompting readers to move from inward change to outward witness. InterVarsity Press uses the chambered nautilus for Formatio, a symbol of spiritual formation because of its continual spiral journey outward as it moves from its center. We believe that each of us is made with a deep desire to be in God's presence. Formatio books help us to fulfill our deepest desires and to become our true selves in light of God's grace.